Lecture Notes in Artificial Inte

Subseries of Lecture Notes in Computer S
Edited by J. G. Carbonell and J. Siekmann

Lecture Notes in Computer Science
Edited by G. Goos, J. Hartmanis and J. van Leeuwen

Springer

Berlin
Heidelberg
New York
Barcelona
Hong Kong
London
Milan
Paris
Tokyo

Soe-Tsyr Yuan   Makoto Yokoo (Eds.)

Intelligent Agents: Specification, Modeling, and Applications

4th Pacific Rim International Workshop
on Multi-Agents, PRIMA 2001
Taipei, Taiwan, July 28-29, 2001
Proceedings

Springer

Series Editors

Jaime G. Carbonell,Carnegie Mellon University, Pittsburgh, PA, USA
Jörg Siekmann, University of Saarland, Saarbrücken, Germany

Volume Editors

Soe-Tsyr Yuan
Fu-Jen University, Department of Information Management
Taipei, Taiwan
E-mail: yuan@tpts1.seed.net.tw

Makoto Yokoo
NTT Communication Science Laboratories
Kyoto, Japan
E-mail: yokoo@cslab.kecl.ntt.co.jp

Cataloging-in-Publication Data applied for

Die Deutsche Bibliothek - CIP-Einheitsaufnahme

Intelligent agents : specification, modeling, and applications ;
proceedings / 4th Pacific Rim International Workshop on Multi-Agents,
PRIMA 2001, Taipei, Taiwan, July 28 - 29, 2001. Soe-Tsyr Yuan ; Makoto
Yokoo (ed.). - Berlin ; Heidelberg ; New York ; Barcelona ; Hong Kong ;
London ; Milan ; Paris ; Singapore ; Tokyo : Springer, 2001
    (Lecture notes in computer science ; Vol. 2132 : Lecture notes in
    artificial intelligence)
    ISBN 3-540-42434-2

CR Subject Classification (1998): I.2.11, I.2., D.2, F.3, C.2.4

ISBN 3-540-42434-2 Springer-Verlag Berlin Heidelberg New York

Springer-Verlag Berlin Heidelberg New York
a member of BertelsmannSpringer Science+Business Media GmbH

http://www.springer.de

© Springer-Verlag Berlin Heidelberg 2001
Printed in Germany

Typesetting: Camera-ready by author
Printed on acid-free paper   SPIN 10840088   06/3142   5 4 3 2 1 0

Preface

The increasing importance of intelligent agents and their impact on industry/business worldwide is well documented through academic research papers and industrial reports. There is a strong affinity between the Web – a worldwide distributed computing environment – and the capability of intelligent agents to act on and through software. The ultimate goal of intelligent agents is to accelerate the evolution of the Web from a passive, static medium to a tuned, highly valued environment.

This volume contains selected papers from PRIMA 2001, the fourth Pacific Rim International Workshop on Multi-Agents, held in Taipei, Taiwan, July 28-29, 2001. In this volume, the papers cover specification, modeling, and applications of intelligent agents.

PRIMA is a series of workshops on autonomous agents and multi-agent systems, integrating the activities in Asia and the Pacific Rim countries. PRIMA 2001 built on the great success of its predecessors, PRIMA'98 in Singapore, PRIMA'99 in Kyoto, Japan, and PRIMA 2000 in Melbourne, Australia.

The aim of PRIMA 2001 was to bring together researchers from Asia and the Pacific Rim and developers from academia and industry to report on the latest technical advances or domain applications and to discuss and explore scientific and practical problems as raised by the participants.

We received 41 submissions to this workshop from more than 10 countries. Each paper was reviewed by at least two internationally renowned program committee members, and 16 papers were selected for this volume. We would like to thank all the authors who submitted papers to the workshop. We are also grateful to our PC members for the terrific job they did in reviewing and in recommending accepted papers. We would also like to thank the invited speakers, Professor Nick Jennings (University of Southampton, UK), Professor Milind Tambe (University of Southern California, USA), and Professor Satoshi Tadokoro (Kobe University, Japan). Finally, we thank the editorial staff of Springer-Verlag for publishing this volume in the Lecture Notes in Artificial Intelligence series.

For more information about PRIMA, please check the following web pages:
PRIMA Web page   http://www.lab7.kuis.kyoto-u.ac.jp/prima/
PRIMA'99 Web page http://www.lab7.kuis.kyoto-u.ac.jp/prima99/
PRIMA 2000 Web page http://www.lab7.kuis.kyoto-u.ac.jp/prima2000/
PRIMA 2001 Web page http://www.lab7.kuis.kyoto-u.ac.jp/prima2001/

This workshop is held in cooperation with:
- Association for Computing Machinery (ACM)
- Ministry of Education, Taiwan
- National Science Council, Taiwan
- National Tsing Hua University, Taiwan
- Taiwanese Association for Artificial Intelligence

June 2001

Soe-Tsyr Yuan
Makoto Yokoo

PRIMA 2001 Committee Members

General Co-chairs

    Jieh Hsiang
    Dean, College of Science and Technology
    National Chi-Nan University
    Puli, Nantou, Taiwan
    E-mail: hsiang@csie.ntu.edu.tw
    http://www.csie.ntu.edu.tw/~hsiang/

    Von-Wun Soo
    Department of Computer Science
    National Tsing Hua University
    Hsin-Chu City, Taiwan
    E-mail: soo@cs.nthu.edu.tw
    http://www.cs.nthu.edu.tw/document/Faculty/vwsoo.html/

Program Co-chairs

    Soe-Tsyr Yuan
    Department of Information Management
    Fu-Jen University
    Taipei, Taiwan
    E-mail: yuans@tpts1.seed.net.tw
    http://bim.im.fju.edu.tw/yuans/

    Makoto Yokoo
    NTT Communication Science Laboratories
    Kyoto, Japan
    E-mail: yokoo@cslab.kecl.ntt.co.jp
    http: www.kecl.ntt.co.jp/csl/ccrg/members/yokoo/

Workshop Web Master

    Yohei Murakami
    Kyoto University
    606-8501 Kyoto, Japan
    Email: yohei@kuis.kyoto-u.ac.jp

Program Committee

Cristiano Castelfranchi (Italy)

Brahim Chaib-draa (Canada)

John Debenham (Australia)

Ed Durfee (USA)

Klaus Fisher (Germany)

Chun-Nan Hsu (Taiwan)

Michael Huhns (USA)

Michael Luck (UK)

Xudong Luo (HK)

John Jules Meyer (NL)

Luc Moreau (UK)

Joerg Mueller (Germany)

Hideyuki Nakashima (Japan)

Ei-Ichi Osawa (Japan)

Toru Ishida (Japan)
Minkoo Kim (Korea)
David Kinny (Australia)
Yasuhiko Kitamura (Japan)
Kazuhiro Kuwabara (Japan)
Jaeho Lee (Korea)
Jimmy H.M. Lee (HK)
Ho-fung Leung (HK)
Chao-Lin Liu (Taiwan)
Jiming Liu (HK)
Jyi-shane Liu (Taiwan)
Rey-long Liu (Taiwan)
Jian Lu (China)

Ichiro Osawa (Japan)
Sascha Ossowski (Spain)
Van Parunak (USA)
Ramakoti Sadananda (Thailand)
Abdul Satter (Australia)
Zhongzhi Shi (China)
Liz Sonenberg (Australia)
Peter Stone (USA)
Toshiharu Sugawara (Japan)
Ron Sun (USA)
Qijia Tian (China)
Makoto Yokoo (Japan)
Xinhuo Yu (Australia)
Chengqi Zhang (Australia)

Table of Contents

The Role of Castes in Formal Specification of MAS

Hong Zhu

School of Computing and Mathematical Sciences, Oxford Brookes University
Gipsy Lane, Headington, Oxford, OX3 0NW, UK
hzhu@brookes.ac.uk

Abstract. One of the most appealing features of multiagent technology is its natural way to modularise a complex system in terms of multiple, interacting and autonomous components. As a natural extension of classes, castes introduced in the formal specification language SLAB provide a language facility that provides modularity in the formal specification of multiagent systems. A caste represents a set of agents of common structural and behavioural characteristics. A caste description defines the tasks that the agents of the caste are capable of, the rules that govern their behaviour, and the environment that they live in. The inheritance relationship between castes defines the sub-group relationship between the agents so that special capabilities and behaviours can be introduced. The instance relationship between an agent and a caste declares that an agent is a member of a caste. This paper discuses how the caste facility can be employed to specify multiagent systems so that the notion of roles, organisational structures of agent societies, communication and, collaboration protocols etc. can be naturally represented.

1   Introduction

From software engineering point of view, one of the most appealing features of multiagent technology is its natural way to modularise a complex system in terms of multiple, interacting, autonomous components that have particular objectives to achieve [1]. Such modularity achievable by multiagent systems is much more powerful and natural than any kind of modularity that can be achieved by existing language facilities such as type, module and class. However, extant multiagent systems are mostly developed without a proper language facility that supports this. We believe that the lack of such a facility is one of the major factors hampering the wide-scale adoption of agent technology. In the formal specification language SLAB [2, 3], a facility called *caste* was introduced as a natural evolution of the notion of type in data type and the notion of class in object-oriented paradigm. In this paper, we further examine the uses of the caste facility in formal specification of multiagent systems.

The remainder of the paper is organised as follows. Section 2 is an introduction to the notion of caste. Section 3 outlines syntax and semantics of the caste facility in the formal specification language SLAB. Section 4 discusses the uses of the caste facility in the formal specification of MAS by some examples. Section 5 is the conclusion of the paper.

S.-T. Yuan and M. Yokoo (Eds.): PRIMA 2001, LNAI 2132, pp. 1-15, 2001.
© Springer-Verlag Berlin Heidelberg 2001

2   The Notion of Caste

This section first reviews our model of multiagent systems. Based on this model, we introduce the notion of castes and discuss its similarity and differences with the notion of classes in object-oriented paradigm.

2.1   A Model of Multiagent Systems

In our model, agents are defined as encapsulations of data, operations and behaviours that situate in their designated environments. Here, data represents an agent's state. Operations are the actions that an agent can take. Behaviour is a collection of sequences of state changes and operations performed by the agent in the context of its environment. By encapsulation, we mean that an agent's state can only be changed by the agent itself, and an agent has its own rules that govern its behaviour. Each agent must also have its designated environment. Constructively, agents are active computational entities with a structure containing the following elements.

- *Agent name*, which is the identity of the agent.
- *Environment*, which consists of a set of agents that interact with the agent.
- *Visible state*, which consists of a set of variables. The values of these variables are visible, but cannot be changed by other agents in the environment.
- *Visible actions*, which are the atomic actions that the agent can take. Each action has a name and may have parameters. When the agent take such an action, it becomes an event visible by the agents in the environment.
- *Internal state*: which consists of a set of variables and defines the structure of the internal state, such as the desires, beliefs and intentions of the agents in the BDI model [4, 5]. The values of visible and invisible states can be the first order or higher order, structural or scalar, symbolic or numeric, etc.
- *Internal actions*: which are the internal actions that the agent can take. Other agents in the environment cannot tell if the agent takes such an action. Actions can have parameters, which may also have first order or higher order, structural or scalar, and symbolic or numeric values.
- *Behaviour rules*: which determine the behaviour of the agent. They should cover the following aspects.
    - *The applicability condition*. The agent takes an action only when the environment and its own state are at the right condition, which is called the applicability condition of the action.
    - *The effects of the action*. An action may have effects on visible and/or internal parts of its own state. It is worthy noting that an agent cannot effect the state of any other agent or object.
    - *None-deterministic and stochastic behaviour*. An agent may have none-deterministic and/or stochastic behaviour. If a number of actions are applicable, choices between the actions may be none-deterministic and/or may have a certain probabilistic distribution.

Agents constructively defined above have a number of features. Firstly, they are autonomous. As Jennings [6] pointed out, autonomous means that agents 'have control both over their internal state and over their own behaviour'. In [7, 8], agents' autonomous behaviour was characterised by two features that an agent can say 'go' (the ability to initiate action without external invocation) and say 'no' (the ability to refuse or modify an external request). Our definition requires that agents have their own rules of behaviour. Hence, they are autonomous.

Secondly, agents defined above are communicative and social. Communication plays a crucial role in multiagent systems. Agents must communicate with each other to collaborate, to negotiate and to compete with each other as well. By dividing an agent's states and actions into visible and invisible parts, we have given agents the capability of communication with each other. We human beings communicate with each other by taking actions. We speak, shout, sing, laugh, cry, and write to communicate. We even make gesture or other body languages to communicate. All these means of communication are 'visible' actions. We also utilise visible states to communicate. For example, the colour of traffic lights indicates whether you should cross the road. We show a smiling face to indicate we are happy and a sad face to indicate unhappy. These means of communication are based on visible states. However, taking a visible action or assigning values to visible state variables is only half of the communication process. The agent at the receiver side must observe the visible actions and/or read the values of the visible state in order to catch the signal sent out by the sender. The details of the protocols and meanings of such actions and state values are of premier importance in the development of multiagent systems. However, they are a matter of design decision and should left for software engineers to design and specify rather than pre-defined by the agent model or the language.

Thirdly, our model emphasizes that agents are situated in their designated environments. The power of agent-based systems can best be demonstrated in a dynamic environment [9, 10]. Characteristics of agents can also be defined in terms of their relationship with the environment. For example, agents are considered as 'clearly identifiable problem solving entities with well-defined boundaries and interfaces'. They are 'situated (embedded) in a particular environment - they receive inputs related to the state of their environment through sensors and they act on the environment through effectors' [1]. Our model requires a explicitly and clearly specification of the boundary and interface between an agent and its environment as well as the effects of environment on the agent's behaviour. Usually, such an environment consists of a set of objects and agents, which include equipment, devices, human beings, software and hardware systems, etc. As argued in [2, 3] and briefly summarised below, all these can be considered as agents as defined above. Therefore, the environment of an agent consists of a set of agents.

Fourthly, the definition implies that objects are special cases of agents in a degenerate form, while agents may be not objects. We consider objects as entities that have no control over their behaviours because an object has to execute a method whenever it receives a message that calls the method. The computational model of object-orientation defines the behaviour of all objects by the default rule of 'if receive a message, then execute the corresponding method'. Therefore, objects are agents with such a simple and uniform behaviour rule. With respect to the relationships with the environment, there are two key differences between objects and agents. First, agents are active in the sense they take initiative actions to effect the environment. In contrast, objects are passive, they are driven by the messages sent by the entities in the environment. Second, an agent selectively observes a part of the environment that it is interested in, while an object is open to the environment in the sense that an object executes a method no matter who sends the message. These highlight the difference in the degrees of encapsulation achieved by objects and agents. Generally speaking, encapsulation means to draw a boundary between the entity and its environment and to control the accesses across the boundary. In object-oriented languages, the boundary enhances the access to object's state via method calls so that the integrity of an object's state can be ensured. However, such a boundary is weak because all entities in the environment can send a message to the object and hence call the method. The object cannot refuse to execute the method. In contrast, agents are able to selectively respond to the actions and state changes of certain entities in the environment. In our definition, each agent can explicitly specify its own subset of entities in the environment that can influence its behaviour.

Finally, our model is independent of any particular model or theory of agents. We believe that specific agent models can be naturally defined in our model. It is also independent of any particular agent communication language or protocol. A formal definition of the model can be found in [3].

2.2   The Notion of Caste

Existing language facilities provided by object-oriented languages cannot solve all the problems that software engineers face in developing agents [11]. New language facilities must be introduced to support agent-oriented software development. We believe that agent-orientation should be and can be a natural evolution of object-orientation so that the so-called agent-oriented paradigm can be build on the bases of object-oriented paradigm. In particular, the notion of caste is a natural evolution of the key notion of class in object-oriented paradigm. However, there are a number of significant differences between classes and castes. The following discusses such similarities and differences.

2.2.1   Structure

In object-oriented languages, a class is considered as the set of objects of common structure and function. Objects are instances of classes. Similarly, we define a set of agents of same structural and behavioural characteristics as a caste, where the term caste is used to distinguish from classes in object-oriented languages. Agents are therefore instances of castes. The agents in a caste share a common subset of state structures and a common subset of visible and internal actions, and some common behaviour characteristics. Similar to class, a caste is a structural template of agents. Therefore, a caste should have the same structural elements as agent.

For example, consider basketball players as agents. The environment of a basketball player in a game consists of the ball, the referee and other players in the game. The state of a player consists of a number of parameters, such as its position in the field, the speed and direction of movement, whether holding the ball, etc. These are the visible state of the agent. Of course, a player should also have invisible internal states, such as its plan and intention of actions, its energy level and skills, etc. The skills of a basketball player often represented by a number of statistics, such as field goal percentage, three-point field goal percentage, etc. Another important state of a basketball player is the team that he/she plays for. In the real world, this state is made explicitly visible by requiring the players of a side to ware clothes of the same distinctive colour. A basketball player should also be able to take a number of basic actions, such as to move, to catch a ball, to pass the ball, to shoot, to dribble, to hold ball, etc. These are the visible actions a player is capable of. A good player should also follow certain basic strategies about when to pass ball and to whom, when to shoot, and how to take a good position in order to catch a rebound, how to steal, etc. These are some of its behaviour characteristics. Such structural and behavioural characteristics are common to all basketball player agents. In a system that simulate basketball games, we can define a caste with these characteristics and declare ten agents as instances of the caste. The following illustrates the caste structure by the example of basketball players.

```
Caste Players
    Environment:
        Ball, All:Players, Referee: Referees;
    Visible State
        Team: string;
        Position: Integer X Integer;
        Direction: Real;   Speed: Real;
        Holding_ball: boolean;
        ... ;
    Visible actions
        Move(direction: real, speed: real);
        Jump(direction, speed, upward: real);
        Pass(direction, speed, upward: real);
        Shoot(direction, speed, upward: real);
        ... ;
    Internal State
        FieldGoalPeercentage: real;
        ThreePointFieldGoalPercentage: real;
        ...;
    Internal action
        ...;
    Behaviour
        If HoldingBall
        & No player within the distance of 4 feet
        & Distance to the goal < 15 feet
        Then shoot(d, s, u).
        ...
End Players
```

Obviously, a caste differs from a class in their structures. A caste contains two essential parts that are not included in a class, the description of environment and the description of behaviours. The dynamic semantics of castes is also different from class. Firstly, for a caste, the visibility of a state variable does not imply that other objects or agents can modify the value of the variable. Secondly, an action in a caste is visible does not imply that it can be invoked by all objects and agents in the system. Instead, it is only an event that can be observed by other entities. Only the agent can decide whether and when to take an action. For the basketball player example, only the agent (i.e. the player) can decide when to shoot and how to shoot. It would not be a basketball game if a player shoot whenever someone (including players of the opposite team) asked it to shoot. Finally, communications between the agents are in the direction opposite to message passing between objects and follow the so-called Hollywood principle: 'You don't call me. I call you'. For the basketball example, a player looks for a teammate to pass the ball, rather than waits for a team-mate's request of the ball.

The example of basketball players shows that agents who play the same role and have the same structural and behavioural characteristics can be specified by a caste. If different roles require taking different actions or have different behaviour, separate castes should be defined for the roles. For example, referees of basketball games should be specified by a caste different from the players.

2.2.2   Inheritance

In a way similar to classes, inheritance relationships can be defined between castes. A sub-caste inherits the structure and behaviour characteristics from its super-castes. It may also have some additional state variables and actions, observe more in the environment and obey some additional behaviour rules if any. Some of the parameters of the super-castes may be instantiated in a sub-caste. The inheritance relationship between castes is slightly different from the inheritance relationship between classes. A sub-caste not only inherits the state and action descriptions of its super-castes, but also the environment and behaviour descriptions. However, a sub-caste cannot redefine the state variables, actions, environment or behaviour rules that it inherits.

For example, the role of basketball players can be further divided into five positions: the inside post players, the left forward players, the right forward players, the left guard players and the right guard players. The behaviour of a basketball player is determined by his position. An inside post player will be responsible for rebounds and attacking from the inside. Therefore, an inside post player will take a position close to the goal. We, therefore, define inside post players as a sub-caste of basketball players with additional behaviour rules. Similarly, we can define the castes of left forwards, right forwards, left guards and right guards as sub-castes of the Players.

```
Caste InsidePosts is Sub-Caste of Players
    Behaviour  (* rules for inside post players *)
        If one of the teammates controls the ball
        Then take the position close to the goal;
        ...
End InsidePosts
Caste LeftForwards is Sub-Caste of Players
    Behaviour (* rules for left forward players *)
    ...
End LeftForwards
Caste RightForwards is Sub-Caste of Players

    Behaviour (*rules for right forward players*)
    ...
End RightForwards
Caste LeftGuards is Sub-Caste of Players
    Behaviour (* rules for left guard players *)
    ...
End LeftGuards
Caste RightGuards is Sub-Caste of Players
    Behaviour (* rules for right guard players *)
    ...
End RightGuards
```

The InsidePosts caste defined above is logically equivalent to the following caste. However, caste InsidePosts2 defined below is not a sub-caste of Players while InsidePosts is.

```
Caste InsidePosts2
    Environment:
        Ball, All:Players, Referee: Referees;
    Visible State:
        Team: string;
        Position: Integer X Integer;
        Direction: Real; Speed: Real;
        Holding_ball: boolean;
        ... ;
    Visible actions:
        Move(direction: real, speed: real);

        Jump(direction, speed, upward: real);
        Pass(direction, speed, upward: real);
        Shoot(direction, speed, upward: real);
        ... ;
    Internal State:
        FieldGoalPeercentage: real;
        ThreePointFieldGoalPercentage: real;
        ...;
    Internal action:
        ...;
    Behaviour
```

If HoldingBall
  & No player within the distance of 4 feet
  & Distance to the goal < 15 feet
Then shoot(d, s, u).
...

(* rules for inside post players *)
If one of the teammates controls the ball
Then take the position close to the goal;
...
End InsidePosts

2.2.3   Instance

The relationship between agent and caste is also an instance relationship. When agent is declared as an instance of a caste, it automatically has the structural and behavioural features defined by the caste. The features of an individual agent can be obtained by initialisation of the parameters of the caste, such as the initial state of the agent. For example, Micheal Jordon was a basketball player for the team Bulls. The following declares such an agent as an instance of the caste Players. In addition to those structural and behavioural common features to all agents of a caste, an agent can also have additional properties of its own. For example, a basketball player may have his own style, which can be considered as additional behaviour characteristics. For instances, Jordon was good at shooting three point goals. Because of the uniqueness of his style, it is more natural to specify such a behaviour rule as a part of the agent's specification rather than to introduce a new caste. Therefore, we would have the following specification for the agent MJordan.

Agent MJordan: Players
  Visible State
    Team = 'Bulls';
  Internal State
    FieldGoalPeercentage= 50;
    ThreePointFieldGoalPercentage= 62;

Behaviour
If HoldingBall
  & No player within the distance of 6 feet
  & Distance to the goal < 30 feet
Then shoot(d, s, u).
End MJordan

This agent declaration is logically equivalent to the following declaration. However, the agent Mjordan2 does not belong to the caste Players.

Agent Mjordan2
  Environment:
    Ball, All:Players, Referee: Referees;
  Visible State
    Team: string = 'Bulls';
    Position: Integer X Integer;
    Direction: Real;   Speed: Real;
    Holding_ball: boolean;
    ... ;
  Visible actions
    Move(direction: real, speed: real);
    Jump(direction, speed, upward: real);
    Pass(direction, speed, upward: real);
    Shoot(direction, speed, upward: real);
    ... ;
  Internal State

    FieldGoalPeercentage: real = 50;
    ThreePointFieldGoalPercentage: real =62;
    ...;
  Internal action
    ...;
  Behaviour
    If HoldingBall
      & No player within the distance of 4 feet
      & Distance to the goal < 15 feet
    Then shoot(d, s, u).
    If HoldingBall
      & No player within the distance of 6 feet
      & Distance to the goal < 30 feet
    Then shoot(d, s, u).
    ...
End Player

3   The SLAB Language

This section briefly reviews the SLAB language. We demonstrate how the caste facility is combined with other language facilities to enhance their expressiveness.

3.1   Agents and Castes

The specification of a multiagent system in SLAB consists of a set of specifications of agents and castes. There is a most general caste, called AGENT, that all castes in SLAB are sub-caste of AGENT.

System ::= {Agent-description | caste-description}⁺

The main body of a caste and agent specification in SLAB contains a structure description of its state and actions, a behaviour description and an environment description. The heads of caste and agent specifications give the name of caste or agent and their inherited castes. In a caste description, the clause 'Caste New_Caste <= Caste$_1$, ..., Caste$_n$' specifies that *New_Caste* is a sub-caste of Caste$_1$, ..., Caste$_n$. Similarly, in an agent description, the clause 'Agent New_agent <= Caste$_1$, ..., Caste$_n$' specifies that the *New-agent* is an instance of the castes Caste$_1$, ..., Caste$_n$. When no inherited caste is given, it is by default a sub-caste of the pre-defined caste AGENT. Every agent must be an instance of a caste. When caste name(s) are given in an agent specification, the agent is an instance of the castes; otherwise, the caste is by default AGENT. All the parameters in the specification of the caste must be instantiated in the specification of the agent. The following gives the syntax of castes and agents in EBNF. It can also be equivalently represented in graphic forms similar to the schema in Z [12].

caste-description ::=
  Caste name [<= { caste-name / , } ;]
    [instantiation ;]
    [environment-description ;]
    [structure-description ;]
    [behavior-description ;]
  end name

Name <= castes (instantiation)	
Visible state-variables and actions	
Invisible state-variables and actions	
Environment description	Behaviour-specification

agent-description ::=
  agent name [: { caste-name / , }]
    [instantiation ;]
    [environment-description ;]
    [structure-description ;]
    [behavior-description]
  end name

Name: castes (Instantiation)	
Visible state-variables and actions	
Invisible state-variables and actions	
Environment description	Behaviour-specification

The SLAB language requires an explicitly specification of the environment of an agent as a subset of the agents in the system that may influence its behaviour. The syntax for the description of environments is given below.

Environment-description ::=
  ENVIRONMENT { (agent-name | *All*: caste-name | variable : caste-name) / , }⁺

where an agent name indicates a specific agent in the system. 'All' means that all the agents of the caste have influence on its behaviour. As a template of agents, a caste may have parameters. The variables specified in the form of "identifier: class-name" in the environment description are parameters. Such an identifier can be used as an agent name in the behaviour description of the caste. When instantiated, it indicates a specific agent in the caste. The instantiation clause gives the details about how the parameters are instantiated.

Instantiation ::= { variable := agent-name / , }+

In SLAB, the state space of an agent is described by a set of variables with keyword VAR. The set of actions is described by a set of identifiers with keyword ACTION. An action can have a number of parameters. An asterisk before the identifier indicates invisible variables and actions.

structure-description ::= [*Var* {[*] identifier: type / ; }+] [*Action* { [*] action / ; }+]

action ::= identifier | identifier ({ [parameter:] type / , }+)

In a caste and agent specification, the additional state variables and actions should not overlap with the state variables, action identifiers and parameter variables defined in the super-castes. Moreover, the castes that it inherits should have no common variables, no common action identifiers, and no common parameters. In other words, no re-definition of state variables and actions are allowed.

3.2   Behaviour Rules

In SLAB, the behaviour of an agent is specified by a set of rules.

Behaviour-rule ::= [<rule-name>] pattern | [prob] –> event, [Scenario] [*where* pre-cond] ;

In a rule, the pattern describes the agent's previous behaviour. The scenario describes the situation in the environment. The where clause is the pre-condition of the action to be taken by the agent. The event is the action to be taken when the scenario occurs and the pre-condition is satisfied. The agent may have a non-deterministic behaviour. The prob is an expression that defines the probability for the agent to take the specified action. When the prob is omitted, it means that the probability is greater than 0 and less than 1.

A scenario is a set of situations that might occur in the operation of a system. Here, in a multiagent system, we consider a scenario as a set of typical combinations of the behaviours of related agents in the system. SLAB's basic form of scenario description is pattern. Each pattern describes the behaviour of an agent in the environment by a sequence of observable state changes and observable actions. A pattern is written in the form of $[p_1, p_2, ..., p_n]$, where $n \geq 0$, and p_i are events. Patterns can be combined together by logic connectives and quantifiers to describe global situations of the whole system. The syntax of patterns and scenarios is given below. Their meanings are given in Table 1.

pattern ::= [{ event [|| constraint] / , }]

event ::= [time-stamp:] [action] [! state-assertion]

action ::= atomic-pattern [^ arithmetic-expression]

atomic-pattern ::= $ | ~ | action-variable | action-identifier [({ arithmetic-expression })]

time-stamp ::= arithmetic-expression

Scenario ::= Agent-Name : pattern | arithmetic-relation

| ∃ [arithmetic-exp] Agent-Var ∈ Caste-Name: Pattern | ∀ Agent-Var ∈ Caste-Name: Pattern

| Scenario & Scenario | Scenario ∨ Scenario | ~ Scenario

where a constraint is a first order predicate. An arithmetic relation can contain an expression in the form of μAgent-var$\in$ Caste.Pattern, whose value is the number of agents in the caste that whose behaviour matches the pattern.

Table 1. Semantics of scenario descriptions

Pattern/Scenario	Meaning
$\$$	The *wild card*, it matches with all actions
$\square$	The *silence* event
Action variable	It matches an action
P^k	A sequence of k events that match pattern P
Action $(a_1, ...a_k)$	An *action* that takes place with parameters match $(a_1, a_2, ...a_k)$
! Predicate	The state of the agent satisfies the *predicate*
$[p_1,..., p_n]$	The previous sequence of events match the patterns $p_1, ..., p_n$
A: P	The situation when agent A's behaviour matches pattern P
$\forall X \in C : P$	The situation when the behaviours of all agents in caste C match pattern P
$\exists_{[m]} X \in C : P$	The situation when there are at least m agents in caste C whose behaviour matches pattern P where the default value of the optional expression m is 1
$\mu X \in C: P$	The number of agents in caste C whose behaviour matches pattern P
S_1 & S_2	The situation when both scenario S_1 and scenario S_2 are true
$S_1 \vee S_2$	The situation when either scenario S_1 or scenario S_2 or both are true
$\neg S$	The situation when scenario S is not true

The following are some examples of scenarios.
(1) $\exists$ p$\in$ Players: [shoot(x, y, z)].
   It describes the situation that there is a player who is shooting.
(2) μ p$\in$ Players: [!position(x, y) || Is-Inside(x,y)] = 3
   It describes the situation that there are 3 players inside the goal area.
(3) MJ: [!position(x,y)] & $\forall$p$\in$ Players: [!position(x', y') || Distance(<x,y>, <x', y'>) > 3 & p$\neq$MJ]
   It is the situation when all players are at a distance more than 3 feet from MJ.
   Obviously, without the caste facility, it is not possible to describe such scenarios.

4   Uses of Castes in Formal Specification

In [2, 3], we have shown how to use SLAB to specify personal assistants such as Mae's Maxims [13], reactive agents like ants, and speech act. This section further illustrates the uses of the caste facility in the specification of communication protocol and organisations of agent societies.

4.1   Organisation of Agent Society

Multiagent systems often divide agents into a number of groups and assign each group a specific role. Such a structure of multiagent system can be naturally specified by using the castes and the inheritance and instance relationships.

For example, in section 2, we have seen how castes are used to specify the roles and the organisational structure of a basketball game simulation system. Fig. 1 below shows the inheritance and instance structure of the example.

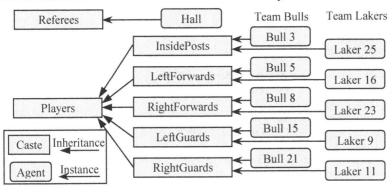

Fig. 1. Castes / agents structure of the basketball example

4.2   A Simple Communication Protocol

A typical example of common behaviour rules that all agents in a multiagent system follow is a communication protocol that defines how agents communicate with each other. Such rules can be specified in a caste and all other castes are then specified as its sub-caste.

For example, the following castes specify a synchronised communication process between agents. If an agent want to send a message to another agent, it signals to the receiver, waits for the receiver to signal back, and then passes the message to the receiver. When an agent saw another agent's signal, it signals back and then receives the message. Here, we have two roles: the senders and the receivers. Each role is specified by one caste.

A sender in the Senders caste has a visible state variable Signal, which indicates whether the sender want to send a message. The process of sending a message is defined by 3 rules. By the <Start sending> rule, the scenario to apply the rule requires that the receiver agent must be in the state of !SignalBack=off, where !pred means that the state of the agent must satisfy the predicate. An agent starts sending a message if its Intention is 'send' and its State is idle, i.e. the assertion !(Intention = 'send' & State=Idle) is true. The result of taking this action is that the state of the agent satisfies the predicate !(Signal = ON & State = Sending). In other words, it will set variable Signal to be ON and State to be Sending. Once this has been done, the agent can take a second action as specified by the <Send message> rule if the receiver's SignalBack turns into

ON. Similarly, the <Finish sending> rule defines the state change for the sender after sending a message.

```
┌══    Senders    ══════════════════════════════════════════┐
│  Var    Signal: {ON, OFF};                                 │
│  Action  Send(AgentName, Message);                         │
│  ─────────────────────────────────────────────────        │
│  Var    State: {Sending, Receiving, Idle} = Idle;          │
│         Intention: String;                                 │
│         Message: String;                                   │
│  - - - - - - - - - - - - - - - - - - - - - - - - - - -     │
│┌─────────────┐                                            │
││ R: Receivers │                                            │
│└─────────────┘                                            │
│  <Start sending>:                                          │
│    [ !(Intention = 'send' & State = Idle)] |–> ! (Signal = ON & State = Sending),│
│                    if R: [!SignalBack = OFF];              │
│  <Send message>:                                           │
│    [ !(Signal = ON & State = Sending)] |–> Send(R, Message),│
│                    if R:[SignalBack = ON];                 │
│  <Finish sending>:                                         │
│    [ Send(R, Message) ! (Signal = ON & State = Sending)]   │
│       |–> Signal = OFF & State = Idle;                     │
└════════════════════════════════════════════════════════════┘
```

```
┌══    Recievers    ════════════════════════════════════════┐
│  Var    SignalBack: {ON, OFF};                             │
│  Action  Receive(AgentName,Message);                       │
│  ─────────────────────────────────────────────────        │
│  Var    State: {Sending, Receiving, Idle} = Idle;          │
│         Intention: String;                                 │
│         Message: String;                                   │
│  - - - - - - - - - - - - - - - - - - - - - - - - - - -     │
│┌───────────┐                                              │
││ S: Senders │                                             │
│└───────────┘                                              │
│  <Start Receiving>:                                        │
│    [!(Intention = 'Receive' & State = Idle)]               │
│       |–> ! (SignalBack = ON & State = Receiving), if S: [Signal = ON];│
│  <Receive message>:                                        │
│    [!(State=Receiving & SignalBack = ON)]                  │
│       |–> Receive(S, x)!(Message=X), if S:[Send(Myself, X) ! Signal = ON];│
│  <Finish receiving>:                                       │
│    [ Receive(S, X) ! (State = Receiving & SignalBack = ON)]│
│       |–> !(Signal = OFF & State = Idle);                  │
└════════════════════════════════════════════════════════════┘
```

The Receivers caste also has three rules, <Start receiving>, <Receiving message> and <Finish receiving>. They define the process of state change for the receiver agent. An agent can be a sender and receiver at the same time. Hence, we define a caste Communicators that inherits both castes of Senders and Receivers as follows.

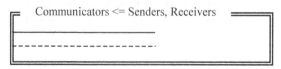

Agents that follow the same communication protocol can be declared as instances of the castes or their sub-castes. For example, the following specifies a system that consists of 3 agents, A, B and C. Here, agent A sends messages to agent B, and B passes the message to agent C. Notice that, the castes Senders, Receivers and Communicators do not specify when an agent will have the intention to send or receive a message. Therefore, additional behaviour rules are added to the specification of agent B so that it repeats the cycle of receiving a message from A, then passing it to agent C.

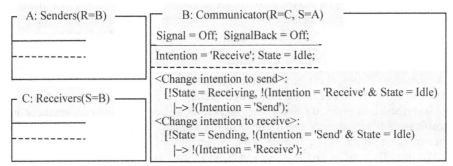

This example shows that the caste and inheritance facilities provide a powerful vehicle to describe the normality of a society of agents. Multiple inheritances enable an agent to belong to more than one society and play more than one role in the system at the same time.

5   Conclusion

The SLAB language integrates a number of novel language facilities that intended to support the development of agent-based systems. Among these facilities, the notion of caste plays a crucial role. A caste represents a set of agents that have same capability of performing certain tasks and have same behaviour characteristics. Such common capability and behaviour can be the ability of speaking the same language, using the same ontology, following the same communication and collaboration protocols, and so on. Therefore, caste is a notion that generalises the notion of types in data type and the notion of classes in object-oriented paradigm. This notion is orthogonal to a number of notions proposed in agent-oriented methodology research, such as the notions of role, team, organisations, but it can be naturally used to implement these notions. A caste can be the set of agents playing the same role in the system. However, agents of the same caste can also play different roles especially when agents form teams dynamically and determines its role at run time. Using the caste facility, a number of other facilities can be defined. For example, the environment of an agent can be described as the agents of certain castes. A global scenario of a multiagent system can be described as the patterns of the behaviours of the agents of a certain caste. The example systems and features of agent-based systems specified in SLAB show that these facilities are powerful and generally applicable for agents in various models and theories.

Our model of agents is closely related to the work by Lesperance, *et al* [14], which also focused on the actions of agents. However, there are two significant differences. First, they consider objects and agents are different types of entities. Consequently, they allow an agent to change the state of objects in the environment, while we only allow an agent to modify its own state. Second, the most important difference is, of course, there is no notion of caste or any similar facility in their system. The notion of agent groups has been used in a number of researches on the multi-modal logic of rationale agents, such as in Wooldridge's work [5], etc. However, such notion of groups of agents is significantly different from the notion of caste, because there is neither inheritance relationships between the groups, nor instance relationship between an agent and a group. The only relationship is the membership relationship. Any subset of agents can form a group regardless of their structure and behaviour characteristics. Many agent development systems are based on object-oriented programming. Hence, there is a natural form of castes as classes in OO paradigm, which is often called agent class. However, as argued in section 2, although agents can be regarded as evolved from objects and castes as evolved from classes, there are significant differences between agents and objects and between castes and classes. Therefore, the notion of caste deserves a new name.

The use of scenarios and use cases in requirements analysis and specification has been an important part of object-oriented analysis; see e.g. [15]. However, because an object must respond in a uniform way to all messages that call a method, there is a huge gap between scenarios and requirements models. As an extension to object-oriented methodology, a number of researchers have advanced proposals that employ scenarios in agent-oriented analysis and design [16, 17, 18]. In the design of SLAB, we recognised that scenarios can be more directly used to describe agent behaviour. The gap between scenarios and requirements models no longer exists in agent-based systems because the agent can controls its behaviour. Its responses can be different from scenario to scenario rather than have to be uniform to all messages that call a method. When the notion of scenario is combined with the caste facility, we obtained a much more powerful facility for the description of scenarios than any existing one.

There are a number of problems related to the caste facility that need further investigation. For example, in SLAB an agent's membership of a caste is statically determined by agent description. Static membership has a number of advantages, especially its simplicity and easy to prove the properties of agents. A question is whether we need a dynamic membership facility in order to specify and implement dynamic team formation. An alternative approach to the problem of team formation is to define aggregate structures of agents and castes. Another design decision about the caste facility that we faced in the design of SLAB was whether we should allow re-definitions of behaviour rules in the specification of sub-castes.

Although the caste facility was first introduced as a specification facility, we believe that it can be easily adopted in an agent-oriented programming language for the implementation of multiagent systems. How to implement the facility is an important issue in the design and implementation of agent-oriented programming languages. It also deserves further research.

References

1. Jennings, N. R., On agent-based software engineering, *Artificial Intelligence*, Vol. 117, 2000, pp277~296.
2. Zhu, H. Formal Specification of Agent Behaviour through Environment Scenarios, *Proc. of NASA First Workshop on Formal Aspects of Agent-Based Systems*, LNCS, Springer. (In press) Also available as Technical Report, School of Computing and Mathematical Sciences, Oxford Brookes University, 2000.
3. Zhu, H., SLAB: A Formal Specification Language for Agent-Based Systems, Technical Report, School of Computing and Mathematical Sciences, Oxford Brookes University, Feb. 2001.
4. Rao, A. S., Georgreff, M. P., Modeling Rational Agents within A BDI-Architecture, in *Proc. of the International Conference on Principles of Knowledge Representation and Reasoning*, 1991, pp473~484.
5. Wooldrighe, M., *Reasoning About Rational Agents*, The MIT Press, 2000.
6. Jennings, N. R., Agent-Oriented Software Engineering, in *Multi-Agent System Engineering, Proceedings of 9th European Workshop on Modelling Autonomous Agents in a Multi-Agent World*, Valencia, Spain, June/July 1999, Garijo, F. J., Boman, M. (eds.), LNAI Vol. 1647, Springer, Berlin, Heidelberg, New York, 1999, pp1~7.
7. Bauer, B., Muller, J. P., and Odell, J., Agent UML: a formalism for specifying multiagent software systems, in *Agent-Oriented Software Engineering*, Ciancarini, P. and Wooldridge, M. (Eds.), LNCS, Vol. 1957, Springer, 2001, pp91~103.
8. Odell, J., Van Dyke Parunak, H., and Bauer, B., Representing Agent interaction protocols in UML, in *Agent-Oriented Software Engineering*, Ciancarini, P. and Wooldridge, M. (Eds.), LNCS, Vol. 1957, Springer, 2001, pp121~140.
9. Jennings, N. R., Wooldridge, M. J. (eds.), *Agent Technology: Foundations, Applications, And Markets.* Springer, Berlin, Heidelberg, New York, 1998.
10. Huhns, M., Singh, M. P. (eds.), *Readings in Agents*, Morgan Kaufmann, San Francisco, 1997.
11. Lange, D. B. and Oshima, M., Mobile agents with Java: the Aglet API, *World Wide Web Journal*, 1998.
12. Spivey, J. M., *The Z Notation: A Reference Manual*, (2nd edition), Prentice Hall, 1992.
13. Maes, P., Agents That Reduce Work And Information Overload, *Communications of the ACM*, Vol. 37, No.7, 1994, pp31~40.
14. Lesperance, Y., levesque, H. J., Lin, F., Marcu, D., Reiter, R. and Scherl, R., Foundations of logical approach to agent programming, in *Intelligent Agents II*, Eds. Wooldridge, M., Muller, J., and Tambe, M., LNAI, Vol. 1037, Springer-Verlag, 1996, pp331~346.
15. Jacobson, I., et al., *Object-Oriented Software Engineering: A Use Case Driven Approach*, Addison-Wesley, 1992.
16. Iglesias, C. A., Garijo, M. Gonzalez, J. C., A Survey of Agent-Oriented Methodologies, in *Intelligent Agents V,* Muller, J. P., Singh, M. P., Rao, A., (eds.), LNAI Vol. 1555. Springer, 1999, pp317~330.
17. Iglesias, C. A., Garijo, M., Gonzalez, J. C., Velasco, J. R., Analysis And Design of Multiagent Systems Using MAS-Common KADS, in *Intelligent Agents IV,* Singh, M. P., Rao, A., Wooldridge, M. J. (eds.), LNAI Vol. 1356, Springer, 1998, pp313~327.
18. Moulin, B. Brassard, M., A Scenario-Based Design Method And Environment for Developing Multi-Agent Systems, in *Proc. of First Australian Workshop on DAI*, Lukose, D., Zhang, C. (eds.), LNAI Vol. 1087, Springer Verlag, 1996, pp216~231.

A Truly Concurrent Model for Interacting Agents

Wieke de Vries[1], Frank S. de Boer[1],
Wiebe van der Hoek[1,2], and John-Jules Ch. Meyer[1]

[1] Utrecht University, Institute of Information and Computing Sciences
PO Box 80.089, 3508 TB Utrecht, The Netherlands
{wieke,frankb,wiebe,jj}@cs.uu.nl
[2] Department of Computer Science, University of Liverpool
Liverpool, United Kingdom

Abstract. We offer a new operational model of agents, which focuses on the *interaction* of agents with each other and with a dynamic environment. We abstract from the inner workings of agents by offering a definable mental lexicon and a flexible cycle of sensing, reasoning and acting. The model incorporates a truly concurrent semantics for physical action, observation, communication and events. The dynamic world and events which can occur in it are explicitly modelled, and actions have a duration. Due to these features, the models offers a realistic view on interacting agents.

1 Introduction

Although agents offer the right level of abstraction for building the complex systems needed nowadays, and interaction is a key concept for agents, interaction issues are not properly treated in many agent programming languages. In this paper, we will identify several interaction aspects and incorporate them in an operational model of agents.

One definition of an agent as given in [10] states:

> "An agent is a computational entity such as a software program or a robot that can be viewed as perceiving and acting upon its environment and that is autonomous in that its behaviour at least partially depends on its own experience."

So, an agent is situated in an environment which can consist of other agents and a physical or virtual world. For example, in robot soccer the environment of an agent consists of the other agents and the physical reality of the playing field and the ball. And a personal agent searching the internet is situated in the environment of the web. In the literature on agent programming, only part of the implications of this agent concept are modelled. Typically, actions are atomic and take zero time, events from the environment aren't explicitly modelled and interference or synergy of actions is impossible. Our model focuses on these aspects.

S.-T. Yuan and M. Yokoo (Eds.): PRIMA 2001, LNAI 2132 , pp. 16–30, 2001.

Although there is a proliferation of agent models, laid down in agent logics, architectures and programming languages, most agents perform the *sense–reason–act cycle*. First the agent *senses* its environment through observation and communication, then it *reasons* to update its local state with new information and to decide which action(s) to perform next, and finally it *acts*, changing the world state, after which the cycle starts again. In [6], it is shown how several architectures for deliberative agents employ some form of this cycle.

Our goal is to find a model for agents that formalises this intuitive notion of multiple agents interacting with their environment via their sense–reason–act cycle, in order to analyse the behaviour of multi-agent systems. The model has to do justice to the complexity of multiple agents interacting with each other and with an external world. So, we focus our model on the interactions of agents with their environment and abstract from their inner processing.

The model we propose is a *skeleton programming language* with a *formal operational semantics*. By instantiating several parameters of the skeleton language, a concrete agent programming language is obtained. Most of the flexibility is related to the internal processing of individual agents. We have:

- A definable range of agent concepts. So, there is no fixed set of modalities (such as beliefs, desires and intentions) that is used to program agents. The set is chosen by the system developer.
- A flexible execution cycle. Our model only fixes that during every round of the cycle reasoning should precede interaction with the environment. As observation in our view is just a special kind of action, we call the cycle the *reason–interact cycle*. The agent programmer has the freedom to decide which (if any) of the observed and communicated information the agent incorporates in its mental state, and also how the mental state of the agent determines the actions that are to be performed next.

By offering this flexibility, we allow the user of the model the freedom to fill in the internal agent according to his/her favourite agent theory or architecture. We abstract from the choices involved.

In order to make the model more realistic with respect to interaction, we include:

- A *world*, which is common to the agents, but only partially controlled by them. So, unexpected changes to the world state (called *events*) are allowed.
- Explicit *actions of observation*. So, the agents' view of the world as represented in its local state doesn't automatically match the state of the world.
- *Actions with duration*. We allow the result of an action to depend on whether other actions or events take place during the execution of the action.
- A treatment of the parallelism relevant to multi-agent executions, in which *true concurrency* plays a vital role. True concurrency means that concurrent actions are semantically treated as happening simultaneously. This contrasts with the common interleaving semantics for parallel actions, where these actions are sequenced in a non-deterministic order. (See [1].)

– Both group actions and individual actions. Group actions are executed synchronously by the group members. We also define a relation between group actions and the individual actions of the participants. A group action results in the synchronised execution of individual actions by the group members.

Many agent programming languages, such as AGENT-0 [9], AgentSpeak [7] and 3APL [4], abstract from an external real world. Agents in these languages maintain an internal database, that represents the state of the world. When the agent acts, this database is changed. As the database always reflects the current state of the world, observations are implicit. Because there is no explicit world, the agent models of these languages also abstract from unexpected events taking place. Also, when multiple agents act, their actions can never interfere with each other, in case they only have private databases modelling mental states.

Another issue is the nature of actions. In our model, each action consists of a number of atomic sub-actions, each taking one unit of time. This way, we model action duration. For the behaviour of a multi-agent system, we combine the effects of all sub-actions and events taking place at some time. In many other agent models, an action is an atomic state transformer, and its semantics is a priori given and independent of other actions or events taking place concurrently.

We think these choices abstract away many problems that can occur when building an actual system with multiple agents. Our target application is a system with a number of robots, situated in some environment. In such an application the dynamic nature of the world and interferences of actions are real problems, as was also shown in [3]. All situated agents have to deal with these issues, but our model is the only agent programming approach that truly incorporates them. So, the contribution we make is *realism* with respect to the dynamics of interaction.

In the next sections, we will explain the syntax and semantics of the skeleton programming language. The aspects of interaction mentioned above will all be formalised during this account. In Section 4 we give an example that demonstrates the new features of this agent model.

2   Syntax

First, we will briefly sketch agent systems as we conceive them. Each agent has a *program* and a *state*. The state of the agent has two parts: the *sense buffer*, where observed and communicated information is received and stored, and the *mental state*, which contains a set of mental formulas. As the program explicitly specifies the reason–interact cycle, it is an iterated statement. A *multi-agent system* consists of a set of agents and an external world, executing in parallel.

2.1   Basic Sets

The basic building blocks of agent programs come from the following sets:

– $\mathcal{P}$ = the set of propositional atoms formalising world conditions

- $\mathcal{I}$ = the set of agent identifiers
- $\mathcal{M}_f$ = the set of modalities applying to formulas (f refers to formula)
- $\mathcal{M}_a$ = the set of modalities applying to actions (a refers to action)
- $\mathcal{A}_s$ = the set of actions agents perform individually (s refers to single agent)
- $\mathcal{A}_g$ = the set of actions which groups of agents perform synchronously (g refers to group of agents)

The sets $\mathcal{P}$ and $\mathcal{I}$ don't need any explanation.

$\mathcal{M}_f$ and $\mathcal{M}_a$ allow the programmer to choose which mental attitudes the agent employs. The mental state of an agent consists of a number of formulas, which (for example) represent the beliefs, goals and desires of the agent held at that moment. Each category of formulas has its own modal operator. The set of modalities is flexible. So, the programmer can decide whether or not the agents should have desires, goals or intentions. The programmer is also allowed to introduce completely new motivational and informational attitudes. By abstracting from these choices, we can focus on aspects of interaction instead of on the internal functioning of the agents.

To instantiate the skeleton language, the programmer specifies two *modality sets*, $\mathcal{M}_a$ and $\mathcal{M}_f$. $\mathcal{M}_a$ contains the modal operators which apply to action (for example intention or request), and $\mathcal{M}_f$ contains the operators which apply to formulas of logic (for example belief or desire). Formulas constructed with these modalities are called *mental formulas*; they can be part of the mental state. The language contains two *mental action constructors*, ins and del, for inserting into and deleting from the mental state.

For example, if $B \in \mathcal{M}_f$, representing belief, then B_i is the belief operator for agent i and $B_i(\varphi)$ (meaning "agent i believes φ") is a formula that can be part of the mental state of agent i. Examples of mental actions are $\mathsf{ins}(B_i(\varphi))$ and $\mathsf{del}(B_i(\varphi))$.

Mental modalities basically are just labels. To give them their intended semantics, mental formulas have to validate a set of axioms. The system developer is responsible for this.

There is another important basic set, namely $\mathcal{E}$, the set of events. These are changes in the world state not caused by any of the agents in the system. Events have no role in the syntax of agent programs, as they are not under control of the agents. The agents can observe the effects of events, and these observations can influence the processing of the agents.

2.2 Group Action and Individual Action

Physical actions take time. For individual actions, we model this by equating each action with a fixed sequence of atomic sub-actions, which each takes one time unit.[1] The length of the time unit is chosen by the system builder. The set $\mathcal{B}$ is the set of atomic sub-actions. For example, if action a takes three units of time, then

---

[1] This has similarities with the way Cohen and Levesque interpret actions in their landmark paper [2].

it corresponds to the sequence $a_1; a_2; a_3$, where $a_1, a_2, a_3 \in \mathcal{B}$ are its sub-actions. Sub-actions never occur in a program; they only play a role in the semantics. As each sub-action can either succeed or fail, depending on circumstances in the environment, we attach a sign to each sub-action to indicate this. Thus, there are four possible executions of action a: $a_{1+}; a_{2+}; a_{3+}$, $a_{1+}; a_{2+}; a_{3-}$, $a_{1+}; a_{2-}$ and a_{1-}. When a sub-action fails, the execution of the action is over.

For group actions, there is more to consider. A group action actually is a multi-set of synchronised individual actions. In order to obtain this synchronisation, the group members need to coordinate their activities. Possibly, they might come to joint mental attitudes, which formalise the agreement of the group on details of the group action. Though this very important, this paper won't go into coordination; we consider it in future research. Here, we just focus on synchronised execution. For example, when four agents are doing the group action LiftTable, then each of these agents is lifting one table-leg. They could do this perfectly synchronised, but the action will probably still succeed when one agent starts lifting one time unit before the others. Also, the agents can lift the table together by lifting a side each, instead of a leg.

In our model, each group action has a fixed number of participants. Each possible realisation of a group action is laid down in a *group action scheme*. If $b \in \mathcal{A}_g$ is a group action with k participants, then a group action scheme $A \sqsubseteq \mathcal{B}^*$ for b is a multi-set with k elements. A group action scheme contains a sequence of atomic actions for each of the participants. To represent different starting times of the actions of the participants, some of the sequences have leading or trailing skip statements. A skip statement means that the agent does nothing for one unit of time. Each atomic sub-action is superscripted with the name of the group action scheme, in order to make it recognisable as a small part of a particular group action realisation. Each atomic sub-action is subscripted with the relative time they are performed. So, all second sub-actions in the sequences of a certain group action scheme are subscripted with 2.

To illuminate this, we extend the example of LiftTable. Lifting a table takes four agents, each lifting a table-leg. LiftLeg $\in \mathcal{A}_s$ is the individual action the four agents perform. This action takes three units of time; during each unit of time, the table-leg can be lifted 15 cm. So, LiftLeg corresponds to the sequence LiftLeg0-15; LiftLeg15-30; LiftLeg30-45. A is a group action scheme for LiftTable:

$$[\text{LiftLeg0-15}_1^A; \quad \text{LiftLeg15-30}_2^A; \quad \text{LiftLeg30-45}_3^A; \quad \text{skip}_4^A; \qquad \text{skip}_5^A,$$
$$\text{skip}_1^A; \qquad \text{skip}_2^A; \qquad \text{LiftLeg0-15}_3^A; \quad \text{LiftLeg15-30}_4^A; \quad \text{LiftLeg30-45}_5^A,$$
$$\text{skip}_1^A; \qquad \text{LiftLeg0-15}_2^A; \quad \text{LiftLeg15-30}_3^A; \quad \text{LiftLeg30-45}_4^A; \quad \text{skip}_5^A,$$
$$\text{skip}_1^A; \qquad \text{skip}_2^A; \qquad \text{LiftLeg0-15}_3^A; \quad \text{LiftLeg15-30}_4^A; \quad \text{LiftLeg30-45}_5^A]$$

In other group action schemes for LiftTable, the LiftLeg-actions could have different relative delays, or be perfectly simultaneous. Also, there can be group action schemes where the four agents each lift a side instead of a leg.

Again, group action schemes are not directly used in the syntax of agent programs. But when semantics is given to an agent program, and a group action is encountered, then this group action is replaced by non-deterministically chosen individual contribution from one of the applicable group action schemes. Like ordinary individual actions, this contribution can fail at any point during execution, so the sub-actions are annotated with $+$ and $-$. In agent programs, group actions are always specified with the group of agents performing them, and this group is also coupled to the each sub-action of the agent's individual contribution in order to synchronise properly with the rest of the group.

For example, discarding success and failure for now, the group action $(\mathsf{LiftTable}, \{i_1, i_2, i_3, i_4\})$ in the program of agent i_2 can be replaced by $(\mathsf{LiftLeg0\text{-}15}_1^A, \{i_1, i_2, i_3, i_4\}); (\mathsf{LiftLeg15\text{-}30}_2^A, \{i_1, i_2, i_3, i_4\});$ $(\mathsf{LiftLeg30\text{-}45}_3^A, \{i_1, i_2, i_3, i_4\}); (\mathsf{skip}_4^A, \{i_1, i_2, i_3, i_4\}); (\mathsf{skip}_5^A, \{i_1, i_2, i_3, i_4\})$ or by $(\mathsf{skip}_1^A, \{i_1, i_2, i_3, i_4\}); (\mathsf{LiftLeg0\text{-}15}_2^A, \{i_1, i_2, i_3, i_4\}); (\mathsf{LiftLeg15\text{-}30}_3^A,$ $\{i_1, i_2, i_3, i_4\}); (\mathsf{LiftLeg30\text{-}45}_4^A, \{i_1, i_2, i_3, i_4\}); (\mathsf{skip}_5^A, \{i_1, i_2, i_3, i_4\}),$ or yet another element from A, modified with the group. If there are more group action schemes for $\mathsf{LiftTable}$, then action sequences from these are also options.

The group action can only succeed if all agents in the group choose the same action scheme, each action sequence in this scheme is performed by exactly one agent and the agents operate in a synchronous way. If these conditions don't hold, for example because there are not enough agents contributing to the group action, the all individual attempted contributions will fail.

Note that it doesn't matter which agent in the group performs some action sequence from a group action scheme. Our present formalism doesn't allow specifying that certain individual contributions to a group action can only be made by agents that have specified abilities and/or authorisations. In other words, we have no roles; all group members are equal. Future research will address this.

2.3   Auxiliary Languages

In order to define the syntax of the programming language, we need several auxiliary languages:

- $\mathcal{L}_w$, the set of formulas describing the state of the world, based on $\mathcal{P}$.
- $\mathcal{L}_{sb(i)}$, the language of the *sense buffer* of agent i. This language defines the set of formulas which can be present in the sense buffer. Basis of the language are formulas like $Od_i(\varphi)$ and $Cd_i(\varphi)$, meaning that φ is observed by i or communicated to i, respectively.
- $\mathcal{L}_{m(i)}$, the mental language, that is, the set of formulas that are allowed in the mental state of agent i. These formulas are constructed with the mental operators from the flexible modality sets.
- $\mathcal{L}_{rep(i)}$, the language of (internal) representations of agent i. Here "representations" is meant to cover both sensory and mental information. A formula of this language can describe a property of the combination of the mental state and the sense buffer of the agent.
- $\mathcal{A}_o$, the set of all actions of observation, defined: $\mathcal{A}_o \equiv \{\mathsf{obs}(\varphi) | \varphi \in \mathcal{L}_w\}$.
- $\mathcal{A}_{c(i)}$, the set of all actions of communication that agent i can perform, defined: $\mathcal{A}_{c(i)} \equiv \{\mathsf{comm}(\varphi, j) | j \in \mathcal{I}, j \neq i, \varphi \in \mathcal{L}_{rep(i)}\}$.

- $\mathcal{A}_{m(i)}$, the set of mental actions of agent i, $i \in \mathcal{I}$, defined:
$$\mathcal{A}_{m(i)} \equiv \{\mathsf{ins}(\varphi)|\varphi \in \mathcal{L}_{m(i)}\} \cup \{\mathsf{del}(\varphi)|\varphi \in \mathcal{L}_{m(i)}\}.$$
- *Interactions$_i$*, the set of composite actions, constructed only from actions of observation and communication and physical actions.
- *Intractions$_i$*, the set of composite actions, constructed only from mental actions.

The auxiliary languages are defined by mutual recursion. Most formal definitions are left. We choose to have a strict separation between internal, mental operations (reasoning, adding and deleting information) and external, interacting operations (observing, communicating, acting). Physical actions only change the state of the world and don't directly affect mental states of agents; for this, the agents must observe first. And even observations and communications don't directly affect the mental state. They arrive in the sense buffer, and the agent can examine this and decide to change its mental state then. Mental actions on the other hand only change mental states.

We introduce the two sets of composite actions *Interactions$_i$* and *Intractions$_i$* to be able to form agent programs which work in reason–interact cycles. For programs, this means that it is forbidden to compose physical actions (including observation and communication) and mental actions in an arbitrary manner. In order to accommodate this, these two kinds of actions are separated into *Interactions$_i$* and *Intractions$_i$*. The set *Interactions$_i$* contains all external actions, that is, actions of interaction with the environment, while *Intractions$_i$* contains all internal, mental actions.

The basic actions in *Interactions$_i$* are skip, actions from $\mathcal{A}_s$, $\mathcal{A}_o$ and $\mathcal{A}_{c(i)}$ and group actions from $\mathcal{A}_g$ (which are specified together with the performing group). Actions may be composed through the conventional operators ';' for sequential composition, '+' for non-deterministic choice and '||' for parallel composition.

The basic actions in *Intractions$_i$* are the mental actions from $\mathcal{A}_{m(i)}$ and the actions that test the local state of the agent. These last actions are of the form $\varphi?$, where $\varphi \in \mathcal{L}_{rep(i)}$. Actions may be composed with the operators ';', '+', '||' and '*' (for iteration).

2.4   Syntax of the Programming Language Itself

We need one more auxiliary language, called $\mathcal{B}_i$, whose elements are valid *behaviours*. A behaviour specifies the body of the reason–interact cycle. In an agent program, one behaviour is iterated, as long as the ultimate objective of the agent is not yet fulfilled. Then $\mathcal{S}_i$, the set of programs for agent i, is the smallest set containing: $(\neg\varphi?; (\gamma))^*; \varphi?$, where $\varphi \in \mathcal{L}_{rep(i)}$ and $\gamma \in \mathcal{B}_i$. This can be read as "while $\neg\varphi$ do γ".
$\mathcal{B}_i$ is the smallest set containing:

- $\alpha; \beta$, where $\alpha \in$ *Intractions$_i$* and $\beta \in \mathcal{B}_i \cup$ *Interactions$_i$*
  or $\alpha \in \mathcal{B}_i \cup$ *Intractions$_i$* and $\beta \in$ *Interactions$_i$*
- $\alpha + \beta$, where $\alpha, \beta \in \mathcal{B}_i$
- $\alpha\|\beta$, where $\alpha, \beta \in \mathcal{B}_i$

The composite statement making up the behaviour (denoted by γ) must be constructed in such a way that all reasoning, mental actions precede all physical actions and actions of observation and communication. So, sequential composition of two actions isn't allowed arbitrarily and iteration isn't allowed at all.

We give some examples of composed statements and indicate whether they are valid agent programs. We use the convention of writing actions in this font, and *logical formulas in this font*. We will use the while ... do notation for the iterated behaviour, as this is more readable.

EXAMPLE 1
while *true* do
$((Od_i(WindowDirty))?; \mathsf{ins}(B_i(WindowDirty));$
$B_i(WindowDirty)?; \mathsf{clean\_window})$
$\parallel$
$(\neg Od_i(WindowDirty)?; \mathsf{skip}))$

This is a (syntactically) valid agent program. Repeatedly, the agent checks whether it observed dirty windows and updates its beliefs accordingly. If there is a dirty window, the agent proceeds to clean it. In this program, each iteration of the cycle first performs some mental actions (updating the beliefs and testing them) and then some physical actions (cleaning windows or doing nothing).

EXAMPLE 2
while *true* do
$((Od_i(WindowDirty))?; \mathsf{ins}(B_i(WindowDirty));$
$B_i(WindowDirty \wedge \neg AtPosition(window))?; \mathsf{goto}(window);$
$B_i(WindowDirty)?; \mathsf{clean\_window})$
$\parallel$
$(\neg Od_i(WindowDirty)?; \mathsf{skip}))$

This program isn't correct, because it allows executions where the agent tests its mental state (which is reasoning) after it performed a physical action of moving. It is very easy to correct the error in the syntax of the previous program, as the second test for a dirty window can just as well be left out.

3   Semantics

3.1   Intuitions

We use two kinds of semantics for the programming language, a local semantics for individual agent programs and a global semantics which composes the local behaviours of the agents and events happening in the world into a global system behaviour, using a form of true concurrency. This global semantics also synchronises the group actions.

The local semantics focuses on the behaviour of one agent at a time. The configuration of an agent i is a triple (σ, δ, π), where σ is the sense buffer, δ the mental state and π the program still to be executed. Here, both σ and δ are sets of formulas; σ is a subset of $\mathcal{L}_{sb(i)}$ and δ is a subset of $\mathcal{L}_{m(i)}$. The local semantics yields a set of local traces. Each trace is a sequence of labelled transitions and local configurations, like this: $S_1 \xrightarrow{l_1} S_2 \xrightarrow{l_2} S_3 \xrightarrow{l_3} S_4$.

Because of the differences between acting and reasoning, we use two different transition functions for the two phases of the reason–interact cycle. As reasoning is a process internal to an agent, we call the transition function for reasoning the *internal* transition function. Interactions are actions in the environment of the agent, so the transition function for interaction is called the *external* transition function. The reason for this split is the way we deal with parallelism.

Parallelism is allowed almost anywhere in the agent program. But we give a different semantics to parallel operations, depending on whether they are mental actions or physical actions. As the agent is the only one altering its own mental state, it is the responsibility of the agent programmer to use parallel reasoning actions in such a way that they never interfere with one other. Assuming this, all parallel actions are independent, so an interleaving semantics is perfectly acceptable for mental actions.

On the other hand, the outcome of observations, communications and physical actions an agent performs depends on the actions of the other agents and on the events happening in the world. This is not under total control of the agent. So, we use a truly concurrent semantics for the interaction part of a reason–interact cycle. This semantics is close to step semantics, as described in [5].

Each internal and external transition step takes one unit of time. This way, we can model that the reasoning process of an agent takes a certain amount of time, and also that physical actions have duration. We assume each atomic mental operation and each action of observing or communication can be executed in one time unit. As explained in Section 2.2, each individual or group action an agent performs is translated into a sequence of atomic sub-actions. Execution of each sub-action takes one time unit.

Fig. 1. Local agent traces

The external and internal transition functions use different arcs with different labels. For internal transitions, we use $(\sigma, \delta, \pi) \xrightarrow{i} (\sigma', \delta', \pi')$. The transitions are labelled only with the identity of the agent. Note that the sense buffer can change. This is because the reasoning process of the agent can be influenced by new information coming in from the environment. Information coming in during reasoning can make it hard to come to definite and consistent decisions. But as we want our model to be realistic with respect to interaction, we allow these disturbances. For external transitions, we use $(\sigma, \delta, \pi) \xrightarrow{i,(O,C,P)} (\sigma', \delta, \pi')$. Here, i again is the agent identifier. The sets O, C and P contain the observations, outgoing communications and atomic physical sub-action steps the agent i performs during a particular time unit. These sets must be part of the label of this transition function in order to be able to arrive at the global transition function. Because observing, communicating and physical action differ in nature, we use three distinct sets for them.

Figure 1 illustrates the two different transition functions and the way the reason–interact cycle is interpreted. Every round of the cycle is rolled out into a sequence of mental, internal actions followed by a sequence of sets of atomic external interactions. For the global transition function, the distinction between the two transition functions is not relevant. Using two different transition arrows in the global transition rule would lead to notational clutter, so we replace each internal transition by an appropriate external transition. This will be explained in the next subsection.

So, the resulting local traces of an agent only use the external transition function. A local trace is a sequence of several ticks of reasoning followed by several ticks of interaction, followed by several ticks of reasoning, etc.

3.2 Local Semantics: Agent Traces

We will only give the transition rules for the local program constructor of parallel composition. Parallel composition in particular is interesting because we want to implement true concurrency in the semantics of parallel executions. Because we have two transition functions now, one for mental actions and one for physical actions, the transition rules are rather subtle. When there are two program fragments in parallel, there are several cases. When the first execution steps of both fragments are internal steps, they are interleaved. When the first steps of both fragments are external, they are taken simultaneously, such that their sets of atomic actions are unified. But when one fragment takes an internal step, and the other an external step, then we give precedence to the internal step. This is because we want the reasoning phase of a round of the reason–interact phase to be totally finished before any interaction with the environment is started.

We assume $\pi \| \sqrt{} = \sqrt{} \| \pi = \pi$ and also $\sqrt{}; \pi = \pi$. These are the transition rules:

$$\frac{(\sigma, \delta, \pi_1) \xrightarrow{i,(O_1,C_1,P_1)} (\sigma', \delta, \pi'_1), \quad (\sigma, \delta, \pi_2) \xrightarrow{i,(O_2,C_2,P_2)} (\sigma', \delta, \pi'_2)}{(\sigma, \delta, \pi_1 \| \pi_2) \xrightarrow{i,(O_1 \cup O_2, C_1 \cup C_2, P_1 \cup P_2)} (\sigma', \delta, \pi'_1 \| \pi'_2)}$$

$$\frac{(\sigma, \delta, \pi_1) \overset{i}{\rightsquigarrow} (\sigma', \delta', \pi'_1)}{(\sigma, \delta, \pi_1 \| \pi_2) \overset{i}{\rightsquigarrow} (\sigma', \delta', \pi'_1 \| \pi_2)} \qquad \frac{(\sigma, \delta, \pi_2) \overset{i}{\rightsquigarrow} (\sigma', \delta', \pi'_2)}{(\sigma, \delta, \pi_1 \| \pi_2) \overset{i}{\rightsquigarrow} (\sigma', \delta', \pi_1 \| \pi'_2)}$$

The local transition rules result in local traces which look like this:

$$(\sigma_0, \delta_0, \pi_0) \overset{i}{\rightsquigarrow} (\sigma_1, \delta_1, \pi_1) \overset{i}{\rightsquigarrow} (\sigma_2, \delta_2, \pi_2) \overset{i}{\rightsquigarrow} \ldots \overset{i}{\rightsquigarrow} (\sigma_n, \delta_n, \pi_n) \xrightarrow{l_1}$$
$$(\sigma_{n+1}, \delta_n, \pi_{n+1}) \xrightarrow{l_2} (\sigma_{n+2}, \delta_n, \pi_{n+2}) \xrightarrow{l_3} \ldots \xrightarrow{l_m} (\sigma_{n+m}, \delta_n, \pi_0) \overset{i}{\rightsquigarrow} \ldots .$$

So, every trace is a finite or infinite alternation of reasoning steps and interaction steps. Note again the separation between internal and external agent behaviour. During the reasoning phase, the mental state (δ) changes. During the interaction phase, it remains the same, as performing physical actions, observations and communications never directly affect the mental state of the agent.

In order to combine the processing of all agents into one system trace, it is convenient to only have one kind of transition arrows. So, after we generated the set of local traces for an agent program, we replace every internal transition $(\sigma, \delta, \pi) \overset{i}{\rightsquigarrow} (\sigma', \delta', \pi')$ in a local agent trace with an external transition $(\sigma, \delta, \pi) \overset{i,(\emptyset,\emptyset,\emptyset)}{\longrightarrow} (\sigma', \delta', \pi')$. The three empty sets labelling the transition indicate that no interactions are done during this reasoning step.

3.3 Global Semantics: System Traces

On the global level, we link up the local traces of all agents in the multi-agent system. Also, we allow events to happen in the world. Because the local behaviour of a single agent is now placed in the context of the behaviours of the other agents and the world, there are several matters that need attention at this level. These are:

- Synchronisation of group actions. A group action can only succeed when all group member simultaneously perform the atomic sub-actions from one group action scheme associated with the action.
- Updating of the sense buffers of the agents. To do this, we introduce a function ρ, which takes a sense buffer and a set of new formulas for the sense buffer, and returns a set of updated sense buffers. The outcome is a set because the revision process might yield several new sense buffers. It is not enough to just add the formulas to the old sense buffer, as new information could contradict older information.
- Changing the world state. Performing actions probably will change the state of the world. We have a function τ, which takes a world state ($\subseteq \mathcal{L}_w$), and a pair consisting of events and annotated atomic single action steps with the identifiers of the agents performing them, and then returns a set of possible new world states.

Note that the function τ, which models world state transformation, incorporates all details about which actions and events interfere with each other, and in which way. To specify this completely is a vast amount of work. The definition of τ is clearly domain dependent and we won't go into this here. Other researchers have tried to give logical formalisations of the effects of actions in a dynamic environment. Issues like the frame, qualification and ramification problems play a role here, as well as theories about concurrent actions. We refer to Sandewall's and Shoham's work for a detailed account of these issues [8].

We define a global system configuration to be a pair $(W, \{S_i | i \in \mathcal{I}\})$, where $W \subseteq \mathcal{L}_w$ is the world state, and the S_i's are local agent configurations. Sub-actions contributing to a group action carry an annotation ($+$ or $-$) and a subscript and superscript (as discussed in Section 2.2). Below, we will need to use variables for the annotation sign. For example, in $\mathsf{b}_k^S x$ the variable x is the sign of the sub-action.

As before, $\mathcal{E}$ is the set of all events possible in the world. For each event $e \in \mathcal{E}$, there is a precondition $\varphi_e \in \mathcal{L}_w$, which expresses in which world states the event could take place. If this condition isn't fulfilled in a world state, the event can't take place in that state. For example, the event GasExplosion can only take place in case someone forgot to turn off the gas or there is a gas leak. If this is the case, it is not certain that there will be a GasExplosion, but it is possible. In the following, $D \subseteq \mathcal{E}$ is the set of events taking place in some time unit.

Now, we have the following global transition rule:

$$\frac{\forall i \in \mathcal{I} : (\sigma_i, \delta_i, \pi_i) \xrightarrow{i,(O_i,C_i,P_i)} (\sigma_i', \delta_i', \pi_i'), \quad W \models \{\varphi_e | e \in D\}}{(W, \{(\sigma_i, \delta_i, \pi_i) | i \in \mathcal{I}\}) \longrightarrow (W', \{(\sigma_i', \delta_i', \pi_i') | i \in \mathcal{I}\})}$$

where the following must hold:

- $\forall i \in \mathcal{I} \; \forall (\mathsf{b}_k^S x, G) \in P_i :$
  $(\neg(\forall \mathsf{a} \in S \; \exists! j \in G \; \exists y \in \{+, -\} : (\mathsf{a}_k^S y, G) \in P_j)) \rightarrow x = -$. This states that an attempt to do a group action according to the scheme S will fail unless there are agents doing all individual contributions from this scheme in a synchronised way.
- $\forall i \in \mathcal{I} : \sigma_i' \in \rho(\sigma_i, \{Od_i(\varphi) | \mathsf{obs}(\varphi) \in O_i \wedge W \models \varphi\} \cup$
  $\{\neg Od_i(\varphi) | \mathsf{obs}(\varphi) \in O_i \wedge W \nvDash \varphi\} \cup \{Cd_i(\varphi) | \exists j \neq i \in \mathcal{I} : \mathsf{comm}(\varphi, i) \in C_j\})$.
  This states that all sense buffers must have been properly updated.
- $W' \in \tau(W, (D, \{(\mathsf{a}, i) | i \in \mathcal{I} \wedge \mathsf{a} \in P_i\} \cup \{(\mathsf{b}, i) | i \in \mathcal{I} \wedge (\mathsf{b}, G) \in P_i\}))$. This computes the next world state.

This transition rule yields the global execution traces of a multi-agent system specified in our programming language. Intuitively, the global transition sums up all actions and events taking place during one unit of time, synchronising the group actions. This is a form of true concurrency.

4   Illustration

The following example serves to illustrate how our model formalises several interaction aspects. Though the domain of the example is totally imaginary, similar interaction takes place in more realistic robotic applications, like in robot soccer.

Figure 2 pictures the scene. Three of the agents are busy doing the group action of skipping (in the sense of jumping over a swinging rope, and not of doing nothing). The fourth agent is skating towards the skipping agents on its skeelers.

The three agents skipping, John, Jack and Sarah, each have the group action SkipRope as part of their programs. In each group action scheme for this action, there are two individual actions SwingRope and one action JumpRope. The two SwingRope actions have to start at the exact same moment; otherwise, the rope

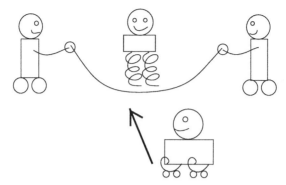

Fig. 2. The robot playground

won't move in the proper way for the jumping agent. The JumpRope action can start somewhat later, but not too late, as the jumping agent would get caught in the rope then. When the group action is executed, each agent chooses one action from a group action scheme, and starts doing its part. If they have chosen the same group action scheme, if each action from the scheme is executed by exactly one agent, and if the individual actions are synchronised properly, the group action potentially succeeds.

Whether the action SkipRope really succeeds depends on other actions and events taking place. In the figure, we see the fourth agent, Mary, moving closer on its skeelers. Mary is executing the individual action Skate. If Mary reaches the other agents, then the skipping action and the skeelering action will interfere and both will end in a clutter of falling robots. The skipping action can also be disturbed by an event. For example, the rope could break.

In Figure 3, one possible scenario is depicted. Here, the marks on the time lines of the agents indicate units of time, and the + and - signs indicate success or failure of the sub-action taking place during that time unit. Solid lines symbolise action parts that actually take place, and dashed lines show parts of actions that would have been done if there hadn't been a disturbance. Recall that global transition steps are computed by taking all sub-actions and events taking place during a time unit and computing the combined effects of these. Failing sub-actions also have effects, though these are disadvantageous.

Jack and John swing the rope perfectly simultaneous, and Sarah starts jumping over the rope one time unit after the rope began to swing. We assume this combination matches a group action scheme for SkipRope. Also, Mary is skating during a time interval which overlaps the interval of the skipping. So, interference of these two actions would be possible. But in this scenario, the disturbance is caused by an event, RopeBreaks. At the moment the rope breaks, the three individual actions contributing to SkipRope fail, and cannot continue any further.

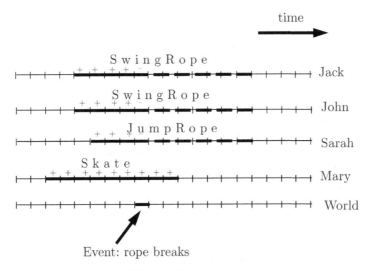

Fig. 3. One scenario

5   Conclusions

We have sketched a model of agents situated in their environment, in which they execute cycles of internal reasoning and external interaction. We focus on faithfully modelling interaction of agents with each other and with their environment. We abstract from the inner functioning of the agents and let the programmer design the mental parts of the agents according to his own view of agents. Our model incorporates features that seem to be missing in other approaches to agents:

- A dynamic world, in which events can occur. We realise this through the incorporation of a separate world state, in which changes can occur without some agent causing them.
- Actions of observation, which agents perform to obtain an internal representation (in their sense buffers) of the state of the world. In other approaches, sensing the environment is done implicitly, resulting in an internal database which is always consistent with the world state. In our approach, the agents need to observe and communicate to maintain accurate information.
- Actions with duration. Both group actions and individual actions take a number of time units. So, interaction of several actions happening during overlapping time frames can be modelled in a natural way.
- The choice between group- and individual actions. Agents can coordinate some of their actions while doing other actions by themselves. Group actions and individual actions are related through group action schemes, which specify the individual actions the group members contribute to the group action and the way these individual actions have to be synchronised.

– The incorporation of true concurrency in the semantics of agent systems. In the global semantic model, two actions of different agents could interfere, yielding results different from the results of some interleaving of the actions. Also, group actions are synchronised by demanding that the individual contributions of the group members follow the scheduling of a group action scheme.

Other approaches of agent programming generally abstract from some of these issues mentioned above. This yields agent models in which important problems can't be studied. Because of the presence of these features, our model is well equipped to analyse the behaviour of diverse systems of agents situated in dynamic environments.

References

1. J. W. de Bakker, W.-P. de Roever and G. Rozenberg (eds.), *Linear Time, Branching Time and Partial Order in Logics and Models for Concurrency*, LNCS 354, Springer, 1989. 17
2. P. R. Cohen and H. J. Levesque, "Intention is Choice with Commitment", *Artificial Intelligence* **42**, pp. 213–261. 19
3. C. M. Jonker, J. Treur and W. de Vries, "Reuse and Abstraction in Verification: Agents Acting in Dynamic Environments", in: *Agent-Oriented Software Engineering, First International Workshop (AOSE-2000)*, (P. Ciancarini and M. Wooldridge, eds.), LNCS 1957, Springer, 2001. 18
4. K. V. Hindriks, F. S. de Boer, W. van der Hoek and J.-J. Ch. Meyer, "Agent Programming in 3APL", *Autonomous Agents and Multi-Agent Systems*, **2** (1999), pp. 357–401. 18
5. J.-J. Ch. Meyer and E. P. de Vink, "Step Semantics for 'True' Concurrency with Recursion", *Distributed Computing* **3** (1989) , pp. 130–145. 24
6. J. Müller, "Control Architectures for Autonomous and Interacting Agents: A Survey", in *Intelligent Agent Systems: Theoretical and Practical Issues* , (L. Cavedon, A. Rao, W. Wobcke, eds.), LNCS 1209, Springer, 1996, pp. 1–26. 17
7. A. S. Rao, "AgentSpeak(L): BDI Agents Speak Out in a Logical Computable Language", in *Agents Breaking Away*, (W. van der Velde and J. W. Perram, eds.), LNAI 1038, Springer, 1995, pp. 341–354. 18
8. E. Sandewall and Y. Shoham, "Non-monotonic Temporal Reasoning", in *Handbook of Logic in Artificial Intelligence and Logic Programming*, vol. 4 on Epistemic and Temporal Reasoning, (D. M. Gabbay, C. J. Hogger, J. A. Robinson, eds.), Clarendon Press, Oxford, 1995. 26
9. Y. Shoham, "Agent-Oriented Programming", *Artificial Intelligence* **60** (1993), pp. 51–92. 18
10. G. Weiss, *Multiagent Systems: a Modern Approach to Distributed Artificial Intelligence*, The MIT Press, 1999, pp. 1–9. 16

Reliable Agent Computation: An Algebraic Approach

David Kinny

Intelligent Agent Laboratory, Department of Information Systems
University of Melbourne, 3010   Australia

dnk@cs.mu.oz.au

Abstract. Agent programming languages based on a sense-compute-act cycle and stored plan execution, such as PRS and dMARS, lack any formal semantics; this and the actual computational models which they employ can make it difficult or impossible to reason about agent behaviour. In this paper we present the Ψ calculus, a novel algebraic language which generalizes and extends these languages and remedies several of their shortcomings. Ψ has a complete operational semantics covering all aspects of agent computation from intention step execution to the top-level control cycle, specified uniformly in process algebraic style, and has certain desirable safety, guarantee and compositionality properties which facilitate reasoning about agent program behaviour.

1   Introduction

An adequate formal semantics is essential for understanding and exact reasoning about agent program behaviour. Agent architectures based on reactive and goal-directed execution of stored plans such as PRS [4] and dMARS [8] lack such a semantics, although simplified treatments exist [3, 16]. The operational semantics of related agent languages such as 3APL [7], SCS [10], ConGolog [5] and Vivid [18] is expressed in ways that cannot concisely and lucidly capture the complexities of plan execution. This paper introduces a novel algebraic language – the Ψ calculus – for the specification of agents which employ a sense–compute–act computation cycle and plan execution as the basis of behaviour.

Ψ generalizes and extends PRS and dMARS in several ways and has a complete operational semantics, specified uniformly in process algebraic style by rewrite rules, covering all aspects of agent computation including control policies which are usually specified algorithmically or by means of a meta-language. In fact, Ψ provides a flexible framework in which many classes of agent languages can be described and the effects of key architectural design decisions on their semantics explored. Importantly, its semantics is based on a notion of *reliable computation* which ensures desirable safety, guarantee and compositionality properties that facilitate reasoning about agent program behaviour.

The presentation here is limited in scope and focuses on individual Ψ agents and how their operational semantics is given, but the approach is easily extended to multi-agent systems. It begins by describing the agent model from an external perspective, and then describes an agent's internal structure and the intention language in which its program is expressed. In Section 3 we develop the operational semantics of Ψ computation and explain the principles upon which it is based, and how its properties lead to a strong notion of *intention* which ensures reliable computation and predictable agent behaviour.

S.-T. Yuan and M. Yokoo (Eds.): PRIMA 2001, LNAI 2132, pp. 31–47, 2001.

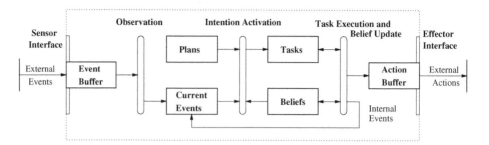

Fig. 1. An Abstract Embedded Agent

2 Ψ Agents

A Ψ (PSI) agent is a strong encapsulation of state and behaviour whose internal elements include *beliefs* (an epistemic component) and *intentions* (a procedural component), the latter including *tasks* and *plans*. (PSI arose as an acronym for Plan System Interpreter.) It interacts with its environment via interfaces of two types: *sensors* from which the agent receives events that carry information from its environment, and *effectors* by which the agent performs actions that are intended to affect its environment. These will be called *external events* and *external actions* to distinguish them from *internal events* which may be generated as a result of changes in the agent's state, of which *goals* are a special case, and from *internal actions* which cause such changes.

Such an agent is depicted in Figure 1. Components of the agent's state are denoted by rectangles, and its computational processes by narrow ovals. The state components are structured aggregations (sequences, sets, multisets, etc.) of elements such as events, actions, beliefs, plans and tasks. A Ψ agent's state is represented formally by an *agent configuration* $\psi = \langle \mathcal{Q}_E, \xi, \beta, \omega, \delta, \mathcal{Q}_A \rangle$ whose elements are respectively an *event queue*, a *signal state*, a *belief state*, an *intention state*, a *response state* and an *action queue*. The set of possible states of an agent is just its *configuration space* Ψ – the direct product of the state spaces of these elements. In the general case, when there are no restrictions on the lengths of queues or the number of intentions in ω, the configuration space is infinite; this is a key feature which distinguishes Ψ from frameworks such as reactive systems [11]. Agent computation is defined in the usual way as a sequence $\psi_0 \longrightarrow_1 \psi_1 \longrightarrow_2 \cdots$ of transitions between agent configurations, and may be captured by a *computation relation*.

2.1 Interaction with the Environment

A Ψ agent's event and action queues are the interfaces between it and its environment, which is taken to include its sensors and effectors. The events generated by sensors, which provide it with information about the state of its environment, and the actions it takes to influence that environment are represented by terms of its *external event languages* $\mathcal{L}_{E_e}$ and $\mathcal{L}_{A_e}$. Individual event and action terms $e = e(v_1, \ldots, v_n)$ and $a = a(v_1, \ldots, v_n)$ consist of a symbol which identifies the *event type* applied to a sequence of value terms which constitute its *properties*. They thus resemble atoms of a first-order logic, but will not be interpreted logically. While that is one possibility, another is as messages in an object-oriented sense or as messages of an agent communication language. The representation captures a minimal set of structural requirements without any semantic baggage.

An agent's event languages allow logical variables, denoted $x, y, x_1, \ldots$, inside terms. Ground terms, denoted $\underline{e}, \underline{a}$, stand for events and actions, whereas non-ground terms are patterns which can match distinct instances of a particular event or action type. We will use E ($\underline{E}$) and A ($\underline{A}$) to denote (ground) *compound events*: sets of events and action terms. In general, T will denote a compound term, $var(T)$ the set of logical variables it contains, $\dot{T}$ a non-empty one, $\ddot{T}$ a non-singleton one, $\star$ an empty one, and $\underline{T}$ a ground one.

Design decisions about interaction determine the expressiveness of an agent model. In Ψ perception is modelled as an external process which inserts ground external events into the event buffer $\mathcal{Q}_E$. We assume in the general case it is uncontrollable: that sensors create events at unpredictable points in time and asynchronously insert them into the event buffer, and do not assume that events carry properties such as timestamps. To enable the preservation of temporal ordering relationships amongst events including simultaneity, the event buffer is modelled as a sequence of compound events, and perception as the atomic concatenation $\otimes$ of a set of events $\dot{E}$ to the end of the queue. As the events in a set are necessarily distinct, an event cannot occur more than once at the same instant. A strict total ordering over events corresponds to the case where each such set is a singleton.

Action is under an agent's control, in the sense that it may initiate an action when it chooses, but the effects of an external action are not; they are determined by its effectors and its environment, and may be immediate or delayed. In Ψ, an agent's effectors, like its sensors, are modelled as an uncontrolled external process, and its action buffer as a sequence of compound external actions $\dot{A}$. Just as the perception process is a producer of events which are consumed by the agent, the external action process is symmetrically a consumer of actions which are produced by the agent. The agent completely controls its consumption of events and its production of actions, but not these external processes.

Abstracting from its internal components and operations, a Ψ agent may thus be characterized as a process which consumes external events and produces external actions, which are produced and consumed by perception and action processes in its environment. Its coupling with its environment is buffered and asynchronous, and so an agent and its environment can be represented symmetrically as a system of directly coupled Ψ agents, by identifying the agent's event queue with the environment's action queue, and *vice versa*. Thus an embedded agent can also be viewed by an observer as a single reduced configuration $\langle \mathcal{Q}_E, \mathcal{Q}_A \rangle$ and two transitions, one representing the observable behaviour of the agent, and the other the observable behaviour of its environment, as in Figure 2. The use of such transition rules to represent behaviour will be described in Section 3.

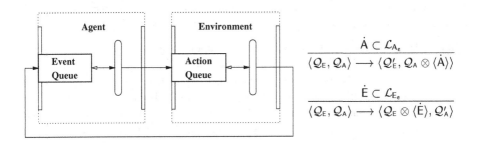

Fig. 2. An Agent embedded in an Environment

2.2   Beliefs, Conditions and Updates

Beliefs A Ψ agent needs beliefs because the events its sensors produce may carry only some quantum of information about some aspect or part of or change in its environment rather than a complete model of it, and because it is computationally less expensive to maintain a cached model than recompute it from scratch every time something changes in the world. One can regard an agent's beliefs as a database, shared by its tasks, supporting basic query and update operations. For our purposes, the details of how beliefs are represented and their exact properties are unimportant, they are viewed quite abstractly, without any commitment to their structure, logical properties, veracity, consistency, etc.; we will merely assume a set $\mathcal{B}$ of belief states $\beta, \zeta, \beta_1, \ldots$, called a *belief space*, and represent queries and updates by transition relations on $\mathcal{B}$. These belief transition relations will constitute the building blocks from which the operational semantics is constructed.

Definition 1 (*Transition relation, Belief transition relation*)

⋄ A *transition relation* on a set S is a binary relation $\rightarrow \subseteq S \times S$.
⋄ The *identity relation* $=$ is defined as $\{ (s, s) : s \in S \}$.
⋄ A transition relation $\rightarrow$ is a *condition* if $\rightarrow \subset =$, and an *update* if $\rightarrow \not\subseteq =$.
⋄ A *belief transition relation* is a transition relation on a belief space $\mathcal{B}$.

We will write transition relations infix, using $r \rightarrow s$ for $(r, s) \in \rightarrow$, $r \rightarrow$ for $\exists s : r \rightarrow s$, $r \not\rightarrow$ for $\neg(r \rightarrow)$, and $\rightarrow^=$ to denote a reflexive closure $(\rightarrow \cup =)$. We will say that a transition $\rightarrow$ is *enabled* in a state s if $s \rightarrow$ and *idle* or *vacuous* in s if $s \rightarrow \{s\}$.

To facilitate examples, beliefs will also be represented as a set of untyped state variables $u, u_1, \ldots$ ranging over a data domain containing booleans, integers, lists and sets. Belief states can then be captured by valuations of these variables in the conventional manner. Their values in particular states will be denoted by $\beta[\![u]\!]$, or when the state is obvious from the context by $[\![u]\!]$, and assignment by $:=$. One could equally take beliefs to be atoms in a first-order language, relational tuples, or untyped object attributes.

Queries Queries are captured by a condition language $\mathcal{L}_C$ whose elements are *atomic conditions* $c, \underline{c}, c_1, \ldots$. Like events these terms may contain logical variables, allowing the representation of non-deterministic conditions such as set membership. Their semantics is given by an interpretation function $[\![\_]\!]$ which maps ground conditions $\underline{c} \in \mathcal{L}_C$ to boolean functions on belief states, whose application to a state β will be written postfix as $\beta[\![\underline{c}]\!]$. *Compound conditions* $C, \underline{C}, C_1, \ldots$ are sets of these, interpreted as conjunctions: the belief transition relation $\xrightarrow{C}$ induced by a condition C is $\{ (\beta, \beta) : \forall c_i \in C, \beta[\![c_i]\!] \}$, and is equivalent to the intersection of the individual relations $\xrightarrow{c_i}$.

Updates The *epistemic effect* of an event or action upon an agent's belief state is similarly given by an interpretation function $[\![\_]\!]$ which associates a belief transition relation with each event $e \in \mathcal{L}_E \cup \mathcal{L}_A$. If an event has no effect the relation is the identity $= (\xrightarrow{\emptyset})$, and in the case of an illegal or non-ground term it is the null relation $\emptyset$. We will write $\beta \xrightarrow{e} \zeta$ for $\beta[\![e]\!]\zeta$, and $\beta \xrightarrow{e}$ for $\exists \zeta : \beta \xrightarrow{e} \zeta$. The epistemic effects of compound events $\xrightarrow{E}$ and actions $\xrightarrow{A}$ are defined by composition of the effects of their elements, and only in the case they *commute*, i.e., their net effect is independent of the order of composition. If not, the associated relation is null and the event or action is *non-executable*.

2.3   Basic transitions, Signals and Responses.

Basic transitions The fundamental construct upon which the Ψ plan language is based is a triggerable, guarded, compound action, referred to as a *basic transition*.

Definition 2 (*Basic transition*)

Let $\mathcal{L}_E$, $\mathcal{L}_C$, and $\mathcal{L}_A$ be respectively an agent's event, condition and action languages. A *basic transition* $X = \langle E, C, A \rangle$ is a tuple of three components:

 - a finite set $E \subset \mathcal{L}_E$ of events, called the *trigger*,
 - a finite set $C \subset \mathcal{L}_C$ of atomic conditions, called the *guard*, and
 - a finite set $A \subset \mathcal{L}_A$ of actions, simply called the *action*.

A basic transition is *complex* if $E \neq \emptyset$ else it is *simple*, and is *guarded* if $C \neq \emptyset$ else it is *unguarded*. If complex or guarded it is *restricted*, and if simple and unguarded it is *free*.

Basic transitions, which are recognizable as elements of formalisms such as Active Databases [19] and Statecharts [6], will be denoted by $\xrightarrow{E[C]A}$ or by ECA. Informally, the *standard semantics* of transition execution is that if the events in E simultaneously occur when the guard condition C holds then the actions in A *must* be performed, atomically. Otherwise, X is disabled and must wait. Any component may be empty: if E is empty the action must be performed when C holds; an empty guard holds vacuously; and an empty action has no effect. The adoption of a *must* rather than a *may* semantics ensures that transition execution has certain strong guarantee and compositionality properties [9].

Signals Transition execution is defined in terms of the *signalling* of events and the belief transition relations associated with conditions and actions. An agent's *signal state* ξ is a set of ground "current" events, called *signals* and distinguished as S rather than E. An event *is signalled* by becoming a member of the signal state, either directly in the case of internal events, or as a result of an *observation* step, which takes the next group of external events from the queue, performs their epistemic effects, and adds them to ξ.

Execution of an enabled transition can consist of up to three stages: *activation*, *liberation*, and *action execution*. Activation, in the basic case, is just simplification: pattern matching between subsets of the signal state and the trigger of a *simplifiable* transition ($\exists \theta : \dot{E}\theta \subseteq \xi$), elimination of the trigger, and application of the substitution that results from the matching to the guard and action. A *satisfiable* guarded transition ($\exists : \beta \xrightarrow{C\theta}$) is liberated by finding a (minimal) substitution satisfying the guard, eliminating the guard, and applying the substitution to the action. Executing the action of an executable free transition ($\beta \xrightarrow{A} \zeta$) consists in performing its effects and eliminating the transition.

Responses One might wonder why it is desirable to discriminate between these stages, rather than just describe an integrated transition execution process that combines them. The answer is that, in order to model concurrent or overlapped execution of transitions by interleaving, one must adopt a suitably fine-grained model of individual transition execution. For example, if several transitions are enabled in a given state, a particular execution semantics may require activating them all before performing the actions of any, or performing their combined actions atomically rather than sequentially. An agent's response state δ is a compound action which permits execution control policies that execute multiple transitions in one computation step by allowing their individual actions to be accumulated and their effects deferred until all have been selected and executed.

2.4   Intentions

The *plan language* $\mathcal{L}_P$ in which agent behaviour is specified is part of a larger *intention language* $\mathcal{L}_\Omega$ whose elements include plans, tasks and processes representing multisets of these. All processes are constructed from basic transitions and the inactive *null process* 0, representing successful termination, by means of the four process combinators:

- $\cdot$ *prefixing*, which joins a transition X and any process π into a *unary task* $\tau = X \cdot \pi$,
- !   *replication*, which transforms a unary task τ into a *plan* $\rho = !\,\tau$,
- +   *choice*, which combines any tasks σ_1 and σ_2 into a *branching task* $\sigma = \sigma_1 + \sigma_2$, and
- ×   *parallel*, which combines any processes π_1 and π_2 into a *multiprocess* $\pi = \pi_1 \times \pi_2$.

As well as using ω and π to denote any process, ρ a plan, and σ an arbitrary task, of which a unary task τ and 0 are special cases, we use ϕ to denote an intention (ρ or σ).

Prefixing is a restricted, asymmetrical form of sequential composition. Replication permits a task to be executed an unbounded number of times without its being consumed; normally this occurs only in response to activation by a signal, i.e., the prefix of a plan, called its *activation transition*, is usually a complex transition. We will omit parentheses if possible, taking the operator precedence order to be $\times < + < ! < \cdot < \langle juxtaposition \rangle$.

Unlike $\cdot$, the operators $+$ and $\times$ are commutative and associative, so one can omit parentheses from nested sums or products, and write any task σ as a sum of unary tasks $\tau_1 + \cdots \tau_n = \sum_{i=1}^{n \geqslant 0} \tau_i$, and any process π as a product of (non-null) intentions $\phi_1 \times \cdots \phi_n = \prod_{i=1}^{n \geqslant 0} \phi_i$. The null process 0 is included, as by definition $0 \stackrel{\circ}{=} \sum_{i=1}^{0} \tau_i \stackrel{\circ}{=} \prod_{i=1}^{0} \phi_i$. This algebraic structure means that a multiprocess π is a multiset of concurrent behaviours, and a task σ is a set of alternative behaviours, each one captured by a particular prefixed process. A unary task consists of just one such alternative, and the null process 0 of none.

Plans and tasks have a natural graphical representation as finite trees. Each transition corresponds to an arc, and each combinator to a node to which the subtrees corresponding to the components are adjoined. The correspondence is formalized as follows.

Definition 3 (*Tree representation of intentions*)

Let $\omega \in \mathcal{L}_\Omega$ be any process. The corresponding tree is defined inductively as follows.

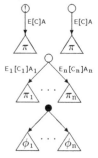

- $\diamond$ A plan $\rho = !\,X \cdot \pi$ is represented by an arc labelled with the transition X from a replication node $\oplus$ to a tree corresponding to π. A unary task $\tau = X \cdot \pi$ is identical except for its root node $\bigcirc$.
- $\diamond$ A branching task $\ddot{\sigma} = \sum_{i=1}^{n>1} X_i \cdot \pi_i$ is represented by joining the roots of the trees corresponding to the summands. An empty summation 0 is represented by a node $\bigcirc$ with no outgoing arcs.
- $\diamond$ A compound multiprocess $\ddot{\pi} = \prod_{i=1}^{n>1} \phi_i$ is represented by a fork node $\bullet$ with outgoing unlabelled arcs to the roots of each of the trees corresponding to the component intentions.

Several examples of types of plans and their corresponding trees appear in Figure 3. A fork node $\bullet$ is a point where execution cannot pause, so all outgoing arcs are executed immediately. The activation transition of a PRS–style plan cannot contain an action, and all its other transitions must be simple and cannot contain guarded actions.

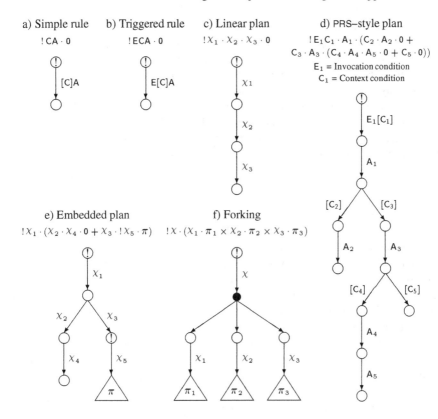

a) Simple rule   b) Triggered rule   c) Linear plan   d) PRS–style plan

!CA · 0   !ECA · 0   !X₁ · X₂ · X₃ · 0   !E₁C₁ · A₁ · (C₂ · A₂ · 0 +
                                                    C₃ · A₃ · (C₄ · A₄ · A₅ · 0 + C₅ · 0))

E₁ = Invocation condition
C₁ = Context condition

e) Embedded plan   f) Forking

!X₁ · (X₂ · X₄ · 0 + X₃ · !X₅ · π)   !X · (X₁ · π₁ × X₂ · π₂ × X₃ · π₃)

Fig. 3. Plans as Trees

Intention execution   The simplest interesting process is the unary task $X \cdot 0$, whose execution is equivalent to the transition X, since 0 represents successful termination. We will call such a process a *rule*, and a nested prefixed process $X_1 \cdot \ldots \cdot X_n \cdot 0$, a *linear task*. Its execution consists in executing its *head* X_1, and then executing the remainder, its *body*, transition by transition. Any substitution applied during the execution of its head is also applied to its body. Exactly the same applies to a unary task $X \cdot \pi$ with an arbitrary body.

Intuitively, a branching task $\ddot{\sigma} = \tau + \dot{\sigma}$ executes by choosing one of its *branches* τ to execute and pruning all the others $\dot{\sigma}$. If many are enabled then one is chosen, non-deterministically in the basic case. It should be clear that disjunction is not needed in guard conditions, since $E[C_1]A \cdot \pi + E[C_2]A \cdot \pi$ implements $E[C_1 \vee C_2]A \cdot \pi$. Choice may also be used to implement more powerful forms of disjunction, such as $X_1 \cdot \pi + X_2 \cdot \pi$.

In the simplest case, a multiprocess or *compound intention* $\ddot{\pi} = \phi \times \dot{\pi}$ executes by choosing some enabled intention ϕ and executing it, retaining all others $\dot{\pi}$ unaffected. When many intentions are enabled an intention selection policy is required; the simplest policy is to choose one non-deterministically. While widespread among agent languages, this policy has many drawbacks [9], not the least of which is that it is not *fair*: some enabled intention might never be chosen if it always has competitors. Ψ allows policies which select in more sophisticated ways and can execute multiple intentions in one step.

Conceptually, a plan $\rho = \, ! \, \tau$ cannot be executed directly, only activated. Technically, its execution consists in replicating instances of it (*sans* replication operator) and executing them, i.e., the creation of one or more new tasks. A key semantic design decision is how this should be done when a plan can be activated in several distinct ways.

A task may contain a parallel or replication operator in its body. In the former case (Figure 3(f)), when it reduces to this point it forks into independent parallel tasks, and in the latter (Figure 3(e)) a new plan is introduced. This does not reflect a general capacity for planning, as such a plan can only specialize a subtree of an existing plan.

Process execution can be captured more formally by *reduction rules*, such as:

$$\frac{\chi \xrightarrow{\theta, \alpha} 0}{\chi \cdot \pi \xrightarrow{\alpha} \pi\theta} \qquad \frac{\tau \xrightarrow{\alpha} \pi}{\tau + \sigma \xrightarrow{\alpha} \pi} \qquad \frac{\phi \xrightarrow{\alpha} \pi}{\phi \times \omega \xrightarrow{\alpha} \pi \times \omega} \qquad \frac{\tau \xrightarrow{\alpha} \pi}{!\,\tau \xrightarrow{\alpha} !\,\tau \times \pi}$$

These sequents capture the contexts in which process execution can occur, the structural changes it causes, and the actions that result. For example, the first rule says that if a transition χ can execute via a substitution θ and perform an action α, then the unary task $\chi \cdot \pi$ can execute and perform α to become $\pi\theta$. Note how plan replication is concisely defined in terms of unary task execution by means of the parallel composition operator.

The reduction approach to representing process execution also has the advantage that it dispenses with the notion of a locus of control and a local environment. A task's locus of control is implicit – it is always its head – and prefixes and branches not chosen are eliminated as it is executed. While a task is indeed an instance of a plan which can be thought of as possessing local state in the form of single-assignment logical variables, these are bound as the task reduces, i.e., it is progressively specialized as it undergoes transformations permitted by the reduction rules. That the state is local is a consequence of the execution semantics of multiprocesses: substitutions are applied only within a task. Parallel processes do, however, share global state, captured by the agent's beliefs.

The intention language $\mathcal{L}_\Omega$ is quite expressive when compared to other agent programming languages, providing triggered guarded action as a primitive, and so allowing a task to wait during its execution not just for conditions but also for events. Many other agent languages can be expressed as restricted, special cases. It is similar in basic structure to Milner's classic π-calculus [13]. The main differences are the absence of names and input/output actions. Signals may be viewed as playing a rôle similar to input and output actions, however the crucial difference is that whereas input and output actions in the π-calculus allow synchronized communication between pairs of processes, signals in Ψ allow broadcast communication between all intentions, i.e., a single signal can trigger many transitions. In this respect Ψ resembles Prasad's broadcast calculus CBS [15].

3   Operational Semantics of Ψ Computation

Having defined the basic structure of a Ψ agent, the task at hand is to give an operational semantics, not just for its intention language, but for all aspects of agent computation. An operational semantics for a language maps terms of a syntactic domain into objects of a semantic domain, providing a complete, unambiguous specification of the meaning of program execution from which an implementation may be constructed or against which one may be validated. These semantic objects are elementary machines of some sort, commonly automata. Here, they will be *transition systems*, which may be viewed as explicit graphs of system behaviour, with nodes denoting system states and labelled, directed edges (transitions) denoting the possibility of particular computation steps.

Transition systems *per se* are not a very practical way of defining a computational model, particularly an infinite one. Structured Operational Semantics (SOS) [14] is a well-known, powerful technique which allows an infinite transition system to be specified as a finite deductive system of axioms and rules of inference by which valid transitions may be derived. However, SOS specifications are still not particularly compact, so we shall use instead *reduction systems*, a variety of conditional term rewrite system [2, 12], which also permit abstraction over the structure of system states.

Definition 4 (*Reduction system*)

A *reduction system* $\mathcal{R}_\Upsilon$ is a calculus $\langle \Gamma, \equiv, \Xi \rangle$ consisting of three elements:

1. a *grammar* Γ of *production rules* which define a language Υ of configuration terms, which are parameterized by a signature of typed *process variables*,
2. a *structural congruence relation* $\equiv$ which partitions Υ into equivalence classes of terms that are considered semantically identical, and
3. a set Ξ of *reduction rules* which define a *reduction relation* $\twoheadrightarrow_\Upsilon$ on configurations.

Terms of the configuration language are usually called processes. Here, configurations will usually be compound, made up of elements of distinct types, e.g., $\langle \beta, \omega \rangle$, represented as $\beta : \omega$, and we will use process as before to refer to atomic or compound intentions ω.

The function of the congruence[1] relation, expressed as a set of equivalences between abstract terms, is to capture algebraic structure, such as associativity of the operators used to construct processes, and so simplify the presentation of the reduction rules, e.g., by eliminating symmetric variants. Formally, rules operate over the quotient space $\Upsilon/\equiv$. Reductions are thus transition relations on sets of equivalence classes of configurations. For example, the reduction $\phi \twoheadrightarrow \varphi$ stands for the relation $\{ (\phi', \varphi') : \phi' \equiv \phi \wedge \varphi' \equiv \varphi \}$.

A reduction rule is a sequent whose premises are reductions or other logical formulae and whose conclusion is a reduction. The conclusion holds, i.e., its reduction may occur, if all its premises hold, i.e., reductions in the premises are possible and logical formulae are satisfied. A rule whose premise is empty is an unconditional reduction: an axiom of the system. A set of reduction rules inductively defines a single-step reduction relation $\twoheadrightarrow_\Upsilon$ upon configurations, namely the union of all the reductions that can be derived.

A particular feature of our approach to defining the operational semantics of Ψ is the construction of a uniform hierarchy of reduction systems, rather than the use an object language and meta-language, cf. [7]. Each level conditionally lifts reductions at lower levels into larger contexts, and has a different notion of a single reduction step, with one step at a higher level often corresponding to many at a lower level. At the lowest level are systems which define the semantics of basic transitions and operate on configurations of belief states and intentions, and at the highest level are those which specify the control cycle and operate upon complete agent configurations. Before presenting such a hierarchy, we shall introduce some principles of intention execution whose adoption ensures a useful and comprehensible semantics that allows reasoning about agent program execution, and avoids some subtle semantic shortcomings of existing languages [9].

---

[1] Recall that a congruence is an equivalence relation over a language that is *functionally reflexive*, so that $r(s_1, \ldots s_n) \equiv r(t_1, \ldots t_n)$ if $\forall i = 1 \ldots n : s_i \equiv t_i$.

3.1 Semantics of Intentions

It should be clear that intentions in Ψ fulfill the basic criterion for their being so named: their execution determines and causes action. Unlike intentions in BDI logics such as [17], intentions in Ψ are a commitment to a means rather than an end, more in the spirit of Bratman's original treatment [1]. More abstract, goal-directed intentions may be defined directly in terms of such concrete ones [9], but we will not explore the semantics of goal-directed intention activation in this paper. A particular intention execution semantics captures a particular strategy for *intention maintenance*, which ideally should reflect some sensible but possibly minimal theory of intentions and their properties. Specifically, plan activation should occur in a way that embodies some set of principles as to how the generic, permanent commitment captured by a plan leads to a more specific, short-term commitment captured by a task. Task execution should similarly reflect principles that decree how intentions should be acted upon and updated as new events occur and beliefs change, and the circumstances under which intention execution terminates should reflect principles that determine when intentions have been fulfilled or should be abandoned.

Beyond correctness and safety properties such as *atomicity* of basic transitions, the most important such principle that we adopt is *reliability*. *Reliable activation* consists in interpreting the activation transition ECA of a plan ! ECA $\cdot$ π as *requiring* that the plan be immediately activated if some signal S $=$ Eθ occurs in a state where Cθ is satisfiable, rather than merely *permitting* it. It applies also to task activation but with a significantly different force, requiring that such a task be activated in one of the ways possible without specifying which way; and generalizes to *reliable execution*: requiring that every enabled task be executed in one of the ways possible. Without this principle, an intention becomes a very weak commitment to action, making it difficult to ensure reaction or reason effectively about the behaviour of plans, of sets of intentions, and thus of agents.

Technically, reliability is a *guarantee property* which requires that certain things do happen, rather than ruling them out. Its adoption means that it is possible to prove that, given a particular set of beliefs, signals and intentions, particular agent computations, and hence actions, will always occur. By contrast, the uncontrolled interleaving of intention execution adopted by other related agent architectures cannot guarantee this, essentially because they do not adequately control and resolve non-determinism that arises when there are multiple plans which may be activated by signals or multiple tasks which may be executed. By failing to, or making poor choices about how to do so, such architectures do not ensure that intended executions actually occur before circumstances change irrevocably. In Ψ such non-determinism can readily be resolved, and a computation sequence which ensures reliability chosen, except in certain cases of error.

An important consequence of reliability is *compositionality*. Informally, this means that the execution of an intention in a given state will be unaffected by the presence of other parallel intentions, except where a set of intentions is in some way inconsistent, i.e., their co-execution is prevented by interference. We have already encountered the possibility that a compound action can be non-executable due to interference between its elements. Interference between the actions (e.g., belief updates) dictated by separate intentions can equally occur, and must somehow be resolved. Compositionality ensures, however, that in the absence of such interference, the behaviour of a compound intention may be understood in terms of the individual behaviours of its components.

Intention execution To construct a reduction system that defines intention execution for the case of simple transitions (those without a trigger), we operate on a partial agent configuration $\psi^2 = \beta : \omega$ containing just belief and intention states. In specifying process reduction rules, we will make much use of syntactic and algebraic structure to distinguish different types of processes. Thus, for example, $\tau + \sigma$ can match any non-null task (as a unary task τ is congruent to $\tau + 0$) but cannot match a compound multiprocess. Similarly, $\tau \times \pi$ can match any multiprocess containing at least one unary task, whereas $\sigma \times \pi$ can match any process, including 0, but $\dot{\sigma} \times \pi$ can only match one containing some task. Such expressions allow rules to non-deterministically select a specific component from a compound process and apply some test or transformation.

Definition 5 (*Simple intention execution*)

The reduction system $\mathcal{R}_{\psi^2} \subset \mathcal{R}_{\Psi}$ is defined by the grammar Γ :

$$\psi^2 ::= \beta : \omega \mid \xi : \sigma \qquad \omega ::= \pi \qquad \pi ::= \phi \mid \pi_1 \times \pi_2 \qquad \phi ::= \sigma \mid \rho \qquad \sigma ::= 0 \mid \tau \mid \sigma_1 + \sigma_2$$

$$\rho ::= !\tau \qquad \tau ::= \chi \cdot \pi \qquad \chi ::= \mathrm{ECA} \qquad \xi ::= S \qquad S ::= \underline{E} \qquad s ::= \underline{e} \qquad \delta ::= \underline{A}$$

$$E ::= \star \mid \dot{E} \qquad \dot{E} ::= e \mid eE \qquad C ::= \star \mid \dot{C} \qquad \dot{C} ::= c \mid cC \qquad A ::= \star \mid \dot{A} \qquad \dot{A} ::= a \mid aA$$

the structural congruence relation $\equiv$ defined by:

$$\pi \times 0 \equiv \pi \qquad \pi_1 \times \pi_2 \equiv \pi_2 \times \pi_1 \qquad \pi_1 \times (\pi_2 \times \pi_3) \equiv (\pi_1 \times \pi_2) \times \pi_3$$

$$\sigma + \sigma \equiv \sigma \qquad \sigma + 0 \equiv \sigma \qquad \sigma_1 + \sigma_2 \equiv \sigma_2 + \sigma_1 \qquad \sigma_1 + (\sigma_2 + \sigma_3) \equiv (\sigma_1 + \sigma_2) + \sigma_3$$

$$E \equiv E\star \qquad ee'E \equiv e'eE \qquad C \equiv C\star \qquad cc'C \equiv c'cC \qquad A \equiv A\star \qquad aa'A \equiv a'aA$$

and the set Ξ of reduction rules:

$$\mathrm{s:} \quad \frac{\exists \theta \, (\, \mathrm{dom}(\theta) = \mathrm{var}(C) \wedge \beta : \xrightarrow{C\theta})}{\beta : \star CA \cdot \pi \xrightarrow{\theta} \star : \star \star A\theta \cdot \pi\theta} \qquad \mathrm{x:} \quad \frac{\beta : \star CA \cdot \pi \xrightarrow{\theta} \star : \tau \qquad \beta \xrightarrow{A\theta} \zeta}{\beta : \star CA \cdot \pi \xrightarrow{A\theta} \zeta : \pi\theta}$$

$$\mathrm{c:} \quad \frac{\beta : \tau \xrightarrow{\alpha} \zeta : \pi}{\beta : \tau + \sigma \xrightarrow{\alpha} \zeta : \pi} \qquad \mathrm{p:} \quad \frac{\beta : \phi \xrightarrow{\alpha} \zeta : \pi}{\beta : \phi \times \omega \xrightarrow{\alpha} \zeta : \pi \times \omega} \qquad \mathrm{r:} \quad \frac{\beta : \tau \xrightarrow{\alpha} \zeta : \pi}{\beta : !\tau \xrightarrow{\alpha} \zeta : !\tau \times \pi}$$

Rule s checks satisfiability of the guard of a transition in the head of a unary task, and rule x combines this test with action execution. Rules c, p, and r allow this reduction to occur beneath the choice, parallel and replication operators. In the first case branches not chosen (σ) are discarded, and in the second parallel intentions (ω) persist unaffected. These rules together define a basic intention execution reduction $\beta : \dot{\pi} \xrightarrow{\alpha} \zeta : \omega$.

Intention activation A key consequence of the reliability principle is to rule out uncontrolled interleaving of intention execution as an acceptable control policy. It also dictates that plan activation should lead to the creation of all possible tasks, while task activation should lead to just one of those possible. The rationale for this is easily seen by considering the case of a plan $! e(\mathrm{x}) \star \star \cdot \pi$. Suppose the events $e(1)$ and $e(2)$, of the same type but with different properties, are signalled on successive cycles. Both will cause plan activation, creating tasks with x instantiated to 1 and 2 respectively. So if by chance the two events are signalled on the same cycle, then both activations should occur. By contrast, if activation is reliable, the task $e(x) \star \star \cdot \pi$ will be activated by the first signal to occur but not by the second, since by then it will already have reduced to $\pi\theta$, hence if they are signalled simultaneously, either but not both activations should occur. Another way to think of this is that a plan with free variables in its activation trigger is equivalent to a parallel composition of all distinct instantiations of these, whereas a corresponding task is equivalent to a choice between all such instantiations.

The key to capturing this semantics formally is to model task activation as a reduction $\sigma \twoheadrightarrow \sigma + \sigma'$ of a task to one whose additional branches represent its possible activations, any one of which may be chosen, and plan activation as a reduction $\rho \twoheadrightarrow \rho \times \pi$ of a plan to one in parallel with its possible activations, all of which may be executed.

Definition 6 (*Intention activation*)

The reduction system $\mathcal{R}_{\Psi^3}$ extends $\mathcal{R}_{\Psi^2}$ to include the signal state ξ and the rules:

$$\text{st:} \quad \frac{X = \mathsf{eECA} \quad \exists\theta \,(\, \mathrm{dom}(\theta) = \mathrm{var}(e) \,\wedge\, s = e\theta\,)}{s : X \cdot \pi \twoheadrightarrow \star : X \cdot \pi + (\mathsf{ECA} \cdot \pi)\theta} \qquad\qquad \text{ut:} \quad \frac{s : \tau \not\twoheadrightarrow}{s : \tau \twoheadrightarrow \star : \tau}$$

$$\text{b:} \quad \frac{s : \tau \twoheadrightarrow \star : \sigma_1 \quad s : \sigma \twoheadrightarrow \star : \sigma_2}{s : (\tau + \sigma) \twoheadrightarrow \star : (\sigma_1 + \sigma_2)} \qquad \text{m:} \quad \frac{s : \sigma \twoheadrightarrow \star : \sigma_1 \quad S : \sigma_1 \twoheadrightarrow^= \star : (\sigma + \sigma_2)}{sS : \sigma \twoheadrightarrow \star : (\sigma + \sigma_2)}$$

$$\psi^3 ::= \xi : \psi^2 \qquad \text{ta:} \quad \frac{\xi : \sigma \twoheadrightarrow \sigma + \sigma_1 + \sum_{i=1}^{n} \tau_i \quad \beta : \sigma_1 \not\twoheadrightarrow \quad \forall \tau_i \,\beta : \tau_i \twoheadrightarrow}{\xi : \beta : \sigma \twoheadrightarrow \star : \beta : \sigma + \sum_{i=1}^{n} \tau_i}$$

$$\text{pa:} \quad \frac{\xi : \beta : \tau \twoheadrightarrow \star : \beta : \tau + \sum_{i=1}^{n} \tau_i}{\xi : \beta : !\tau \twoheadrightarrow \star : \beta : !\tau \times \prod_{i=1}^{n} \tau_i} \qquad \text{a:} \quad \frac{\xi : \beta : \phi \twoheadrightarrow \star : \beta : \pi_1 \quad \xi : \beta : \pi \twoheadrightarrow \star : \beta : \pi_2}{\xi : \beta : \phi \times \pi \twoheadrightarrow \xi : \beta : \pi_1 \times \pi_2}$$

Rules st and ut define successful and unsuccessful *triggering* of a unary task $\tau = X \cdot \pi$ by a single signal s; in the former case the task reduces to a choice between itself and a derivative to which the matching substitution has been applied and whose head has been (perhaps only partially) simplified, in the latter case it remains unchanged. Rule b extends triggering to branching tasks by recursively performing it in parallel on all branches. Unlike typical reductions under choice, all alternatives are retained. Rule m defines multiple triggering, recursively applying all signals in a single step. The branches of the resulting task are, at minimum, just those of the original ($\sigma_2 = 0$) when none of the signals can match any events in the trigger; otherwise, a choice between the original task and all of its (possibly partially) simplified derivatives. For example, letting e and o be distinct events:

$$e(3)\,e(2)\,o() : e(x)\,o()\star a(x) \twoheadrightarrow_m$$
$$\star : e(x)\,o()\star a(x) \;+\; e(x)\star a(x) \;+\; o()\star a(2) \;+\; \star\star a(2) \;+\; o()\star a(3) \;+\; \star\star a(3)$$

Here an unguarded unary task (in fact, a rule $X \cdot 0$ written as X) with a binary trigger is triggered by a compound signal $e(3)\,e(2)\,o()$ which can match it in two distinct ways.

Triggering as defined by these four rules generates a branching task that preserves all possible choices arising from non-determinism due to multiple signals, including the choice "none of the above" represented by the original task. However, it may generate incompletely simplified branches which are not valid choices and must be discarded.

Rule ta defines task activation, lifting triggering into Ψ^3 and filtering out incompletely simplified branches, and those not enabled in the current belief state (not reducible in Ψ^2).

Extending the example to add a guard condition, and assuming $[\![u]\!] = 2$, we obtain:

$$e(3)\,e(2)\,o() : \beta : e(\mathsf{x})\,o()[\mathsf{x} > \mathsf{u}]a(\mathsf{x}) \;\twoheadrightarrow_{\mathsf{ta}}\; \star : \beta : e(\mathsf{x})\,o()[\mathsf{x} > \mathsf{u}]a(\mathsf{x}) \;+\; \star[3 > \mathsf{u}]a(3)$$

i.e., a choice between the original task and its only satisfiable activation. The effect of this rule is to transform a task in one step into one which is a choice between the original and all possible enabled, complete simplifications of any branch of the original. Rule pa defines plan activation, i.e., the behaviour of activation beneath replication. Finally, rule a extends activation to compound multiprocesses by activating all intentions in parallel.

These rules are a remarkable example of the expressive power of reduction systems. The reduction defined by $\mathcal{R}_{\Psi^3}$ is of the general form $\xi : \beta : \dot{\pi} \twoheadrightarrow \star : \beta : \omega$, requiring a non-empty signal state and a non-null intention, is unconditional in this case, and consists in merely consuming the signal state when no matches occur (a vacuous activation). To establish its reliability, three important properties are noteworthy:

Proposition 1 *Activation is deterministic.*
Proof sketch: The two possible sources of non-determinism are the order that branches are considered, and the order in which elements of the signal are matched with triggers. The former is avoided by triggering all branches in parallel, and the latter by the fact that as each matching atomic signal is applied by to a branch by rule s, both the original and its simplification are included in the result, hence the final result is order independent.

Proposition 2 *Activation is monotonic with respect to addition of signals:*
$$\xi : \beta : \sigma \twoheadrightarrow \star : \beta : \sigma_1 \;\wedge\; \xi \subset \xi' \;\Rightarrow\; \exists \sigma_2,\; \xi' : \beta : \sigma \twoheadrightarrow \star : \beta : \sigma_1 + \sigma_2$$
$$\xi : \beta : \rho \twoheadrightarrow \star : \beta : \pi_1 \;\wedge\; \xi \subset \xi' \;\Rightarrow\; \exists \pi_2,\; \xi' : \beta : \rho \twoheadrightarrow \star : \beta : \pi_1 \times \pi_2$$

Proposition 3 *Activation is compositional with respect to choice and parallel:*
$$\xi : \beta : \sigma_1 \twoheadrightarrow \star : \beta : \sigma_3 \;\wedge\; \xi : \beta : \sigma_2 \twoheadrightarrow \star : \beta : \sigma_4 \;\Rightarrow\; \xi : \beta : \sigma_1 + \sigma_2 \twoheadrightarrow \star : \beta : \sigma_3 + \sigma_4.$$
$$\xi : \beta : \pi_1 \twoheadrightarrow \star : \beta : \pi_3 \;\wedge\; \xi : \beta : \pi_2 \twoheadrightarrow \star : \beta : \pi_4 \;\Rightarrow\; \xi : \beta : \pi_1 \times \pi_2 \twoheadrightarrow \star : \beta : \pi_3 \times \pi_4.$$

Proofs of these properties may be established by straightforward structural inductions. Given determinism and the easily established correctness of rule s, the result follows.

Theorem 1 *Activation in $\mathcal{R}_{\Psi^3}$ is reliable.*

The intention execution reduction $\beta : \dot{\pi} \twoheadrightarrow \zeta : \omega$ in $\mathcal{R}_{\Psi^2}$ has rather different properties.

Proposition 4 *Execution in $\mathcal{R}_{\Psi^2}$ is non-deterministic and unreliable.*
Proof: Non-determinism arises because an arbitrary enabled branch of an arbitrary intention is selected under $+$ and $\times$, and because guard elimination itself is potentially non-deterministic. Unreliability arises because at most one enabled intention is executed.

Perhaps unsurprisingly, reliable execution is impossible to ensure in the general case.

Proposition 5 *No universally reliable execution reduction exists.*
Proof: The process $\mathsf{u} := 1 \cdot 0 \times \mathsf{u} := 2 \cdot 0$ can never be reliably executed.

This process constitutes a simplest *inconsistent intention state*, where an inherent conflict between actions prevents reliable intention execution. We consider such a situation to be a specification error. But can reliable execution be achieved when there is no such unavoidable conflict? Although space limitations preclude a proof here, the answer is yes. To do so requires a more complex intention execution policy, one which can intelligently resolve the several sources of non-determinism aand potential conflicts that can arise.

3.2 Agent Computation

Having defined the semantics of intention activation and individual intention execution, we can now assemble a framework for agent computation based upon these reductions, extending the configuration to include the response state and the event and action queues.

Definition 7 (*Agent computation system* $\mathcal{R}_\Psi$)

The agent computation system $\mathcal{R}_\Psi$ extends $\mathcal{R}_{\Psi^3}$ with the following rules:

$$\psi ::= \psi^6 \mid \psi^4 \mid \psi^3 \mid \psi^2 \qquad \psi^6 ::= Q_E : \psi^4 : Q_A \qquad Q_E ::= \underline{E_e}^* \qquad Q_A ::= \underline{A_e}^*$$

$$\psi^4 ::= \psi^3 : \delta \qquad \text{min:} \ \frac{\xi : \beta : \pi \twoheadrightarrow^= \ \star : \beta : \pi_1 \quad \beta : \pi_1 \xrightarrow{A} \zeta : \omega \quad \beta \xrightarrow{\delta \cup A}}{\xi : \beta : \pi : \delta \longrightarrow \star : \beta : \omega : \delta \cup A}$$

$$\text{int:} \ \frac{\xi : \beta : \pi : \star \longrightarrow \star : \beta : \omega : \delta \quad \beta \xrightarrow{\delta} \zeta \quad E = \delta \cap \mathcal{L}_{E_i} \quad A = \delta \cap \mathcal{L}_{A_e}}{Q_E : \xi : \beta : \pi : \delta_0 : Q_A \xrightarrow{A} Q_E : E : \zeta : \omega : \delta : Q_A \otimes \langle A \rangle}$$

$$\text{obs:} \ \frac{\beta \xrightarrow{E} \zeta}{\langle E \rangle \otimes Q_E : \xi : \beta : \omega : \delta : Q_A \longrightarrow Q_E : \xi \cup E : \zeta : \omega : \delta : Q_A}$$

Rule int defines an entire computation cycle, lifting reductions of ψ^4, performing belief update on the basis of the response state δ, placing any external actions on the action queue and extracting and directly signalling any new internal events. Rule obs performs *observation*, taking a group of perceived events from the event queue, performing their epistemic effects and signalling them. Here, there are no constraints on when observation occurs and some *observation policy* is likely required; two possibilities are that it should only occur when the signal state is empty, i.e., no internal events have occurred on the previous cycle, or when in addition there are no enabled intentions; such constraints may easily be imposed by adding appropriate premises to rule obs.

Reduction in ψ^4, here defined by the single rule min, constitutes an agent's control policy for internal computation, determining when and which intention activations and executions occur. Rule min defines a typical *minimal* execution policy which composes activation of all intentions with execution of just one. Such a policy, while widespread amongst existing agent architectures, has undesirable properties.

Proposition 6 *Every control policy based on minimal execution is unreliable.*

Proof: The consistent process $[u > 0]\{u := 0, u_1 := 1\} \cdot 0 \times [u > 0]\{u := 0, u_2 := 2\} \cdot 0$ can never (when enabled) be reliably executed by a minimal execution policy.

The problem here is not inconsistency of the intention state, but a lack of serializability which arises because whichever intention is executed first immediately disables the other. Yet disabling the condition which activates such condition-action rules is crucial for their correct behaviour, to avoid their being repeatedly activated in successive states. Both intentions are individually correct, their actions are consistent, and they could both be executed, but not by any minimal policy, which, no matter how it selects enabled intentions, requires that guards are re-evaluated after each and every action.

The system $\mathcal{R}_\Psi$ above can serve as a basis for a variety of systems employing different control policies, specified by adding suitable rules to replace rules min and obs. There are many distinct policies possible for both computation and observation, and the choice made has profound effects upon the intention execution semantics. Elsewhere, we have formally defined reliability and notions of intentions consistency, explored which types of policies can guarantee desirable semantic properties such as reliability under what circumstances, and constructed ones which can achieve reliable agent computation whenever it is possible. Space limitations unfortunately prevent an exposition of these more complex policies here; the details may be found in [9].

Comparison, Conclusions and Future Work

The most important ways in which Ψ extends and generalizes the architectures which are its direct ancestors, PRS and dMARS, are as follows.

- It provides triggered, guarded action as a primitive which can appear anywhere in an intention. In PRS and dMARS triggers cannot be compound and occur only in the initial transitions of plans, which also lack an action, and transitions in plan bodies may be guards or actions but not guarded actions. Guarded action allows intentions in Ψ to implement synchronization constructs such as semaphores and regions directly, and the ability to wait for events at points within intentions permits a flexible style of communication and coordination between intentions not previously possible.
- By allowing but not requiring epistemic effects (belief updates) to be associated with individual external events, Ψ enables both the *direct update* style of observation of PRS, and the *indirect update* style of observation of dMARS, where new external events have no effect other than to activate intentions. The former is more efficient, whereas the latter allows flexible control of if, how and when belief updates occur.
- In Ψ the event queue is a sequence of sets of events, allowing simultaneity of events to be preserved without requiring the introduction of timestamps, and allowing their subsequent processing to occur in unison. Compound triggers allow the detection by intentions of simultaneous events. In dMARS and many other architectures the event queue is a sequence of events, i.e., an arbitrary order is imposed on simultaneously perceived events. In PRS all events in the event queue are processed on each cycle, so there is no possibility of controlling when observation and belief update occurs. Both these approaches can lead to many subtle sources of error [9].
- Ψ provides a uniform treatment of plans and tasks as types of intentions, treating plan and task activation as related cases of intention execution. Unlike PRS and dMARS, it also allows them to contain embedded plans and parallel processes. Embedded plans are useful for building recognizers for *episodes* – complex sequences of events and conditions – and embedded parallel operators allow a direct expression of concurrent computations at the programming level.

Beyond these differences, Ψ has an operational semantics for all aspects of agent computation, from basic transition execution to the top-level control cycle, defined compactly and uniformly, whereas PRS and dMARS have no operational semantics other than partial, simplified treatments [3, 16]. This permits both verifying the correctness of a Ψ implementation and formal reasoning about the behaviour of Ψ agents.

More distantly related agent languages such as ConGolog [5], 3APL [7], SCS [10] and Vivid [18] also have a complete operational semantics, but it is expressed in ways that cannot concisely and lucidly capture all the complexities of reactive and goal-directed plan execution. They also impose architectural or language constraints absent in Ψ, and generally employ computation policies based on uncontrolled interleaving of intentions that lead directly to unreliability, in the sense we have defined it here. 3APL, for example, lacks guarded action, has only PRS-style direct update perception, employs a minimal computation policy for execution of reactive rules, hence activation is unreliable, and solves the intention selection problem by assuming the existence of an ordering over the (infinite) space of possible tasks and plans. Vivid, by contrast, allows guarded action and avoids minimalism, but permits only one-step rules, requires a similar fixed preference ordering over them, and avoids interference problems by requiring that the effects of all actions commute.

Viewed abstractly, Ψ is a broadcast calculus with shared mutable state and buffered asynchronous interfaces for perception of and action upon an external environment. Its semantics is specified, not in a typical logic framework, but in a uniform, algebraic style as is traditional in concurrency theory [12, 13], which may help to make the study of plan execution systems accessible to a wider audience in Computer Science. The semantics of computation in Ψ, defined by reduction systems, is kept quite separate from the program of a particular agent, captured by its plans. In contrast, 3APL allows and even relies upon an agent's program, captured by a set of rules, to override the natural execution semantics of intentions in order to perform basic execution functions such as means-end reasoning and failure handling, which are absent from the language itself and hence must be implemented by the programmer. While expressive, this approach provides a less abstract programming environment, and means that the semantics of a 3APL program is defined in a non-compositional way by a part of the program itself, opening the door to many possibilities for unreliability and programmer error.

Ψ provides a framework in which the semantics of a general class of plan-based agent programming languages may be specified, and variants evaluated. We hope that it will provide a basis for our and others' research in this area. We have presented here its fundamental structures, assumptions and constraints, and defined reduction systems which capture a particular semantics for intention activation and execution. Activation has desirable semantic properties such as reliability and compositionality, whereas the minimal execution policy presented here, on account of its simplicity, does not. Elsewhere [9], we have defined more sophisticated execution policies which achieve these properties whenever it is possible, and shown how the semantics of more abstract language concepts such as subgoals, maintenance conditions and exceptions can be specified in terms of the basic language presented here. A reference implementation of Ψ is being developed, and research is being undertaken on the analysis and formal verification of Ψ programs.

Acknowledgements

Thanks to Frank Dignum, Bob Kowalski and Chris Wright for their feedback and suggestions, and especially to Noriko Hayashi and Liz Sonenberg for their unfailing encouragement and support.

References

1. Michael E. Bratman. *Intentions, Plans, and Practical Reason*. Harvard University Press, 1987.
2. N. Dershowitz and J.-P. Jouannaud. Rewrite systems. In J. van Leeuwen, editor, *Handbook of Theoretical Computer Science Vol. B*, pages 243–320. MIT Press/Elsevier, 1990.
3. M. d'Inverno, D. Kinny, M. Luck, and M. Wooldridge. A formal specification of dMARS. In *Intelligent Agents IV: Proceedings of ATAL-97*, Providence, RI, 1997. Springer LNAI 1365.
4. Michael P. Georgeff and Felix Ingrand. Decision-making in an embedded reasoning system. In *Proceedings of IJCAI-89*, pages 972–978, Detroit, MI, 1989.
5. G. De Giacomo, Y. Lesperance, and H. J. Levesque. ConGolog, a concurrent programming language based on the situation calculus. *Artificial Intelligence*, 121:109–169, 2000.
6. D. Harel and C. Kahana. On statecharts with overlapping. *ACM Transactions on Software Engineering and Methodology*, 1(4), 1992.
7. Koen V. Hindriks, Frank S. de Boer, Wiebe van der Hoek, and John-Jules Ch. Meyer. Control structures of rule-based agent languages. In *Intelligent Agents V: Proceedings of ATAL-98*, pages 381–396, Paris, 1998. Springer LNAI 1555.
8. David Kinny. *The Distributed Multi-Agent Reasoning System Architecture and Language Specification*. Australian Artificial Intelligence Institute, Melbourne, Australia, 1993.
9. David Kinny. *Fundamentals of Agent Computation Theory: Semantics*. PhD thesis, Department of Computer Science, University of Melbourne, Australia, 2001.
10. Jaeho Lee and Edmund H. Durfee. On explicit plan languages for coordinating multiagent plan execution. In *Intelligent Agents IV: Proceedings of ATAL-97*, pages 113–126, Providence, RI, 1997. Springer LNAI 1365.
11. Zohar Manna and Amir Pnueli. *The Temporal Logic of Reactive and Concurrent Systems*. Springer Verlag, 1992.
12. Jœse Meseguer. Conditional rewriting logic as a unified model of concurrency. *Theoretical Computer Science*, 96(1):73–155, 1992.
13. Robin Milner. The polyadic π-calculus: A tutorial. Technical Report LFCS report 91-180, University of Edinburgh, Edinburgh, 1991.
14. G. Plotkin. A structural approach to operational semantics. Technical Report DAIMI FN-19, Aarhus University, 1981.
15. K. V. S. Prasad. A calculus of broadcasting systems. *Science of Computer Programming*, 25, 1995.
16. Anand Rao. AgentSpeak(L): BDI agents speak out in a logical computable language. In *Agents Breaking Away: Proceedings of MAAMAW '96*, Eindhoven, The Netherlands, 1996. Springer LNAI 1038.
17. Anand S. Rao and Michael P. Georgeff. Modeling rational agents within a BDI-architecture. In *Proceedings of the Second International Conference on Principles of Knowledge Representation and Reasoning, KR '91*, pages 473–484, Cambridge, MA, 1991.
18. Gerd Wagner. A logical and operational model of scalable knowledge- and perception-based agents. In *Agents Breaking Away: Proceedings of MAAMAW '96*, pages 26–41, Eindhoven, The Netherlands, 1996. Springer LNAI 1038.
19. Jennifer Widom and Stefano Ceri. *Active Database Systems*. Morgan Kaufmann, 1996.

An Argument-Based Agent System with KQML as an Agent Communication Language

Yoshirou Toda, Masashi Yamashita, and Hajime Sawamura

Department of Information Engineering and Graduate School of
Science and Technology, Niigata University
8050, 2-cho, Ikarashi, Niigata, 950-2181 Japan
{toda,masashi,sawamura}@cs.ie.niigata-u.ac.jp

Abstract. Argumentation = Computation + Communication (A = 2C). Argumentation is a novel and prominent apparatus to attain both communication and computation in a unifying manner since they are intrinsically related to each other. In this paper, we propose an argument-based agent system which has two unique features: (i) Reconciliation in argumentation based on the dialectical logics, and (ii) Cooperation in argumentation. In doing so, we introduce KQML-like agent communication language which is augmented by some performatives proper to the communication with which agents can make arguments, better or stronger arguments, and make cooperation to reach an agreement. We evaluate our system using argumentative dialogues.

Keywords: argumentation, agent, dialectics, dialectical logic, Aufheben, KQML

1 Introduction

There have been many approaches to building multi-agent systems [6]. Among other things, we have been promoting argumentation as a basic and uniform mechanism for both computation and communication among interacting agents [17,18,22,16]. We have viewed argumentation as yielding a social computing paradigm that is a most primary concern in agent-oriented computing [22]. More specifically, argumentation is inherently closely related to the following concepts that are all essential in agent-oriented computing [17,22,16].

- Negotiation, compromise, concession, cooperation, coordination, collaboration, conflict resolution, consensus attainment, etc. supporting a societal view of computation
- Interaction among agents
- Reasoning method for agents
- Resolution method of conflict, difference and contradiction

Argumentation is tolerant of inconsistencies in the world as well as in data and knowledge base, in contrast to traditional logics. This is extremely suitable for dealing with the computer-networked world as well as our actual and dynamic world, in which our knowledge is incomplete, contradictory, not closed,

S.-T. Yuan and M. Yokoo (Eds.): PRIMA 2001, LNAI 2132 , pp. 48–62, 2001.

distributed, always changing, developing and so on. The more closely and widely our world is informationalized and interconnected by the computer network with the advance of the internet, the more conflicts emerges. Reaching an agreement or understanding through argumentation is a most important aspect of decision making in our real society. This would not be exceptional in a virtual society as well, which is now very rapidly being formed over the computer network. As a matter of fact, much attention has been paid to argumentation by researchers in computer science [9,13,12,17,18,22,16] as well as by informal logicians, philosophers, linguists, sociologist and so on [1,5,19,14].

It is also the case that the concept and phenomena expressed in terms of conflict, contradiction, opposite, difference, etc. in thought, nature, and society are the motive force both of natural and of human history, leading to a further phase of development. That is, they play the central role in the logical development of thought or reality through thesis and antithesis to a synthesis of these opposites if borrowed from Hegel [4]. The Hegelian dialectic accepts the contradiction as a real aspect of the world, which is continually overcome and continually renews itself in the process of change. In agents' world, therefore, we should pay attention to the most important aspects of Hegelian dialectics such as (1) Aufheben through synthesis from thesis and antithesis and (2) the law of the negation of the negation as a development process of thought, reality (nature, history), etc. where an operational force of development is viewed as negation. Negation plays a role of destruction and amplified renewal that lead to something better and more various (see Figure 1 for these interrelated aspects of dialectics).

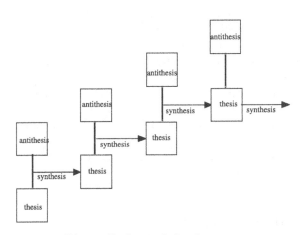

Fig. 1. Dialectical development

It should be noted that in the recent books of computer science [11,20], we can observe the similar thought to us, "The term 'conflict' induces negative feelings in human contexts. Conflicts produce uncertainty and fear, and people interpret conflicts as harassment or at least as something unpleasant which should better not occur. Most people are proud of having no conflicts at all, because then they are in balance with their environment. However, the evolution of people, teams, and organizations needs conflicts. Most of the radical changes in the human society stem directly from massive conflicts. Hence, conflict avoidance is not always the best choice. Conflicts might also be seen as a chance for improvement and as an indication for invoking learning processes."

The paper is organized as follows. In Section 2, we describe two basic components of our argument-based agent system. One is a dialectical reasoning method based on the dialectical logics **DL** and **DM** by Routley and Meyer [15], which attains an agreement by allowing for changing issues alternatively. The other is KQML-like agent communication language [7][2] that allows agents to make flexible communication in cooperating with other agents as well as argumentation. In Section 3, we propose the argumentation protocol with the two components above integrated. In Section 4, we illustrate applications of the system to a contemporary topic using an argumentative dialogue in e-commerce, and an argumentative but cooperative conversation. Final section includes concluding remarks and future work that need further deep insights.

2   Two Basic Components of the Argument-Based Agent System that Allows for Issue Changes

Arguments usually proceeds with mutually casting arguments and counterarguments constructed under each agent's knowledge base, and result in 'justified' (sort of 'win') or 'overruled' (sort of 'lose') of the either side [9,13,18,22]. In addition to such a simple structure of argumentation, we are further concerned with the following aspects of argumentation which can be seen in our ordinary argumentation very often: (i) (Reconciliation in argumentation) if an argument has not been settled, it might be better or necessary for the both sides to attain an agreement (consensus) satisfactory to some extent rather than leaving it unsettled, and (ii) (Cooperation in argumentation) if an agent can not make arguments or counter-arguments due to the lack or insufficiency of his knowledge, he can call for cooperation so that he can supply his lacking knowledge from other agents.

For (ii) we introduce KQML-like communication language among agents in the subsection 2.1, and for (i) we introduce dialectics in the subsections 2.2 and 2.3.

2.1   KQML with Performatives for Arguing Agents

KQML (Knowledge Query and Manipulation Language) [7] aims at a high-level communication standard based on speech acts. It allows cognitive and deliberate agents to cooperate.

For argumentation, we added to KQML some performatives proper to the communication with which agents can make arguments, better or stronger arguments, and make cooperation to reach an agreement. The performatives of

KQML that have been most useful in our argument-based agent system are *stream-about, stream-all, tell, eos and sorry.*

- *stream-about*: This is used when an agent wishes to ask other agents multiple responses in order to supply lacking knowledge that might be useful for making counterarguments.
- *stream-all*: This is used when an agent wishes to ask other agents multiple responses in order to make his incomplete knowledge complete, with which he could not make counterarguments.
- *tell*: This is used when agents tell answers to the requests by stream-about and stream-all.
- *eos*: This denotes the end of a sequence of responses by *tell.*
- *sorry*: This is used when agents can not supply any information to the requests by stream-about and stream-all.

In addition, we introduced some specially tailored KQML-like performatives proper to the progress and the acceptability of argumentation.

- *start*: This is a performative for initiating an argument.
- *argue-for*: An agent puts forward an argument.
- *argue-against*: An agent makes a counterargument to the issue or counterargument put forward from other parties.
- *backtrack*: An agent makes a counterargument to the past argument.
- *abandon*: An agent gets the issue abandoned when he could not make a counterargument to the counterargument from other parties.
- *agree*: An agent agrees the argument from other parties when the argument can be also made in terms of his own knowledge.
- *accept*: An agent accepts the argument from other parties when he cannot make a counterargument to it, reaching an understanding.

Figure 2 illustrates an example of a KQML message which has been sent to *Jiro* from *Taro* in reply to the message *abc*, in order to call for knowledge of the form $c < -X$. In Section 4, we illustrate argumentative example in which these performatives are effectively used.

2.2 Dialectical Principles for Reconciling Argumentation

The dialectical logics **DL** and **DM** by Routley and Meyer [15] possesses some preferable properties. For example, the absolute consistency, three fundamental principles for logic by Aristotle: (1) $A = A$ (Law of identity), (2) $\neg(A \wedge \neg A)$ (Law of contradiction) and (3) $A \vee \neg A$ (Law of the excluded middle). Furthermore, the following properties are held as proper requirements for dialectical logics.

- The refusal of the proposition $A \wedge \neg A \to B$ (ex falso quodlibet [3]).

> performative stream-all
>
> : sender Taro
> : receiver Jiro
> : ontology car
> : reply-with null
> : in-reply-to abc
> : aspect X
> : content c <- X
> : language Prolog

Fig. 2. A KQML message

- The refusal of the proposition $A \rightarrow \neg\neg A$ (required only in **DM**). This rejection reflects the law of the negation of the negation by Engels [4], satisfying that $A \neq \neg A \neq \neg\neg A \neq \neg\neg\neg A \neq \neg\neg\neg\neg A \neq \cdots$.
- The admissibility of the proposition $p_0 \wedge \neg p_0$, for some propositional constants p_0 such as 'God exist' and 'God do not exist'.

2.3   Elementary Dialectical Inference Rules on Top of DL and DM

We here give a breath of dynamism to the static dialectical logics, **DL** and **DM** above by introducing the following elementary dialectical inference rules with Aufheben flavor, as to the logical connective $\wedge$ (similarly for other connectives). These dialectical inference rules play a significant role in the argumentation protocol of the argument-based agent system that allows for issue changes.

- $\vdash A , \vdash \neg A \Rightarrow \vdash A$
- $\vdash A , \vdash \neg A \Rightarrow \vdash \neg A$
- $\vdash A \wedge B , \vdash \neg B \Rightarrow \vdash A \wedge \neg B$
- $\vdash A \wedge \neg B , \vdash \neg A \wedge B \Rightarrow \vdash A \wedge B$

Readers might have noticed that they are considered to represent sort of compromise, concession, reconciliation and so on that constitute a part of the important computational concepts for multi-agent systems (cooperation, coordination, collaboration, competitiveness, conflict management, etc. are others). Generally these may be considered as elementary dialectical inferences in the sense that the consequent are sort of syntheses from confrontational antecedents: thesis and antithesis. We can also observe similar concepts of Aufheben in other more specific terms such as sublime, enlightenment in Buddhism, nirvana in Sanskrit (meaning 'isolate oneself from all trouble'), etc. Here we situate the significances of those dialectical inferences above by introducing the comprehensive definitions for Aufheben as follows.

Definition 1 (Aufheben). *Given two conflicting propositions, A and B, a proposition C is said to be a higher-order agreement (Aufheben) lifted up from A and B (diagrammatically see Figure 3) if (i) neither ⊢ A → C nor ⊢ B → C, and (ii) C shares some atomic propositions with A or B.*

The condition (i) is placed to represent that the content of the synthesis from the thesis and antithesis in the dialectical inference is supposed to be logically richer than the thesis and antithesis alone. The condition (ii) is placed to represent the relevance of the thesis and antithesis to the synthesis, similarly to the variable sharing property in relevant logics [3].

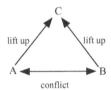

Fig. 3. Aufheben

For example, $Java \wedge Prolog$ is an agreement lifted up from the conflicting propositions, $Java \wedge Lisp$ and $Prolog$, assuming $Lisp = \neg Prolog$. Actually, it is not the case that ⊢ $Java \wedge Lisp \rightarrow Java \wedge Prolog$ and ⊢ $Prolog \rightarrow Java \wedge Prolog$ in the dialectical logics DL and DM, and even in classical logic. Note that the Aufheben shares the atomic propositions $Java$ and $Prolog$ with the two contradictory propositions respectively.

Definition 2 (Weaker Aufheben). *Given two conflicting propositions, A and B, a proposition C is said to be a higher-order agreement (compromise, concession, etc.) lifted up from A and B if it is not the case that ⊢ A → C and it is the case that ⊢ B → C, or it is the case that ⊢ A → C and it is not the case that ⊢ B → C, and C shares some atomic propositions with A or B.*

3   The Argumentation Protocol

Taking into account two components described in the previous section, we will describe the argumentation protocol that allows to manage, control, and mediate arguments.

The argumentation protocol described below proceeds following two logics: the logic of the extended logic programming [13] with which arguments and counterarguments are made, possibly producing contradictory propositions (see Figure 4 for an example of argument process), and the dialectical logics above where existence of conflicting arguments are justified from scratch and they turn out to trigger dialectical reasoning.

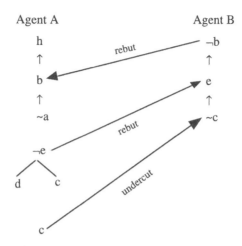

Fig. 4. An argument process by Prakken and Sartor

The argumentation protocol also allows for reaching an understanding with other agents concerned, through argumentative dialogue. Reaching an understanding is attained by allowing for changing issues to be settled alternatively. The final issue (consensus) is agreed by agents under the dialectical inferences of **DL** and **DL**.

For simplicity, we describe the argumentation protocol only for arguments between three agents in this paper. It consists of three phases: (i) Phase 1: proposing an issue (agenda) and making Aufheben or weak Aufheben if needed, (ii) Phase 2: making an argument or counterargument. As to the second phase, we basically follow our former paper [21] [22], and Phase 3: Calling for knowledge for counterarguments. These three phases are interleaved each other as follows.

[Phase 1: Proposing an issue (agenda) and making Aufheben or weak Aufheben]

Step 1 An issue (agenda) to be settled is first passed to Agent a.

Step 2 Agent a tries to make an argument for the issue. If it succeeds, then go to Step 3 to start arguing with another agent Agent b. Otherwise, Agent a attempts to make Aufheben or Weaker Aufheben by incorporating Agent b's desire. If it succeeds, then Agent a tries to make an argument for this new issue, and go to Step 3, otherwise if Agent a and Agent b have failed in making a new issue consecutively, then the system terminates in the failure of this negotiation, else Agent a passes her/his right of proposing a new issue to Agent b, and go to Step 4.

Step 3 Letting Agent a be a proponent and Agent b an opponent, invoke the **Phase 2**. As the result, if Agent a's argument for the issue is justified, then the issue becomes a final agreement between Agent a and Agent b, and the system terminates. If the issue is overruled, then Agent b can have a right to make a new proposal.

Step 4 Agent b tries to make an argument for the issue. If it succeeds, then Agent b tries to make an argument for the issue, and go to Step 5. Otherwise Agent b attempts to make Aufheben or Weaker Aufheben by incorporating Agent a's desire. If it succeeds, then Agent b tries to make an argument for the issue, and go to Step 5, otherwise if Agent a and Agent b have failed in making a new issue consecutively, then the system terminates in the failure of this negotiation, else Agent b passes her/his right of proposing a new issue to Agent a, and go to Step 6.

Step 5 Letting Agent b be a proponent and Agent a an opponent, invoke the **Phase 2**. As the result, if Agent b's argument for the issue is justified, then the issue becomes a final agreement between Agent a and Agent b, and the system terminates. If the issue is overruled, then Agent a can have a right to make a new propose.

Step 6 Repeat from Step 2 to Step 5.

[Phase 2: Making an argument or counterargument]

Step 1 The issue is passed to the opponent.

Step 2 The opponent analyzes the issue that the proponent desires.

Step 3 The opponent examines if s/he can agree with the issue. If so, the issue is viewed as justified and return to the corresponding step of the **Phase 1**. Otherwise, go to Step 4.

Step 4 The opponent tries to make a counterargument for the issue. If it succeeds or **Phase 3** leads to the success, go to Step 5, else the issue is viewed as justified and return to the corresponding step of the **Phase 1**.

Step 5 The proponent tries to make a counterargument for the counterargument. If it fails or **Phase 3** leads to the failure, then the issue is viewed as overruled and return to the corresponding step of the **Phase 1**, else go to Step 4.

[Phase 3: Calling for knowledge for making counterarguments]

Step 1 An agent calls for knowledge usable to make counterarguments, to other agents.

Step 2 If the agent can obtain the knowledge, Phase 3 successfully terminates. Otherwise Phase 3 fails.

The system has been implemented in Java for the part of the communication control among agents, and in Prolog for the part of the construction of arguments and counterarguments. It is, however, not easy for us to follow and debug argument processes made by the above argumentation protocol since it is apt to produce complicated argument flows. We have developed a subsystem for the argument-based agent system so that argument processes taken into account issue changes are visualized. In Figure 5, the lower right window displays two argument process trees in which the issue and its argument located in the top node of the left tree has changed into the right one, and the upper window displays an argument tree located in a node of argument process tree.

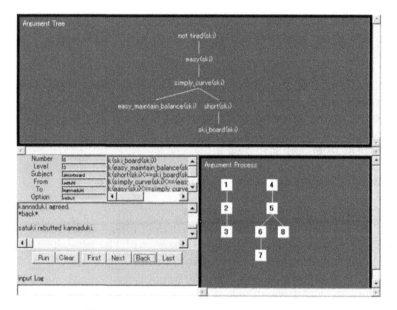

Fig. 5. Visualizing an argument process

4   Argumentative Dialogue Examples

We have dealt with various kinds of realistic argument examples that cannot go well without dialectical resolution, and are not easy for us to foresee which side is predominant, immediately from the knowledge bases. They include an argument on right and wrong or propriety of the nuclear power plant, an argument on design choices occurring in the software design, an argument on the scheduling of the time and place for a meeting, a traveling salesman agent who negotiates by argumentation, and so on.

Here we specifically describe an application to E-Commerce of our agent system with dialectical reasoning. It would be an intriguing question how the argument-based agent system can be applied to such a contemporary topic as electronic commerce with a high demand. Let us consider the following argumentative dialogue between a salesclerk and a customer at a PC shop.

(Issue) Customer: I want to buy a pc with 700 Mhz cpu ($1,500) and a 17-inch monitor ($500).

(Counterargument) Salesclerk: That type of a pc is now out of stock.

Customer: No counterargument and hence the issue is overruled.

(Issue change) Salesclerk: What about a popular 19-inch monitor ($1,500) and a pc with 600 Mhz cpu ($600)?

(Counterargument) Customer: The total price is two high and I can't afford it.

Salesclerk: No counterargument and hence the issue is overruled.

(Issue compromised) Customer: I will take such a combination of a pc with 600 Mhz cpu (a part of the customer's original desire) and a 17-inch monitor (a part of the clerks suggestion) because it does not exceed my estimate.

Salesclerk: No counterargument and the customers issue has been justified. Both will be happy, reaching an agreement!

What they have attained in the argumentative dialogue is such a dialectical agreement, CPU(600Mhz)∧Monitor(17inch) that

(i) not ⊢ CPU(700Mhz) ∧ Monitor(17inch) → CPU(600Mhz) ∧ Monitor(17inch) and

(ii) not ⊢ CPU(600Mhz) ∧ Monitor(19inch) → CPU(600Mhz) ∧ Monitor(17inch),

subject to the variable sharing condition. Diagrammatically, we depict it as in Figure 6.

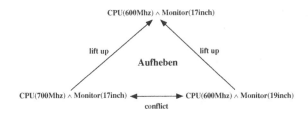

Fig. 6. Forming a dialectical agreement (Aufheben)

Next, we illustrate a cooperative conversation in which two agents, Kannazuki and Satsuki talk about which is enjoyable, skiing or snowboarding, and then another agent, Megumi helps Satsuki with some knowledge. The dialogue proceeds as follows.

1. Kannazuki talks to Satsuki that snowboarding is safer than skiing because we do not need ski poles and hence allow us a free hand.

2. Satsuki simply has believed that snowboarding is dangerous without having any reason. So, he asks his friend Megumi why it is dangerous.

3. Megumi knows the reason and tells Satsuki that snowboarding is dangerous because people suffer injuries to the head very often.

4. Megumi tells Satsuki that this is all she knows.

5. Satsuki retorts against Kannazuki in terms of his knowledge united with Megumi's knowledge.

6. Kannazuki overrules his argument because he cannot make a counterargument to Satsuki's counterargument. 7. Satsuki talks to Kannazuki that skiing is easier than snowboarding because it is easy for us to walk and glide on two skis. (an issue change)

8. Kannazuki retorts against Satsuki that it is cumbersome for us to carry pairs of skis and ski poles and hence we get tired from skiing.

9. Satsuki again asks Megumi because he cannot make a counterargument to Kannazuki's counterargument.

10. Megumi tells Satsuki that we do not get tired from skiing because ski binding is easy to handle.

11. Megumi also tells Satsuki that we do not get tired from skiing because there are various types of skis such as curving skis, short skis and so on.

12. Megumi tells Satsuki that these are all she knows.

13. Satsuki successfully makes a counterargument with the first knowledge from Megumi in 10. above.

14. Kannazuki argues against this, saying that a snowboard has an easy to handle step-in binding.

15. Satsuki cannot argue against this, and backtracks to the past argument to which he can make a counterargument with the second knowledge obtained from Megumi in 11. above.

16. Kannazuki cannot argue against this, and finally accepts Satsuki's argument (see Figure 7 for the overall communication flow of this polylogue).

In this argumentative conversation, Satsuki reaches an understanding with Kannazuki, with the help of Megumi's knowledge without which Satsuki could not continue arguing with Kannazuki.

5   Limitations and Reflections

Dialectics is worthy to challenge but not an easy subject both philosophically and computationally. It would be informative to see other different types of dialectical phenomena that can be seen in everyday life very often but have not been dealt with in the manner of this paper, and hence discuss their possible solutions.

Example 1. A strip of comics by Tomato appeared in the Japanese newspaper.
Child: I want to keep a parrot.
Grandfather: A hen is better because it lays eggs.
Child and Grandfather: A parrot, a hen, a parrot, a hen (a conflict forever)
Grandmother: As a compromise, what about a parrot mocking a hen?

This suggests us that for such a dialectical proposal, agents and we have to have a versatile knowledge and experience that can persuade them to mutually accept it.

Example 2. Kowalski's reconciliation example [8].
The issue is concerned with the composition of a new resources committee. Two

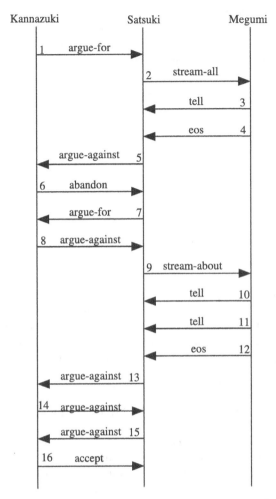

Fig. 7. Communications flow-chart of the argumentative and cooperative dialogue

conflicting arguments are put forward by the director of administration and the director of research.

(i)The director of administration says composition of resources-c is of type non-elected for efficiency (denoted as $\neg A(a)$).

(ii)The director of research says composition of resources-c is of type elected for democracy (denoted as $A(a)$).

Then we could have such a reconciliation (after a (possibly) long argument) as

- Resources-c administers resources (denoted as E),
- Composition of resources-c is of type non-elected (denoted as $\neg A(a)$),
- Head-of-sections-c makes policy about resources (denoted as D), and

- Composition of head-of-sections-c is of type elected (denoted as A(b)).
We can depict this reconciliation like in Figure 8, where $(\neg A(a) \wedge E) \wedge (A(b) \wedge D)$
is an agreement lifted up from $\neg A(a)$ and $A(a)$ in the sense of our Definition
1. Actually, it is not the case that $\vdash \neg A(a) \rightarrow \neg A(a) \wedge E \wedge A(b) \wedge D$ and
$A(a) \rightarrow \neg A(a) \wedge E \wedge A(b) \wedge D$ in the dialectical logics DL and DM, and even in
classical logic.

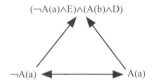

Fig. 8. Kowalski's example

Such an Aufheben is beyond the forms of the dialectical inference rules taken
up in this paper. Hence we now can have no justification for it, although it lies
within our definition. In order to reach such a kind of consensus, agents will need
the ability to further understand the problem and acquire the deeper knowledge
surrounding the problem, via dialogue, and uncover deeper and more meaningful
issues.

6   Concluding Remarks and Future Work

We have proposed an argument-based agent system featuring (i) reconciliation
in argumentation and (ii) cooperation in argumentation. For (i), we based the
dialectical logics **DL** and **DM**. For (ii), we introduced KQML agent communication language with some performatives added for argumentation that allowed
for a flexible communication among arguing agents. The illustrative example
showed its potential and practical usefulness.

There are many important directions to be pursued further. We will touch
upon some of them.

Social validation As far as we confine ourselves to logical dialectics, validation
of dialectical conclusions is guaranteed. However, this is not sufficient for agents
situated in an environment interacting with other agents. The problem of social
validation emerges and we are particularly interested in formulating it in relation
to argumentation.

Nature of opposites, conflicts and differences All the logics mentioned
above are only concerned with negation-inconsistency in the sense of strict opposites. As a matter of course, there seems to be opposites with other meanings,
as discussed in [10], where the principle of the unity of opposites is interpreted

in six ways. Likewise, there can be seen many aspects of conflicts in the daily life, which are not necessarily of the sense in formal logics [11]. Being influenced by these insights, we think that we have to proceed to computational dialectics that takes into account these concepts, for a fruitful theory and practice of argument-based agent with dialectics.

various aspects of cooperation Actually, there are so many aspects and situations in which cooperation is involved (see [22] for the other use of cooperation). We will make cooperation more versatile in the framework of argumentation as a next step. Then, it would be an important question how agents can beg cooperation and to whom. For this, we would need to introduce an agent society and agent relationship in it, or a way to discover the existence of other agents who can cooperate, through a directory agent, broker agent, and so on.

Acknowledgements

We are grateful to R. Meyer, J. Slaney, R. Gore and J. Lloyd of Computer Sciences Laboratory, Research School of Information Sciences and Engineering, Australian National University for their invaluable discussions and our research collaborations.

References

1. Benthem, J. van et al. (eds.): *Logic and Argumentation*, Proc. of the Colloquium 'Logic and Argumentation', Royal Netherlands Academy of Arts and Sciences, 1994. 49
2. Chang, M. K. and Woo, C. C.: *A Speech-Act based Negotiation Protocol: Design, Implementation, and Test Use*, ACM Transactions on Information Systems, Vol. 12, No. 4, pp. 360-382, 1994. 50
3. Dunn, J. M.: *Relevance Logic and Entailment*, in Gabbay, D. and Guenthner, F. (eds.): Handbook of Philosophical Logic, Vol. III, D. Reidel Publishing Company, pp. 117-224, 1986. 51, 53
4. Edwards, P. (ed.): *The Encyclopedia of Philosophy*, Vol. 1, The Macmillan Company and The Free Press, 1967. 49, 52
5. Eemeren, F. H., Grootendorst, R., Henkmans, A. F. S., et al.: *Fundamentals of Argumentation Theory, A Handbook of Historical Backgrounds and Contemporary Developments*, Lawrence Erlbaum, 1996. 49
6. Ferber, J.: *Multi-Agent Systems*, Addison-Wesley, 1999. 48
7. Finn, T., Labrou, Y. and Mayfield, J.: *KQML as an Agent Communication Language*, in Bradshaw, M. (ed.): Software Agents, AAAI Press/The MIT Press, pp. 291-316, 1997. 50
8. Kowalski, R. A. and Toni, F.: *Argument and Reconciliation*, FGCS Workshop on Application of Logic Programming to Legal Reasoning, ICOT, pp. 9-16, 1994. 58
9. Krause, P., Ambler, S., Goransson, M. E. and Fox, J.: *A Logic of Argumentation for Reasoning under Uncertainty*, Computational Intelligence, Vol. 11, No. 1, pp. 113-131, 1995. 49, 50

10. McGill, V. J. and Parry, W. T.: *The Unity of Opposites: A Dialectical Principle*, Science and Society, Vol. 12, pp. 418-444, 1948. 60

11. Müller, H. J. and Dieng, R. (eds.) : *Computational Conflicts*, Springer, 2000. 49, 61

12. Parsons, S., Sierra, C. and Jennings, N.: *Agents that Reason and Negotiate by Arguing*, J. of Logic and Computation, Vol. 8, No. 3, pp. 261-292, 1998. 49

13. Prakken, H. and Sartor, G.: *Argument-based Extended Logic Programming with Defeasible Priorities*, J. of Applied Non-Classical Logics, Vol. 7, No. 1-2, pp. 25-75, 1997. 49, 50, 53

14. Rescher, N.: *Dialectics - a controversy-oriented approach to the theory of knowledge* -, State University of New York Press, 1977. 49

15. Routley, R. and Meyer, R.: *Dialectical Logic, Classical Logic, and the Consistency of the World*, Studies in Soviet Thought, Vol. 16, pp. 1-25, 1976. 50, 51

16. Sawamura, H., Yamashita, M., Inagaki, M. and Umeda,Y.: *Agents Meet Dialectics*, Proc. of International ICSC Symposium on Multi-Agents and Mobile Agents in Virtual Organizations and E-Commerce (MAMA2000), ICSC Academic Press, pp. 354-360, 2000. 48, 49

17. Sawamura, H., Umeda, Y. and Meyer, R. K.: *Computational Dialectics for Argument-based Agent Systems*, Proc. of the Fourth International Conference on MultiAgents Systems (ICMAS2000), IEEE Computer Society, pp. 271-278, 2000. 48, 49

18. Sawamura, H. and Maeda, S.: *An Argumentation-Based Model of Multi-Agent Systems*, in Kangassalo, H., Jaakkola, H. and Kawaguchi, E. (editors): Information Modelling and Knowledge Bases XII, IOS Press, pp. 137-150, 2001. 48, 49, 50

19. Toulmin, S.: *The Uses of Argument*, Cambridge Univ. Press, 1958. 49

20. Tessier, C., Chaudron, L. and Müller, H. J. (eds.): *Conflicting Agents*, Kluwer Academic Pub., 2001. 49

21. Umeda, Y. and Sawamura, H.: *Towards an Argument-based Agent System*, Proc of 3rd Int. Conf on Knowledge-Based Intelligent Information Engineering Systems, IEEE, pp. 30-33, 1999. 54

22. Umeda, Y., Yamashita, M., Inagaki, M. and Sawamura, H.: *Argumentation as a Social Computing Paradigm*, Proc. of 3rd Pacific RIM Int. Workshop on Multi-Agents (PRIMA2000), Lecture Notes in AI, Vol. 1881, pp. 46-60, 2000. 48, 49, 50, 54, 61

On Fairness in an Alternating-Offers Bargaining Model with Evolutionary Agents

Norberto Eiji Nawa[1,2], Katsunori Shimohara[1,2], and Osamu Katai[2]

[1] ATR International - Information Sciences Division
2-2-2 Hikari-dai, Seika-cho, Soraku-gun, Kyoto 619-0288, Japan
[2] Dept. of Systems Science, Graduate School of Informatics, Kyoto University
Yoshida-honmachi, Sakyo-ku, Kyoto 606-8501, Japan

Abstract. The emergence of agents that play fair strategies is investigated in a simple bargaining model. The strategies played by the agents are constructed by evolutionary algorithms. Agents make offers to each other describing possible ways to share a certain commodity, until an offer is accepted. Finite-horizon bargaining models give an advantage to the first or last part making an offer, depending on the discount factor incurred by the players in each transaction. By introducing uncertainty regarding the playing order, i.e., who makes the first or last offers, experimental results show that evolutionary agents abandon greedy strategies, that attempt to obtain the whole commodity without sharing, for those that lead to more just divisions of the commodity.

1 Introduction

Recently, there has been an intense exchange between the areas of economics and computer science [6], which has opened new and interesting possibilities to the development of both fields. Though the use of computational models in economics research is rather a natural consequence of the widespread computational power available nowadays, the possibilities that arise with the introduction of decision-making models and machine learning methods, mainly investigated in the field of artificial intelligence (AI), are still to be fully appreciated. By doing so, economics can loosen up the assumption of perfectly rational agents that have been molding in a great extent their models. Indeed, many researchers have already started exploring these new possibilities [1,19].

On the other hand, as the number of market institutions in the Internet grows, there is an imminent possibility that computational agents will play an increasingly important role in the determination of the market dynamics [23,10]. Since the field of economics has dedicated much of its efforts to the study of coordination of decentralized systems populated with self-interested individuals, from the computer science point of view such knowledge represents a valuable source of ideas for the design of innovative approaches to deal with distributed systems. Therefore, it is important that multi-agent systems (MAS) practitioners pay close attention to the theoretical results achieved in economics when

S.-T. Yuan and M. Yokoo (Eds.): PRIMA 2001, LNAI 2132 , pp. 63–77, 2001.

designing new market institutions, and the behavioral mechanisms of the agents that will take part on them.

Negotiation mechanisms coordinate the interaction of two or more parties with heterogeneous, possibly conflicting preferences, who search for a compromise that is satisfactory and mutually beneficial, so to be accepted by all participants. Many of these mechanisms have drawn the interest of the AI community due to their direct implications in the implementation of MAS. Bargaining models are one of the most well studied negotiation mechanisms in the field of economics, since it describes a situation that underlies several instances of socioeconomic interactions. Rubinstein's alternating-offers model [18], among others, has served as the basic framework for much of the research in the field of bargaining models. There, two players have to agree on the division of a certain commodity, represented by a "pie", by directly making offers to each other. The offers describe possible ways to split the pie, such as "Player 1 receives 0.7 and Player 2 receives 0.3". When an offer is accepted, a deal is sealed according to the division described by that offer.

Remarkably, though, it has been noticed that there is a considerable gap between the game theoretic predictions of bargaining outcomes and observations performed in experiments with human subjects. It is frequently observed that besides deviating from theoretic predictions, there is a tendency for humans to aim for divisions that hover around the equal split of the commodity at stake, even in cases where they would be strictly better off by not doing so. This indicates that other factors besides payoff maximization may influence the decision-making processes of the players. (A more detailed explanation of bargaining games follows in Section 2.) Though still the reasons that originate this phenomenon in human societies are not completely clarified, it is clear that this question has deep implications in the realm of MAS design and agent design. More specifically, it is related to the question of finding general design principles, both in the system and agent levels, that guarantee or induce certain global properties, despite the heterogeneity, selfishness, and learning capabilities presented by the collective of agents.

This paper reports on experiments performed with a simple alternating-offers bargaining model, with agents who build their strategies using evolutionary algorithms. Bargaining games of finite duration give an advantage to the agent who makes the first or last offer, depending on the value of the discount factor incurred in each exchange. By introducing uncertainty regarding the playing order, i.e. in the definition of the agent that makes the first or last offers, experimental results show that the evolutionary agents abandon greedy strategies for those that lead to a more equal split of the pie. This situation resembles the hypothetical framework presented by Rawls [16] for the generation of fair compromises, and examined fully by Binmore in bargaining settings [3]. There, uncertainty is considered to play a crucial role in the generation of fair compromises. A clear distinction should be made, however, between the game theoretical results regarding uncertainty in bargaining models and the experimental results presented in this paper. Despite the similarities they may share, here the evolutionary agents learn the strategies from scratch, while playing the game with their opponents. The learning dynamics, therefore, is a key component in the definition of the system outcomes.

The rest of the paper is organized as follows. Section 2 revises the portions of bargaining theory that are relevant to the context of this work; Section 3 gives a brief overview of related work on evolutionary algorithms applied to the construction of negotiation strategies. Section 4 describes the model, the experiments performed and the obtained results. Finally, the conclusions are presented in Section 5.

2   Bargaining Models

A bargaining situation consists of two or more players trying to engage in a mutually beneficial agreement over a set of issues. The players, or agents, have a common interest to cooperate; the question that remains open is which one of the possibly several compromise settings will be chosen by the players [12]. That decision should be deliberated by the participating agents, in the light of their conflicting, and perhaps incompletely revealed, preferences. In the alternating-offers bargaining model, the path towards an agreement involves the direct interaction of the players, who will make offers and counteroffers to each other through several stages, until a compromise that is accepted by all the parties is achieved.

The seminal work by Rubinstein [18] set the dominant tone in the systematic analysis of bargaining games. Rubinstein started by illustrating the typical situation using the following scenario: two players have to reach an agreement on the partition of a "pie". For this purpose, the players alternate offers describing possible divisions of the pie that they would like to settle. The player that receives the offer at a certain stage of the game decides whether to accept it or not. If the offer is accepted, the process ends, and each player receives the share of the pie determined by the engaged contract. Otherwise, the receiving player makes a counteroffer, and all the steps above are repeated until a solution is reached or the process is aborted due to some other reason (e.g., one of the parties leaves the negotiation process).

Explaining the model in more details, there are two agents in the game, A_1 and A_2. Let the pair (x, t) represent a partition of the pie at stake, a general offer from one agent to the other, denoting "A_1 receives x and A_2 receives $1 - x$ at time t". For the sake of simplicity, x is in the unit interval $[0, 1]$. In addition to the pie itself, time is also a relevant commodity. Interactions between the players are not "frictionless"; every additional time step in the bargaining process reduces the utility obtained by the agents from the acquired pie's share. Thus, for the agents, the longer the process takes, the more severe is the discount in the obtained utilities; time pressure makes it advantageous to set a deal in earlier stages. The discount factor due to time is usually calculated as follows. Let y be the share received by agent A_s; the time t in which the contract is set reflects in the obtained payoff U_s by means of a fixed discount factor, such as $U_s = y \cdot \delta_s^t$, where $0 \leq \delta_s \leq 1$ is the discount factor of agent A_s. The lower the δ_s, the stronger is the time pressure.

In an infinite-horizon scenario, if the transactions are frictionless, rational agents would most likely get trapped in a impasse, since the offering side at a certain time would attempt to obtain the whole pie for itself, in an endlessly effort to maximize its payoff. Thus, costs due to time constitute an incentive for mutual concessions and agreements.

The most significant result introduced in [18] is that under the assumptions that (1) the discount factors are common knowledge to the players and (2) the number of stages to be played is infinite, the solution for the game is unique, i.e., there is a *perfect equilibrium partition (P.E.P)*. In other words, in an exchange between rational agents, the first proposer should (calculate and) offer the P.E.P in the very first stage; the rational responder should then accept the offer right away, making an instantaneous deal with no need of further interaction. In a setting where agents A_1 and A_2 have discount factors δ_1 and δ_2, respectively, and assuming that A_1 is granted the first offer, the composition of the P.E.P contract is that player A_1 receives a share of the pie which returns her a utility of $U_1 = (1 - \delta_2)/(1 - \delta_1\delta_2)$, whereas player A_2 gets a share that returns him a utility of $U_2 = \delta_2(1 - \delta_1)/(1 - \delta_1\delta_2)$.

It is possible to perform a similar analysis for the finite-horizon case. Say the total number of steps in the game, n, is common knowledge to the players. In the case where $n = 1$ (also known as the *ultimatum game*), agent A_1 makes the only offer; A_2 can accept it or refuse it; in either case the negotiation process ends. If the offer is refused, both agents receive nothing. For a rational agent "anything is better than nothing"; consequently, A_1, aware of the size of the game and the rationality of its opponent, attempts to keep the whole pie to herself, offering only a minimum share to A_2; conscious that there are no further stages to be played in the game, rational A_2 would inevitably accept such tiny offer. By applying a backward induction reasoning on the preceding situation, it is possible to calculate the P.E.P for $n > 1$. As one may notice, finite-horizon alternating-offers bargaining games can give a great advantage to the party offering in the last turn (depending on the value of the discount factors), since it becomes an ultimatum game.

2.1   Fairness

Rubinstein is careful enough to emphasize the difference between what would be the just agreement and what would be the reached agreement assuming that the players behave rationally. The latter is the question originally addressed by him. In other words, the parties in the model are interested only in maximizing their own payoffs; considerations of moral nature are not made by the players. Under that model, unless the utility functions explicitly specify that it pays to be fair, rational players will only seek to promote their own good.

Experiments with human subjects, however, show discrepancies between the theoretic predictions of such games and the actual contracts that the subjects engage during the simulated situations [21]. Very often, the players agree to divide the prize in more fair ways, even in situations where one of the parties could benefit from an advantageous position and receive a higher payoff. Several experiments and models have been reported [4,13,14,7,5] to explain the mechanisms underlying the decision-making processes employed by humans in bargaining situations, in order to clarify the influence of other factors that are not captured by conventional economic models.

This leads in fact to a much larger question, which is whether the game theory postulates on rationality are suitable descriptions of human behavior. This question has been exhaustively discussed in the literature [20] and indeed it is still an unresolved matter surrounded by fierce argumentation. Harsanyi (p.16, [9]) comments on the rationality assumption as follows:

> The basic reason for this often quite remarkable explanatory power of rational behavior theories lies in a general and fundamental *empirical* characteristic of human behavior, viz., in its goal-directedness, its goal-seeking orientation; in effect, what we mean by "rational behavior" is essentially behavior showing this goal-directedness to a particular high degree and in a particularly consistent manner.

Interestingly enough, the above description could as well describe the characteristics of autonomous agents. In fact, consistent goal-seeking behavior is one of the aspects, if not the only one, where the envisioned computational agents could possibly excel humans. Being free, in principle, from the influence of social, emotional or psychological factors (assuming that these factors can be accounted for the deviations from rational behavior), computational agents would be closer approximations of the perfect rational *homo economicus* portrayed in economic models. This line of thought has been also explored in [17]. Computational agents strive for the accomplishment of clearly described goals in a more consistent way than humans, but may not be able to take the most suitable action in every situation, as they learn the behaviors that maximize their payoffs on the run. Being halfway between humans and the *homo economicus*, they can be considered *quasi* rational entities.

The question that arises then is how outcomes regarding moral criteria, such as fairness could be achieved in a scenario populated with *quasi* rational agents? Would it be possible to devise a system that leads to fair outcomes, even though the agents solely aim to increase their own welfare, and for this purpose try to act rationally to the best of their efforts? In an open world such as the Internet, it would be unrealistic to rely on the agents' goodwill, or in the goodwill of their designers in order that fair divisions be achieved. Truly, there are several other incentives in the opposite direction. In an ideal situation, fairness should be a side effect of the rational actions of imperfect players.

3   Evolutionary Computation and Economic Agents

The dissertation by Oliver [15] was the first work that succeeded to show that evolutionary algorithms could design strategies for agents playing multi-issue negotiation games. Oliver's motivation has its origins in the observation that negotiation problems are rather inefficiently resolved by humans, who not rarely settle in suboptimal agreements. The negotiation process is framed as a search problem for a mutual agreement, in a scenario where the parties dispute shares of items that revert to utilities, according to their private valuations. In that framework, a strategy consists of a vector of numerical parameters that represent offers and thresholds; offer values indicate the portion that the proposer is willing to share with its opponents; threshold values denote the minimum value a received offer should have in order to be accepted. Bargaining occurs with agents alternating offers to each other. The offers are checked against the threshold values, and as soon as one offer satisfies an opponent's threshold, the bargaining is considered successful.

Matos et. al. take a different approach [11] evolving tactics with higher level "flavors", such as the time-dependent tactics, where an agent concedes more rapidly as the negotiation deadline approaches, or the behavior-dependent tactics, where an agent's action is determined by the actions taken by their opponents. An evolutionary algorithm evolves the parameters of linear and non-linear functions that determine the negotiation behaviors. Combinations using several functions allow one to represent variations on the base tactics.

The works by van Bragt, Gerding and La Poutré [22] and Gerding, van Bragt and La Poutré [8] have a different spirit from the previous ones; they perform an interesting and detailed game-theoretic analysis of the evolved trading strategies. Using the Rubinstein's alternating-offers bargaining game with a finite-horizon as a base model, they perform several numerical experiments with traders that evolve strategies shaped on the ones presented in [15], i.e., sequences of offer and threshold values. The results show that despite the bounded rationality of the traders, since they are only aware of their own profits and discount factors, their behavior is surprisingly aligned with what is predicted by game theory.

In [22], it is noted that if $\delta_1 = \delta_2 = 1.0$, a last-offer advantage arises in the end of the finite game, i.e., the agent allowed to make the last offer, be it A_1 or A_2, quickly perceives its advantageous position and offers very small shares of the pie in the last stage. Consequently, the strategies of the agent receiving the last offer have their values adjusted so to accept the tiniest shares. This leads to a situation where the last proposer gets almost the whole prize, an ultimatum game in the last exchange. However, when more severe discounts ($\delta_1 \rightarrow 0, \delta_2 \rightarrow 0$) are applied, the situation reverts, as the cost incurred by each additional step becomes very heavy. Therefore, the first stage becomes an ultimatum game, and the last proposer is no longer able to explore its advantageous position. van Bragt et al. conjecture that rejecting the first offer has a too strong impact in the payoff obtained afterwards by the first responder, leading it to accept the first offer, no matter how small it is. The first proposer perceives this situation and explores it accordingly. Obviously, when one is concerned with fairness, these two extreme situations are undesirable.

4   Model Description and Experiments

The framework used in [8,22] is the basis for the model applied in this paper. Two bargaining agents, A_1 and A_2, each one equipped with its own evolutionary algorithm, optimize the numerical parameters of the negotiation strategies. The strategies consist of sequences of floating point numbers in the interval $[0, 1]$, encoding offers and thresholds, similarly to the strategies used in [15]. The maximum number of offers that can be exchanged between the traders is limited to n. If n is even, each trader will be allowed to make at most $n/2$ offers. In this case, the last offer is granted to the agent that does not make the first offer. If n is odd, the last offer is granted to the same agent that makes the first offer. If the maximum number of offers is reached and no agreement is accomplished, both traders receive a null payoff.

Each agent holds a set of strategies, which are optimized by a conventional $(\mu + \lambda)$ evolution strategies (ES) [2]. In one complete iteration, all the strategies are evaluated and ordered according to their fitness values. In an $(\mu + \lambda)$-ES, the best μ strategies (*parents*) remain in the set from one iteration to the next; in addition, λ new strategies (*offspring*) are produced at each iteration. Offspring is generated by applying operators such as *mutation* and *recombination* in the set of parents.

In the experiments, only the mutation operator was employed when generating offspring. In an ES, mutation consists of adding or subtracting samples from a Gaussian distribution with standard deviation σ to the parameters of a certain parent strategy. The role of the control parameter σ is critical, as it determines the strength of the mutation, and therefore the range of the search in the space of strategies (which is ultimately related to the convergence speed of the algorithm, and in this context, to the learning performance of the agents). Each strategy keeps the σ value of the Gaussian distribution from which it was generated; at each iteration, the average of the standard deviations in the parents set is calculated to produce the Gaussian distribution that generates the offspring.

When there are no costs due to time, even though the agents are not informed about the length of the game, the evolutionary processes quickly perceive the absence of time pressure, leading to the construction of greedy strategies that take the system to an all-or-nothing situation, where one of the parties gets the whole pie to itself, as predicted by game theoretic models. Figure 1 shows the result of a representative run when both discount factors are set to $\delta_1 = \delta_2 = 1.0$. In that situation, A_1 has the first offer, and A_2 has the last offer. As explained before, the average payoff obtained by A_2's strategies converges to 1, whereas A_1's payoff converges to 0. Analyzing the number of steps taken until a deal is closed, it is clear that A_2 is making use of its last-offer advantage, as the negotiation process tends to finish in the very last offer at each confrontation. Figure 2 shows the average strategies played by A_1 and A_2 over 20 runs in such situation. It should be noted that the agents are not perfectly rational, as assumed in game theoretic models, but learn to play the game by experimenting different strategies. Nevertheless, they are able to reproduce the results predicted in theoretical models.

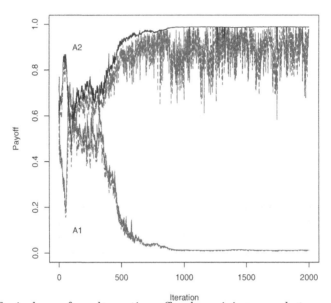

Fig. 1. Typical run of an alternating-offers bargaining game between A_1 and A_2, with $\delta_1 = \delta_2 = 1.0$; the graph shows the development through time of the payoff obtained by A_1 and A_2 (for each agent, the payoff obtained by the best strategy is displayed by the full line; the mean payoff for all the strategies in the set is displayed by the dashed line). The horizontal axis shows the iteration number; the vertical axis is the payoff; maximum number of steps $n = 10$, total of 2000 iterations. The system reaches an equilibrium where A_2 acquires nearly the whole pie, leaving only a minimum amount to A_1

The fact that agents A_1 and A_2 have fixed roles during a run, as the first to make or respond to an offer, clearly enables them to learn the best strategies for the setting. In such situation, it is hopeless to expect the agents to develop any other kind of strategy but the one in accordance with the game theoretic analysis. In fact, the incentive for one agent to take part in a bargaining game, knowing in advance that the role reserved to him is under a serious handicap compared to his opponent, is minimum, as the chances to get a considerable share of the pie are negligible[1]. However, it is reasonable to presume that different strategies

---

[1] In [12] it is argued that the finite-horizon version of an alternating-offers bargaining model is indeed implausible, as it is not conceivable that two players that are better off bargaining are prevented to do so simply because a given number of offers have been rejected. Even though the number of offers that can be exchanged is limited, the influence of such restriction in the model is avoided by using values of $\delta_s < 1.0$,

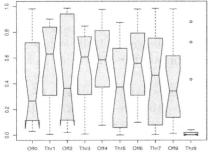 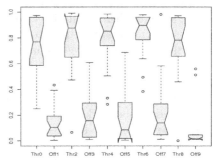

Fig. 2. Average strategies (over 20 runs) evolved in a 10-stage bargaining game, where A_1 is the first proposer (left) and A_2 is the last proposer (right). $\delta_1 = \delta_2 = 1.0$. For each run, the mean strategy of each agent was calculated by averaging the offers and threshold values over all the strategies in the set at iteration 750. These values were then grouped into box-and-whisker graphs: the box indicates the range between the lower and upper quartiles; the central notch in the box indicates the median, and the whiskers indicate lower and upper extremes. The legends show whether the parameter is an offer (Off$n$) or a threshold (Thr$n$). Note that A_2 clearly attempts to take the negotiation until the last stage by alternating high threshold values and low offers, until it gives a last very low offer (Off9, right) which is accepted by A_1, who has a very low threshold value at the last stage (Thr9, left). The large spread observed in A_1's parameters can be justified as an artifact of the evolutionary algorithm underlying the learning process; it samples different values of offer and threshold, in a fruitless attempt to increase its payoff by making a better deal

would be devised if the agents were uncertain at each confrontation about the roles reserved to them in the game.

Indeed, such a situation resembles Rawls's "veil of ignorance" [16]. In his view, the institutions and laws that comprise a society should be, above all, just. The question that arises then is how people in a group or society can ever reach a common agreement about the definition of justice, since they occupy different positions and have distinct abilities, needs, incomes, and so forth. In a thought experiment, he proposed that such an agreement would be possible if all the members of the group meet and define all the governing rules before they actually enter the society and know the positions they will occupy. At this point, called "original position", since all the members are equally empowered and unaware of their future positions (i.e., behind a "veil of ignorance"), the design criteria for the rules would be based solely on justice and fairness. The

---

so as to make it indifferent from the agents' point of view to close a deal in the last stage or receive a null payoff. In other words, the time pressure badly penalizes those deals that are settled in the last stage. (In fact, in the experiments here described, it was noticed that the large majority of the deals are closed before the last stage, neutralizing any influence the finite-horizon may have in the agents' learning processes.)

members would take in consideration how the rules affect every position in the society, as all of them would have equal chances to be assigned to any position. Rawls's criterion therefore maximizes the utility of the worst-off member of the group, the one that receives the minimum share in the group. If the members of a group follow this rationale, fairness should permeate the agreements and the governing rules of such society.

A bargaining setting inspired by such thought was investigated in the experiments described below. At every confrontation, the role of the agents in the game, i.e., whether the first to make or respond an offer, was defined according to a certain probability, Γ_{A_s}. That means that a strategy could be used once when an agent was assigned to be the first proposer, and later on, in the same iteration, when it was assigned to be the first responder. Hence, the agents can never be secure of what role they will play in the game, and have to devise strategies to cope with such situation. This uncertainty introduces a high degree of noise in the evaluation of strategies and consequently in the ES underlying the learning processes.

Computational experiments with this model were performed[2] and the results are presented next. In all the experiments $\delta_1 = \delta_2 = 0.7$, and $(\mu, \lambda) = (25, 25)$, unless otherwise stated. The discount factor values give an advantage to the first proposer, as they penalize the payoffs obtained in subsequent steps (the first offer is the only one exempted from the discount). The parameter σ was initialized at 0.5 in all the runs. The random number generator was seeded with different values in each of the 50 runs performed in each session; for each run, 2000 iterations were completed. In each iteration, each one of the 50 strategies owned by A_1 had to confront with a randomly chosen subset of size 25 of A_2's strategies, and vice versa. The fitness value of a strategy was calculated as the mean value over the payoffs obtained in all confrontations contained in one iteration. The payoff in one confrontation was the share obtained in the final agreement, for the successful cases, discounted by $\delta_i^\tau, i = 1, 2$, where τ is the index of the accepted offer ($\tau = 0, \cdots, n-1$). Unsuccessful confrontations returned null payoff. The objective of the optimization process is to maximize the strategies' payoffs. Threshold and offer values were only accepted in the range $[-1, 1]$ (negative values were used in their absolute form); any strategy that contained a value out of the range had a penalty added to the fitness, if the respective parameter was demanded in a confrontation.

In the first session of experiments, the probability that A_1 becomes the first proposer, Γ_{A_1}, was set to 0.0, i.e., A_2 is always the first proposer. Figure 3 shows the first offer and threshold of A_1 (right) and A_2 (left). The solid square over the box-and-whisker plot indicates the mean value; the solid vertical line in the middle of the box indicates the range of the standard deviation of the parameters. Only the parameters relative to the first two stages are shown (namely,

---

[2] The system was implemented using the Swarm Simulation System, developed by the Swarm Development Group. Detailed information about the software can be found at www.swarm.org. The source code used in the experiments described in this paper is available upon request.

first proposer's offer → first responder's threshold; first responder's offer → first proposer's threshold), as the large majority of the deals are settled in the first two stages. As it can be clearly seen, A_2 explores its first-proposer advantage and offers small values to A_1, which are almost entirely accepted, as A_1 evolves very low first threshold values. Interestingly, the dominance of A_2 over A_1 extends to the second stage. As A_2 has a high threshold value, A_1 can only make a bad deal, being forced to offer a high value to cover A_2's threshold. A_1 could also take the negotiation to the third stage, but this increases the losses due to the discount factor (which are applied to both players). All in all, A_1 usually accepts the A_2's first offer in this situation.

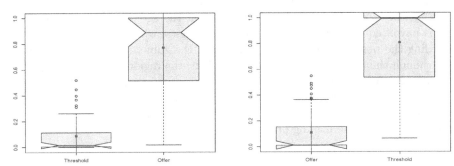

Fig. 3. Average strategies (over 50 runs) evolved in a 10-stage bargaining game by A_1 (left) and A_2 (right). A_1 is always the first responder ($\Gamma_{A_1} = 0.0$), and $\delta_1 = \delta_2 = 0.7$. For each run, the mean strategy of each agent was calculated by averaging the parameters over all the strategies in the set at iteration 2000. The figure shows the box-and-whisker plots for the first offer and threshold evolved by each of the agents; the solid square over the box-and-whisker plot indicates the mean value; the solid vertical line in the middle of the box indicates the range of the standard deviation of the parameters

Figures 4, 5 and 6 show the results for $\Gamma_{A_1} = 0.25, 0.50, 0.75$. The most noticeable aspect is that by introducing uncertainty about the roles played by the agents in each confrontation makes the deals hover around the region of fair splits of the pie.[3] Again, as in the previous case, the majority of the deals are closed in the first two stages due to the effect of the discount factor. Interestingly enough, similar strategies are prepared by both agents. They make offers that aim an equal split of the commodity more often than when the roles played in the game are fixed throughout the run.

For the situation where $\Gamma_{A_1} = 0.5$, at least, if both agents play all the time greedy strategies that attempt to get the whole pie, the same payoff should

---

[3] Unpaired t-tests for each one of the parameters in consideration were realized between the results for $\Gamma_{A_1} = 0.25$ and 0.50. The p-values were 0.027, 0.062, 0.20, and 0.2676 for the first offer and threshold of A_1 and A_2, respectively. For the pairs $\Gamma_{A_1} = 0.50$ and 0.75, and $\Gamma_{A_1} = 0.25$ and 0.75, the largest p-value obtained was 0.013.

be obtained as when fair strategies are played. This would happen because, by structure, half the time agent A_1 would be assigned the first offer (therefore, getting the whole pie), and half the time A_2 would be assigned the first offer. However, due to the uncertainty in the game setting, the ES are not able to converge to that state, converging to the area of fair divisions instead.

Figure 7 shows the results for $\Gamma_{A_1} = 1.0$, where A_1 dominates A_2, in symmetry to the results shown in Figure 3.

The influence of the time pressure introduced by the discount factor in the results was also verified. Similar experiments were ran for $\delta_1 = \delta_2 = 1.0$ and $\Gamma_{A_1} = 0.5$. Usually, the agents would oscillate between the two extremes of complete success and complete loss, until eventually stabilizing in one of the extreme configurations, failing to evolve fair strategies, as shown in Figure 8.

What these results show, in summary, is that the agents converge to a state that is payoff equivalent to playing greedy strategies, when there is uncertainty regarding the position they will be assigned in the game. Making a conjecture, even though the two states are payoff equivalent, the region of fair strategies, as a focal point, is stronger than the region of greedy strategies. In other words, it is "easier" to the learning processes to take the set of strategies to the fair division region than to keep them in the greedy strategy region, when there is uncertainty about the playing order.

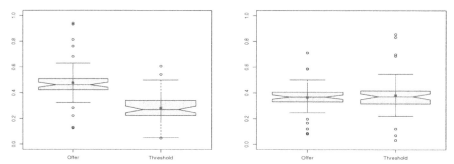

Fig. 4. Average strategies (over 50 runs) evolved in a 10-stage bargaining game by A_1 (left) and A_2 (right). $\Gamma_{A_1} = 0.25$, and $\delta_1 = \delta_2 = 0.7$

5   Conclusions

Experiments were realized with a simple bargaining with agents using strategies constructed by evolutionary algorithms. The agents only aim the maximization of their payoffs, and they were able to successfully explore asymmetries in the game, such as the last-proposer advantage, when they were present. However, the emergence of fair strategies was observed as a result of the introduction of uncertainty regarding the playing order in the bargaining game. Such situation resembles Rawls's idea of the "veil of ignorance", that advocates that fair rules

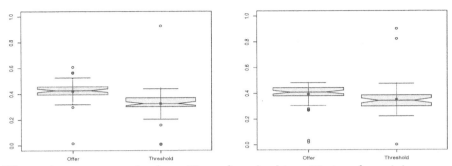

Fig. 5. Average strategies (over 50 runs) evolved in a 10-stage bargaining game by A_1 (left) and A_2 (right). $\Gamma_{A_1} = 0.5$, and $\delta_1 = \delta_2 = 0.7$

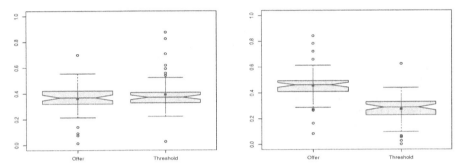

Fig. 6. Average strategies (over 50 runs) evolved in a 10-stage bargaining game by A_1 (left) and A_2 (right). $\Gamma_{A_1} = 0.75$, and $\delta_1 = \delta_2 = 0.7$

and institutions would emerge in a society if their members had no knowledge of the positions they would occupy in the social structure in the future, and in that situation, the "original position", had to devise the governing rules of a society.

Unraveling the mechanisms that systematically lead to fair agreements in a scenario with selfish agents is a question of fundamental importance in the design of multi-agent systems. Future work includes a game theoretic analysis of the simulated model presented here, in order to compare the obtained results in the light of a formal framework, in the lines presented in [3]. Moreover, it is necessary to verify if agents equipped with different learning algorithms, such as reinforcement learning, lead to the same results, in order to detect eventual artifacts introduced by the evolutionary algorithms underlying the agents' learning mechanisms.

Acknowledgments

Thanks to the reviewers for their helpful comments. The first author receives partial financial support from CNPq, the Brazilian agency for the development of science and technology, under grant number 200050/99-0.

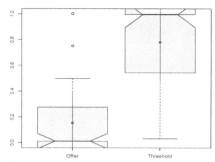 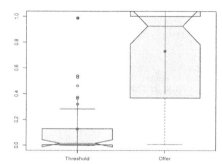

Fig. 7. Average strategies (over 50 runs) evolved in a 10-stage bargaining game by A_1 (left) and A_2 (right). A_1 is always the first proposer ($\Gamma_{A_1} = 1.0$), and $\delta_1 = \delta_2 = 0.7$

References

1. W. B. Arthur, J. H. Holland, B. LeBaron, R. Palmer, and P. Tayler. Asset pricing under endogenous expectations in an artificial stock market. In W. B. Arthur, S. N. Durlauf, and D. A. Lane, editors, *The Economy as an Evolving Complex System II*, pages 15–44. Addison-Wesley, 1997. 63
2. T. Bäck, G. Rudolph, and H.-P. Schwefel. Evolutionary programming and evolution strategies: Similarities and differences. In D. B. Fogel and W. Altmar, editors, *Proc. the 2nd Annual Evolutionary Programming Conference*, pages 11–22, February 1992. 69
3. K. Binmore. *Game Theory and the Social Contract - Volume 2: Just Playing*. MIT Press, 1998. 64, 75
4. K. Binmore, A. Shaked, and J. Sutton. Testing noncooperative bargaining theory: A preliminary study. *American Economic Review*, 75(5):1178–1180, December 1985. 67
5. G. E. Bolton. The rationality of splitting equally. *Journal of Economic Behavior and Organization*, 32:365–381, 1997. 67
6. C. Boutilier, Y. Shoham, and M. P. Wellman, editors. *Artifical Intelligence*, volume 94 (1-2). Elsevier, July 1997. Special Issue on Economic Principles of Multi-Agent Systems. 63
7. R. Forsythe, J. L. Horowitz, N. E. Savin, and M. Sefton. Fairness in simple bargaining experiments. *Games and Economic Behavior*, 6:347–369, 1994. 67
8. E. H. Gerding, D. D. B. van Bragt, and J. A. L. Poutré. Multi-issue negotiation processes by evolutionary simulation: Validation and social extensions. Technical Report SEN R0024, CWI, Centre for Mathematics and Computer Science, 2000. 68, 69
9. J. C. Harsanyi. *Rational Behavior and Bargaining Equilibrium in Games and Social Situations*. Cambridge University Press, 1977. Paperback edition: 1986. 67
10. J. O. Kephart, J. E. Hanson, and J. Sairamesh. Price and niche wars in a free-market economy of software agents. *Artificial Life*, 4(1):1–23, 1998. 63
11. N. Matos, C. Sierra, and N. R. Jennings. Determining successful negotiation strategies: An evolutionary approach. In *Proc. 3rd Int. Conf. on Multi-Agent Systems (ICMAS 98)*, pages 182–189, 1998. 68
12. A. Muthoo. *Bargaining Theory with Applications*. Cambridge University Press, 1999. 65, 70

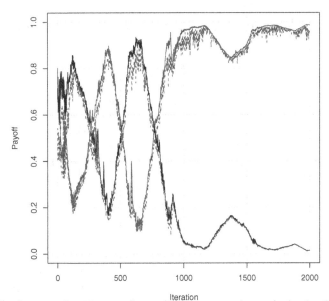

Fig. 8. Single run of a 10-stage bargaining game where A_1 is the first proposer and A_2 is the last proposers, $\Gamma_{A_1} = 0.5$, and $\delta_1 = \delta_2 = 1.0$. The agents' payoffs fluctuate between the two extreme situations, until eventually converging to one of them

13. J. Neelin, H. Sonnenschein, and M. Spiegel. A further test of noncooperative bargaining theory: Comment. *American Economic Review*, 78(4):824–836, September 1988. 67
14. J. Ochs and A. E. Roth. An experimental study of sequential bargaining. *American Economic Review*, 79(3):355–384, June 1989. 67
15. J. R. Oliver. *On Artificial Agents for Negotiation in Electronic Commerce*. PhD thesis, University of Pennsylvania, 1996. 67, 68, 69
16. J. Rawls. *A Theory of Justice*. Belknap Press, 1999. Revised Edition. 64, 71
17. J. S. Rosenschein and G. Zlotkin. *Rules of Encounter: Designing Conventions for Automated Negotiation among Computers*. MIT Press, 1994. 67
18. A. Rubinstein. Perfect equilibrium in a bargaining model. *Econometrica*, 50(1):97–109, January 1982. 64, 65, 66
19. T. J. Sargent. *Bounded Rationality in Macroeconomics*. Oxford University Press, 1993. 63
20. H. A. Simon. *Models of Bounded Rationality: Behavioral Economics and Business Organization*, volume 2. MIT Press, 1982. 67
21. R. H. Thaler. The ultimatum game. *Journal of Economic Perspectives*, 2(4):195–206, 1989. 66
22. D. D. B. van Bragt, E. H. Gerding, and J. A. L. Poutré. Equilibrium selection in alternating-offers bargaining models: The evolutionary computing approach. In 6th *Int. Conf. of the Society for Computational Economics on Computing in Economics and Finance (CEF'2000)*, July 2000. 68, 69
23. H. R. Varian. Economic mechanism design for computerized agents. In *Proceedings of the First Usenix Conference on Electronic Commerce*. July 1995. 63

Sealed Bid Multi-object Auctions with Necessary Bundles and its Application to Spectrum Auctions

Tomomi Matsui[1] and Takahiro Watanabe[2]

[1] Department of Mathematical Informatics,
Graduate School of Information Science and Technology,
University of Tokyo, Bunkyo-ku, Tokyo 113-0033, Japan,
tomomi@misojiro.t.u-tokyo.ac.jp,
WWW home page: http://www.misojiro.t.u-tokyo.ac.jp/~tomomi/
[2] Department of Policy Studies, Iwate Prefectural University,
twatanab@iwate-pu.ac.jp,
WWW home page: http://www.anna.iwate-pu.ac.jp/~twatanab/

Abstract. In this paper, we consider multi-object auctions in which each bidder has a positive reservation value for only one special subset of objects, called a necessary bundle. In the auction, each bidder reports its necessary bundle and its reservation value. The seller solves the assignment problem of objects which maximizes its revenue and decides the winning bidders who can purchase their necessary bundles for their reporting prices. We show that this auction leads to an efficient allocation through Nash equilibria under complete information when the bid-grid size is sufficiently small. We apply our results to spectrum auctions satisfying the conditions that necessary bundles are intervals of discretized radio spectrum. We show that the revenue maximization problem for the seller can be solved in polynomial time for the above auctions. The algorithm also indicates a method to choose an accepted bidder randomly when the revenue maximization problem has multiple optimal solutions. Lastly, we introduce a linear inequality system which characterizes the set of Nash equilibria.

1 Introduction

In this paper, we deal with the multi-object auctions under a specified class of preferences. Multi-object auctions have been used in trading important commodities such as oil leases, treasury securities, furniture and so on. Recently, important applications arise such as pollution rights, airport time slots, assignment of spectrum licenses and delivery routes. As increasing new remarkable applications of multi-object auctions, investigations of them have been developed enormously. These models of multi-object auctions can be characterized by assumptions on bidders' preferences, auction forms and information among the bidders' preferences. Initially, most of the literatures consider the case where objects are identical. The simplest assumption on bidders' preferences is that

S.-T. Yuan and M. Yokoo (Eds.): PRIMA 2001, LNAI 2132, pp. 78-92, 2001.
© Springer-Verlag Berlin Heidelberg 2001

each bidder demands only one unit of the objects. Weber's paper [20], a pioneer work of multi-object auctions, considered this case.

In other studies, bidders have positive or negative marginal utilities of items, or complementary or substitution of objects, since it is an important feature to consider the new area of remarkable auctions. Gale [8], Krishna and Rosenthal [10], Levin [12] and Rosenthal and Wang [16] investigated multi-object auctions with synergies or complementarity. Engelbrecht-Wiggans and Kahn [7] and Noussair [14] investigated the case that each bidder has two independent values for objects.

In this paper, we consider multi-object auctions in which each bidder has a positive reservation value for only one special subset of objects, called a necessary bundle. We assume that any object in the set is necessary and sufficient to the bidder. If the bidder misses any object in the set, the bidder has no value for other objects in the set. We also assume that the bidder has no value for objects outside of the set. This is an extreme case of preferences with synergies or complementarities among objects. We assume that the seller knows that each agent has such a preference, and consider the following auction: each bidder reports its necessary bundle and the reservation value for the bundle. The seller solves the assignment problem of the objects which maximizes its revenue and decides the winning bidders who can purchase their necessary bundles for their reporting prices. We call it an auction with necessary bundles. It is applicable to the recent remarkable multi-object auctions as stated above. We study that it leads to an efficient allocation through Nash equilibria under complete information.

Our motivation of this paper is derived from the applications and the sequence of studies listed above, and strongly related to Bikhchandani [3]. The paper [3] analyzed general preferences in which each bidder's reservation value for any subset is given by a real valued function defined on the power set of objects. Many articles on auctions, including multi-object auctions, focus on incomplete information games because auctions can achieve efficient allocations under complete information, but they do not under incomplete information. Bikhchandani [3] also showed that a sealed bid first price auction, in which each object is sold independently, implements Walrasian equilibrium allocations by pure strategy Nash equilibria, when the bid grid-size in the auction is sufficiently small. The sealed bid first price auction, in which each object is sold independently, is also discussed in [4].

Auctions in which each bidder reports its reservation values for any subset of objects may achieve efficient allocations, even if no Walrasian equilibrium exists. Such models are investigated as combinatorial auctions, which have received much attention recently. Vries and Vohra [5] survey articles about combinatorial auctions. Since computing winning bids and allocations is very hard in combinatorial auctions, there are many studies about computational aspects of combinatorial auctions [17]. However, combinatorial auctions have another problem. As the number of objects increases, the number of subsets of the objects increases exponentially. Hence, revealing reservation values for all the subsets is very hard in practice, when the number of objects is large. On our restriction on preferences such that each bidder has a necessary bundle, our auction form is simple and practically implementable.

In this paper, we discuss the existence of a Nash equilibrium of the multi-objective auctions with necessary bundles. We show that reporting necessary bundles and a minimal price vector in a specified set is a pure strategy Nash equilibrium. This result implies that when the bid grid-size is small enough, a pure strategy Nash equilibrium exists. We apply our results to spectrum auctions analyzed in Krishna and Rosenthal [10] and Rosenthal and Wang [16]. In that auction, necessary bundles are intervals of discretized radio spectrum. We show that the revenue maximization problem for the seller can be solved in polynomial time for the above auctions. The algorithm also indicates a method to choose an accepted bidder randomly when the revenue maximization problem has multiple optimal solutions. Lastly, we introduce a linear inequality system which characterizes the set of Nash equilibria.

This paper is organized as follows. In Section 2, we describe our model and auctions with necessary bundles. In Section 3, we discuss the existence of pure Nash equilibria. In Section 4, we discuss some problems related to spectrum auctions. Section 5 concludes.

2   The Model

2.1   Notation and Definitions

In this paper, we denote the n dimensional vector whose ith component is y_i by $\boldsymbol{y} = (y_1, y_2, \ldots, y_n)$ and the $n - 1$ dimensional vector $(y_1, \ldots, y_{i-1}, y_{i+1}, \ldots, y_n)$ by $\boldsymbol{y}_{-i}$. For convenience, the n dimensional vector $(y_1, \ldots, y_{i-1}, z_i, y_{i+1}, \ldots, y_n)$ is denoted by $(z_i, \boldsymbol{y}_{-i})$.

There are n bidders and m indivisible objects. Let $N = \{1, 2, \ldots, n\}$ be the set of bidders, and $M = \{1, 2, \ldots, m\}$ the set of objects. Each subset of objects is called a *bundle*. Each bidder i has a nonnegative reservation value $V_i(S)$ for each bundle $S \subseteq M$. We assume that the reservation value to the empty set is zero for any bidder i, i.e., $V_i(\emptyset) = 0$ for any $i \in N$. We also assume that for any bundle, the reservation value of the seller is equal to zero.

In this paper, we assume that each bidder has a positive reservation value only for one special bundle. This bundle is called the *necessary bundle*. If the bidder misses any object in the bundle, other objects in the bundle are not valuable to the bidder at all. We also assume that the objects in the bundle are also sufficient to the bidder, so the bidder has no value for any object out of the necessary bundle. We denote the necessary bundle of the bidder i by T_i and its value for T_i by $v_i > 0$. Hence, the reservation value $V_i(S)$ is written as follows:

$$V_i(S) = \begin{cases} v_i & (T \subseteq S), \\ 0 & (\text{otherwise}). \end{cases}$$

Throughout this paper, we assume that each reservation value is a positive multiple of δ, the *unit of reservation values*, i.e., we assume that $v_i \in \{\delta, 2\delta, 3\delta, \ldots\}$ for any $i \in N$.

2.2   Auctions with Necessary Bundles

We propose the sealed bid simultaneous auctions with necessary bundles. At the beginning of the auction, each bidder $i \in N$ submits a bid (B_i, b_i) where B_i is a bundle and the nonnegative real number b_i is the amount it is willing to pay for the bundle B_i. We assume that there exists a positive integer number I such that each bid is a multiple of $\frac{\delta}{I}$. We write the bid unit as ε, i.e., $\varepsilon = \frac{\delta}{I}$. The set of integer multiples of the bid unit is denoted by $Z_\varepsilon \stackrel{\text{def.}}{=} \{\varepsilon k \mid k \text{ is a nonnegative integer}\}$. Thus, $b_i \in Z_\varepsilon$ for each $i \in N$. In the following, we write a profile of bids $((B_1, b_1), (B_2, b_2), \ldots, (B_n, b_n))$ as $(\boldsymbol{B}, \boldsymbol{b})$ by changing the order of components where $\boldsymbol{B} = (B_1, B_2, \ldots, B_n)$ and $\boldsymbol{b} = (b_1, b_2, \ldots, b_n)$.

The seller solves the following integer programming problem, called the Bundle Assignment Problem (BAP), which maximizes the revenue:

$$\text{BAP}(\boldsymbol{B}, \boldsymbol{b}): \quad \text{maximize} \sum_{i \in N} b_i x_i = \boldsymbol{b} \cdot \boldsymbol{x}$$

$$\text{subject to} \sum_{i: B_i \ni j} x_i \leq 1 \quad (\forall j \in M),$$

$$x_i \in \{0, 1\} \quad (\forall i \in N),$$

where $\boldsymbol{x} = (x_1, x_2, \ldots, x_n)$. We denote the set of all the optimal solutions of BAP$(\boldsymbol{B}, \boldsymbol{b})$ by $\Omega(\boldsymbol{B}, \boldsymbol{b})$. The seller solves the problem BAP$(\boldsymbol{B}, \boldsymbol{b})$ and obtains an optimal solution $\boldsymbol{x}^*$. If the problem BAP$(\boldsymbol{B}, \boldsymbol{b})$ has multiple optimal solutions, the seller chooses an optimal solution $\boldsymbol{x}^* \in \Omega(\boldsymbol{B}, \boldsymbol{b})$ at random. The bid by the bidder i is *accepted* if and only if $x_i^* = 1$. Papers [2, 17] discuss some algorithms for solving the problem BAP$(\boldsymbol{B}, \boldsymbol{b})$.

If the bidder i is accepted, the bidder gets the bundle B_i and pay the price b_i. Given the problem BAP$(\boldsymbol{B}, \boldsymbol{b})$, we partition the set of bidders by P$(\boldsymbol{B}, \boldsymbol{b})$, Q$(\boldsymbol{B}, \boldsymbol{b})$ and R$(\boldsymbol{B}, \boldsymbol{b})$ as follows:

$$\text{P}(\boldsymbol{B}, \boldsymbol{b}) \stackrel{\text{def.}}{=} \{i \in N \mid x_i = 1, \ \forall \boldsymbol{x} \in \Omega(\boldsymbol{B}, \boldsymbol{b})\},$$

$$\text{R}(\boldsymbol{B}, \boldsymbol{b}) \stackrel{\text{def.}}{=} \{i \in N \mid x_i = 0, \ \forall \boldsymbol{x} \in \Omega(\boldsymbol{B}, \boldsymbol{b})\},$$

$$\text{Q}(\boldsymbol{B}, \boldsymbol{b}) \stackrel{\text{def.}}{=} N \setminus (\text{P}(\boldsymbol{B}, \boldsymbol{b}) \cup \text{R}(\boldsymbol{B}, \boldsymbol{b})),$$

where each member in P$(\boldsymbol{B}, \boldsymbol{b})$, Q$(\boldsymbol{B}, \boldsymbol{b})$ and R$(\boldsymbol{B}, \boldsymbol{b})$ is called a *passed* bidder, a *questionable* bidder, and a *rejected* bidder, respectively.

For the given profile $(\boldsymbol{B}, \boldsymbol{b})$, the expected utility of the bidder i denoted by $U_i(\boldsymbol{B}, \boldsymbol{b})$ is defined as follows:

$$U_i(\boldsymbol{B}, \boldsymbol{b}) \stackrel{\text{def.}}{=} \begin{cases} V_i(B_i) - b_i & (i \in \text{P}(\boldsymbol{B}, \boldsymbol{b})), \\ (V_i(B_i) - b_i) \dfrac{|\{\boldsymbol{x} \in \Omega(\boldsymbol{B}, \boldsymbol{b}) \mid x_i = 1\}|}{|\Omega(\boldsymbol{B}, \boldsymbol{b})|} & (i \in \text{Q}(\boldsymbol{B}, \boldsymbol{b})), \\ 0 & (i \in \text{R}(\boldsymbol{B}, \boldsymbol{b})), \end{cases}$$

where $|\{\boldsymbol{x} \in \Omega(\boldsymbol{B}, \boldsymbol{b}) \mid x_i = 1\}| / |\Omega(\boldsymbol{B}, \boldsymbol{b})|$ is the probability that the bidder i is accepted.

3   Pure Strategy Nash Equilibria

In this section, we discuss the existence of pure strategy Nash equilibria. We say that a profile $(\boldsymbol{B}^*, \boldsymbol{b}^*)$ is a *Nash equilibrium* when $(\boldsymbol{B}^*, \boldsymbol{b}^*)$ satisfies the conditions that for each bidder $i \in N$, $U_i(\boldsymbol{B}^*, \boldsymbol{b}^*) \geq U_i((B_i, \boldsymbol{B}^*_{-i}), (b_i, \boldsymbol{b}^*_{-i}))$ for any bid (B_i, b_i) where $B_i \subseteq M$ and $b_i \in Z_\varepsilon$.

Let us consider the following set:

$$
\mathcal{F}_\varepsilon(\boldsymbol{B}, \boldsymbol{v}) \overset{\text{def.}}{=} \left\{ \boldsymbol{b} \in Z_\varepsilon^N \middle| \begin{array}{l} b_i = v_i \quad (\forall i \in \mathrm{R}(\boldsymbol{B}, \boldsymbol{v}) \cup \mathrm{Q}(\boldsymbol{B}, \boldsymbol{v})), \\ b_i \leq v_i - 2^n \varepsilon \ (\forall i \in \mathrm{P}(\boldsymbol{B}, \boldsymbol{v})), \\ \Omega(\boldsymbol{B}, \boldsymbol{b}) = \Omega(\boldsymbol{B}, \boldsymbol{v}) \end{array} \right\}
$$

which is a subset of bid price vectors satisfying that the set of optimal solutions does not change. Given a subset of bid price vectors $X \subseteq Z_\varepsilon^N$, a vector $\boldsymbol{b} \in X$ is called a *minimal vector in X* if and only if for any $\boldsymbol{b}' \in Z_\varepsilon^N$, the condition $[\boldsymbol{b}' \leq \boldsymbol{b}$ and $\boldsymbol{b}' \neq \boldsymbol{b}]$ implies $\boldsymbol{b}' \notin X$.

Theorem 1. *If $\mathcal{F}_\varepsilon(\boldsymbol{T}, \boldsymbol{v})$ is non-empty, then for any minimal vector $\boldsymbol{b}^*$ in $\mathcal{F}_\varepsilon(\boldsymbol{T}, \boldsymbol{v})$, $(\boldsymbol{T}, \boldsymbol{b}^*)$ is a Nash equilibrium.*

To prove this theorem, we need the following two lemmas whose proofs appear in Appendix.

Lemma 1. *Let $\boldsymbol{B}$ be any bundle vector satisfying $T_i \subseteq B_i$ for any $i \in N$. Suppose $\mathcal{F}_\varepsilon(\boldsymbol{B}, \boldsymbol{v})$ is non-empty and let $\boldsymbol{b}^*$ be a minimal vector of $\mathcal{F}_\varepsilon(\boldsymbol{B}, \boldsymbol{v})$. Then, on a profile of bid $(\boldsymbol{B}, \boldsymbol{b}^*)$, any bidder $i \in N$ can not improve its payoff by changing its price b_i^* to any price $b_i \in Z_\varepsilon$, i.e., $U_i(\boldsymbol{B}, \boldsymbol{b}^*) \geq U_i(\boldsymbol{B}, (b_i, \boldsymbol{b}^*_{-i}))$ for any $b_i \in Z_\varepsilon$.*

Lemma 2. *Let $(\boldsymbol{B}, \boldsymbol{b})$ be any profile of bidding. If the bidder $i \in N$ satisfies $b_i \leq v_i$, then its expected utility of reporting (T_i, b_i) is greater than or equal to reporting (B_i, b_i), i.e., $U_i((T_i, \boldsymbol{B}_{-i}), \boldsymbol{b}) \geq U_i(\boldsymbol{B}, \boldsymbol{b})$.*

Proof of Theorem 1 We have to show that for each bidder $i \in N$, $U_i(\boldsymbol{T}, \boldsymbol{b}^*) \geq U_i((B_i, \boldsymbol{T}_{-i}), (b_i, \boldsymbol{b}^*_{-i}))$ for any bundle B_i and any price b_i. If $T_i \setminus B_i \neq \emptyset$, then $U_i(\boldsymbol{T}, \boldsymbol{b}^*) \geq 0 \geq U_i((B_i, \boldsymbol{T}_{-i}), (b_i, \boldsymbol{b}_{-i}))$ and we have done. If $b_i > v_i$, then we also have $U_i(\boldsymbol{T}, \boldsymbol{b}^*) \geq 0 \geq U_i((B_i, \boldsymbol{T}_{-i}), (b_i, \boldsymbol{b}_{-i}))$.

Suppose $T_i \subseteq B_i$ and $b_i \leq v_i$. Lemma 1 implies $U_i(\boldsymbol{T}, \boldsymbol{b}^*) \geq U_i(\boldsymbol{T}, (b_i, \boldsymbol{b}^*_{-i}))$ and Lemma 2 implies $U_i(\boldsymbol{T}, (b_i, \boldsymbol{b}^*_{-i})) \geq U_i((B_i, \boldsymbol{T}_{-i}), (b_i, \boldsymbol{b}^*_{-i}))$. Hence, we can conclude that $(\boldsymbol{T}, \boldsymbol{b}^*)$ is a Nash equilibrium. $\qquad \|$

The following theorem shows the non-emptiness of $\mathcal{F}_\varepsilon(\boldsymbol{T}, \boldsymbol{v})$.

Theorem 2. *If ε is a sufficiently small positive number, $\mathcal{F}_\varepsilon(\boldsymbol{T}, \boldsymbol{v})$ is non-empty.*

Proof. If $\mathrm{P}(\boldsymbol{T}, \boldsymbol{v}) = \emptyset$, then $\mathcal{F}_\varepsilon(\boldsymbol{T}, \boldsymbol{v}) = \{\boldsymbol{v}\}$ and so $\mathcal{F}_\varepsilon(\boldsymbol{T}, \boldsymbol{v})$ is non-empty. When $\mathrm{P}(\boldsymbol{T}, \boldsymbol{v}) \neq \emptyset$, put

$$
d = \min \left\{ (\boldsymbol{v}\boldsymbol{x}' - \boldsymbol{v}\boldsymbol{x}'') \middle| \begin{array}{l} \text{solutions } \boldsymbol{x}', \boldsymbol{x}'' \text{ are feasible to BAP}(\boldsymbol{T}, \boldsymbol{v}), \\ (\boldsymbol{v}\boldsymbol{x}' - \boldsymbol{v}\boldsymbol{x}'') > 0 \end{array} \right\}.
$$

Now assume that $\varepsilon \leq d/(n2^n + 1)$. Let $\boldsymbol{b}$ be the vector defined by,

$$b_i = \begin{cases} v_i & (i \in \mathrm{Q}(\boldsymbol{T}, \boldsymbol{v}) \cup \mathrm{R}(\boldsymbol{T}, \boldsymbol{v})), \\ v_i - 2^n\varepsilon & (i \in \mathrm{P}(\boldsymbol{T}, \boldsymbol{v})). \end{cases}$$

Let $\boldsymbol{x}^*$ be a solution in $\Omega(\boldsymbol{T}, \boldsymbol{v})$. Clearly, the equality $\boldsymbol{b} \cdot \boldsymbol{x}^* = \boldsymbol{v} \cdot \boldsymbol{x}^* - 2^n\varepsilon|\mathrm{P}(\boldsymbol{T}, \boldsymbol{v})|$ holds.

In the rest of this proof, we show that $\Omega(\boldsymbol{T}, \boldsymbol{b}) = \Omega(\boldsymbol{T}, \boldsymbol{v})$. If $\boldsymbol{x}'$ is a solution satisfying $\boldsymbol{v} \cdot \boldsymbol{x}' < \boldsymbol{v} \cdot \boldsymbol{x}^*$, then

$$\boldsymbol{b} \cdot \boldsymbol{x}' \leq \boldsymbol{v} \cdot \boldsymbol{x}' \leq \boldsymbol{v} \cdot \boldsymbol{x}^* - d \leq \boldsymbol{v} \cdot \boldsymbol{x}^* - (n2^n + 1)\varepsilon \leq \boldsymbol{v} \cdot \boldsymbol{x}^* - (|\mathrm{P}(\boldsymbol{T}, \boldsymbol{v})|2^n + 1)\varepsilon$$
$$< \boldsymbol{v} \cdot \boldsymbol{x}^* - 2^n\varepsilon|\mathrm{P}(\boldsymbol{T}, \boldsymbol{v})| = \boldsymbol{b} \cdot \boldsymbol{x}^*,$$

and so $\boldsymbol{b} \cdot \boldsymbol{x}' < \boldsymbol{b} \cdot \boldsymbol{x}^*$. If $\boldsymbol{v} \cdot \boldsymbol{x}' = \boldsymbol{v} \cdot \boldsymbol{x}^*$, then $\boldsymbol{x}' \in \Omega(\boldsymbol{T}, \boldsymbol{v})$ and so

$$\boldsymbol{b} \cdot \boldsymbol{x}' = \boldsymbol{v} \cdot \boldsymbol{x}' - 2^n\varepsilon|\mathrm{P}(\boldsymbol{T}, \boldsymbol{v})| = \boldsymbol{v} \cdot \boldsymbol{x}^* - 2^n\varepsilon|\mathrm{P}(\boldsymbol{T}, \boldsymbol{v})| = \boldsymbol{b} \cdot \boldsymbol{x}^*.$$

Thus, we have $\Omega(\boldsymbol{T}, \boldsymbol{b}) = \Omega(\boldsymbol{T}, \boldsymbol{v})$.

From the above, $\boldsymbol{b} \in \mathcal{F}_\varepsilon(\boldsymbol{T}, \boldsymbol{v})$ and so $\mathcal{F}_\varepsilon(\boldsymbol{T}, \boldsymbol{v})$ is non-empty.

For characterizing Nash equilibria in practice, we need to describe the set $\mathcal{F}_\varepsilon(\boldsymbol{B}, \boldsymbol{v})$ in a tractable form. The following lemma gives an alternative description of $\mathcal{F}_\varepsilon(\boldsymbol{B}, \boldsymbol{v})$, which enables us to separate conditions related to the discretization with bid unit ε. For any $\mathcal{G} \subseteq \mathrm{R}^N$, $\mathrm{int}\mathcal{G}$ denotes the set of relative interior points in $\mathcal{G}$. When $\mathcal{G}$ is a singleton, we define that $\mathrm{int}\mathcal{G} = \mathcal{G}$.

Lemma 3. *Let $\overline{\mathcal{F}}(\boldsymbol{B}, \boldsymbol{v})$ be the set defined by*

$$\overline{\mathcal{F}}(\boldsymbol{B}, \boldsymbol{v}) \stackrel{\mathrm{def.}}{=} \left\{ \boldsymbol{b} \in \mathrm{R}^N \left| \begin{array}{l} b_i = v_i \ (\forall i \in \mathrm{R}(\boldsymbol{B}, \boldsymbol{v}) \cup \mathrm{Q}(\boldsymbol{B}, \boldsymbol{v})), \\ b_i \leq v_i \ (\forall i \in \mathrm{P}(\boldsymbol{B}, \boldsymbol{v})), \\ \Omega(\boldsymbol{B}, \boldsymbol{b}) \supseteq \Omega(\boldsymbol{B}, \boldsymbol{v}) \end{array} \right. \right\}.$$

Then, $\mathcal{F}_\varepsilon(\boldsymbol{B}, \boldsymbol{v}) = \mathrm{int}\overline{\mathcal{F}}(\boldsymbol{B}, \boldsymbol{v}) \cap \{\boldsymbol{b} \in Z_\varepsilon^N \mid b_i \leq v_i - 2^n\varepsilon \ (\forall i \in \mathrm{P}(\boldsymbol{B}, \boldsymbol{v}))\}$.

The above lemma gives an idea for describing the set of Nash equilibria in a tractable form. We apply the above lemma to an application setting later.

4   Spectrum Auctions

In this section, we consider a spectrum auction. An auctioneer wants to sell licenses for radio spectrum $M = \{1, 2, \cdots, m\}$. Each spectrum license $j(\geq 2)$ is adjacent to $j - 1$ on the right. Kirishna and Rosenthal [10] and Rosenthal and Wang [16] analyzed models in which each object has two neighboring objects on the right and the left, and "global" bidders want to purchase the object together with its neighbor on the left or the right. We consider the case of the preferences in which each bidder i requires any spectrum license j satisfying $\ell_i \leq j \leq h_i$ but no spectrum license outside of it. This setting is applied to our model, auctions with necessary bundles, where agent i's necessary bundle is an interval $T_i = \{j \in M \mid \ell_i \leq j \leq h_i\}$.

In this case, we show that the related bundle assignment problem (BAP) is polynomially solvable. We also discuss a method to choose an optimal solution randomly, when BAP has multiple optimal solutions. Lastly, we describe a linear inequality system which includes the set of Nash equilibria as the set of feasible minimal vectors.

4.1   Bundle Assignment Problem and Longest Path Problem

Here we denote BAP by $\max\{b \cdot x \mid Ax \leq 1, \; x \in \{0,1\}^N\}$. Then the coefficient matrix $A \in \mathrm{R}^{M \times N}$ belongs to the class of consecutive one matrices, where each column vector $(a_{1i}, a_{2i}, \ldots, a_{mi})^\top$ satisfies the condition that there exists a pair of row indices (ℓ_i, h_i) satisfying that

$$a_{ji} = \begin{cases} 0 \; (j < \ell_i), \\ 1 \; (\ell_i \leq j \leq h_i), \\ 0 \; (h_i < j). \end{cases}$$

It is well-known that the consecutive one matrices are totally unimodular, i.e., the determinant of each square submatrix is either 0, -1 or 1 (see [18] for example). And so, the linear relaxation problem of BAP, $\max\{b \cdot x \mid Ax \leq 1, \; 0 \leq x \leq 1\}$, has a 0-1 valued optimal extreme point solution for any vector b. Thus, when we solve the above linear programming problem by polynomial time method, we can obtain an optimal solution to BAP in polynomial time. In the following, we show that the above problem is essentially equivalent to the longest path problem and we can solve the problem by CPM (critical path method) for PERT (Program Evaluation and Review Technique).

First, we construct a directed graph $G = (V, A)$ with the vertex set $V = \{0\} \cup M = \{0, 1, 2, \ldots, m\}$ and the directed arc set $E = E_1 \cup E_2$ defined by

$$E_1 \overset{\text{def.}}{=} \{(0,1), (1,2), \ldots, (m-1, m)\} \quad \text{and} \quad E_2 \overset{\text{def.}}{=} \{(\ell_i - 1, h_i) \mid i \in N\}.$$

For any directed path P in G, we define the corresponding set of bidders $N(P)$ by

$$N(P) \overset{\text{def.}}{=} \{i \in N \mid \text{ the arc } (\ell_i - 1, h_i) \text{ is contained in } P\}.$$

Then, for any directed path P from 0 to m in G, $N(P)$ satisfies the property that bundles in $\{T_i \mid i \in N(P)\}$ are mutually disjoint. Conversely, for any set of mutually disjoint bundles $\{T_{i_1}, T_{i_2}, \ldots, T_{i_k}\}$, there exists a path P' from 0 to m in G satisfying that $N(P') = \{i_1, i_2, \ldots, i_k\}$. For each arc $e \in E$, we define its arc weight $w(e)$ by;

$$w_b(e) \overset{\text{def.}}{=} \begin{cases} b_i \; (e = (\ell_i - 1, h_i) \in E_2), \\ 0 \; (e \in E_1 \setminus E_2). \end{cases}$$

Since BAP finds a set of mutually disjoint bundles which maximizes the total revenue, the problem is essentially equivalent to the problem for finding a longest directed path from 0 to m in G. The critical path method, which is equivalent to the ordinary dynamic programming technique, finds a longest path from 0 to m in G in $O(n + m)$ time (see [1, 6, 11] for example). The method also finds the longest distance from 0 to j for every vertex $j \in V$ without increasing the time complexity.

4.2   Random Selection from Multiple Optimal Solutions

When BAP has multiple optimal solutions, seller needs to choose an optimal solution at random. Here we describe a polynomial time method for choosing a longest path in G randomly. In the following, we denote the longest distance from vertex 0 to vertex j in G by d_j for each vertex $j \in V$. The *admissible graph* is a directed subgraph $G^* = (V, E^*)$ of G where $E^* = \{e' = (j', j'') \in E \mid d_{j''} - d_{j'} = w(e')\}$. Then it is easy to show that a directed path P from 0 to m in G is a longest path if and only if P is contained in the admissible graph G^*. Thus, the seller only needs to choose a path from 0 to m in G^* at random. For each vertex j in G^*, α_j denotes the number of directed paths in G^* from j to m. We can calculate α_j for each vertex $j \in V$ by solving the following recursive equality system;

$$\alpha_m = 1,$$
$$\alpha_j = \sum_{(j,j') \in E^*} \alpha_{j'} \quad (j \in V \setminus \{m\}).$$

Since each arc (j, j') satisfies $j < j'$, we can obtain the vector $(\alpha_0, \alpha_1, \ldots, \alpha_m)$ in decreasing order of indices. The above procedure requires $O(n + m)$ time. Then, seller can choose a path in G^* randomly, as follows.

<u>Randomized Path Selection</u>

Step 0: Set $P := (0)$ and $j := 0$.
Step 1: If $j = m$, then output the path corresponding to P and stop.
Step 2: Set $J := \{j' \in V \mid (j, j') \in E^*\}$ and choose a vertex $j^* \in J$ with the probability that $\Pr[j^* = j'] \stackrel{\text{def.}}{=} \alpha_{j'} / \sum_{j'' \in J} \alpha_{j''}$. Add the vertex j^* to the tail of the vertex sequence P. Set $j := j^*$ and go to Step 1.

If we can choose a vertex j^* in Step 2 in a constant time, then the time complexity of the above algorithm is bounded by $O(m + n)$ time.

4.3   Nash Equilibria

Here we show an inequality system for describing the region $\overline{\mathcal{F}}(B, v)$ of the spectrum auction defined above.

First, we consider the sets of passed, questionable and rejected bidders. As described in the previous subsection, we can calculate α_j, the number of directed paths in G^* from j to m, in linear time. Put $E_3 \stackrel{\text{def.}}{=} \{(j, j') \in E^* \mid \alpha_{j'} > 0\}$. Then, for each arc $e \in E_3$, there exists at least one path from 0 to m in G^* including e, it is because G^* contains a path from 0 to j for each vertex $j \in V$. It implies that the set of rejected bidders is equivalent to $\{i \in N \mid (\ell_i - 1, h_i) \notin E_3\}$. An arc e is called 0-m *cut-arc* of (V, E_3), if every 0-m path in (V, E_3) contains the arc e. It is clear that each arc $(\ell_i - 1, h_i) \in E_3$ corresponds to a passed bidder if and only if the arc is a 0-m cut-arc of (V, E_3). The ordinary depth-first search on directed graph finds all the 0-m cut-arcs in linear time [19]. From the above, we can construct the sets of passed, questionable and rejected bidders in $\mathrm{O}(n + m)$ time.

For any subset of bidders N', we denote the arc subset $\{(\ell_i - 1, h_i) \mid i \in N'\}$ by $E(N')$. In the following, we denote the set of passed bidders by $\mathrm{P}(\boldsymbol{B}, \boldsymbol{v}) = \{p_1, p_2, \ldots, p_s\}$ where $\ell_{p_1} < \ell_{p_2} < \cdots < \ell_{p_s}$. The definition of 0-m cut-arc implies that $\ell_{p_1} \le h_{p_1} < \ell_{p_2} \le h_{p_2} < \cdots < \ell_{p_s} \le h_{p_s}$. A subset N' of passed bidders is called an *interval of passed bidders*, when there exists a pair of indices (k, k') satisfying that $N' = \{p_k, p_{k+1}, \ldots, p_{k'}\}$. The family of all the intervals of passed bidders is denoted by $\mathcal{I}(\boldsymbol{B}, \boldsymbol{v})$. For each interval of passed bidders $N' \in \mathcal{I}(\boldsymbol{B}, \boldsymbol{v})$, we choose a longest 0-m path in the graph $(V, E \setminus E(N'))$ with arc weight $w_{\boldsymbol{v}}$ if it exists, and denote the path by $P(N')$. In case of non-existence, we set $P(N') = \emptyset$. We choose a longest path in the graph G with respect to $w_{\boldsymbol{v}}$ and denote the path by P^*. Then we have the following lemma.

Lemma 4.

$$\overline{\mathcal{F}}(\boldsymbol{B}, \boldsymbol{v}) = \left\{ \boldsymbol{b} \in \mathrm{R}^N \left|
\begin{array}{ll}
b_i = v_i & (\forall i \in \mathrm{R}(\boldsymbol{B}, \boldsymbol{v}) \cup \mathrm{Q}(\boldsymbol{B}, \boldsymbol{v})), \\
b_i \le v_i & (\forall i \in \mathrm{P}(\boldsymbol{B}, \boldsymbol{v})), \\
\displaystyle\sum_{i \in N(P^*)} b_i \ge \sum_{i \in N(P(N'))} b_i & (\forall N' \in \mathcal{I}(\boldsymbol{B}, \boldsymbol{v}))
\end{array}
\right. \right\}.$$

Proof.

$$\text{Put } \mathcal{F}' = \left\{ \boldsymbol{b} \in \mathrm{R}^N \left|
\begin{array}{ll}
b_i = v_i & (\forall i \in \mathrm{R}(\boldsymbol{B}, \boldsymbol{v}) \cup \mathrm{Q}(\boldsymbol{B}, \boldsymbol{v})), \\
b_i \le v_i & (\forall i \in \mathrm{P}(\boldsymbol{B}, \boldsymbol{v})), \\
\displaystyle\sum_{i \in N(P^*)} b_i \ge \sum_{i \in N(P(N'))} b_i & (\forall N' \in \mathcal{I}(\boldsymbol{B}, \boldsymbol{v}))
\end{array}
\right. \right\}.$$

First, we show that $\overline{\mathcal{F}}(\boldsymbol{B}, \boldsymbol{v}) \subseteq \mathcal{F}'$. For any $\boldsymbol{b}^* \in \overline{\mathcal{F}}(\boldsymbol{B}, \boldsymbol{v})$, $\boldsymbol{b}^*$ satisfies the inequality $\sum_{i \in N(P^*)} b_i^* \ge \sum_{i \in N(P')} b_i^*$ for each 0-m path P' in G, since $\Omega(\boldsymbol{B}, \boldsymbol{b}) \supseteq \Omega(\boldsymbol{B}, \boldsymbol{v})$. Thus, we have $\boldsymbol{b}^* \in \mathcal{F}'$.

Next, we show the converse. Let $\boldsymbol{b}^*$ be a vector in $\mathcal{F}'$. Assume on the contrary that $\boldsymbol{b}^* \notin \overline{\mathcal{F}}(\boldsymbol{B}, \boldsymbol{v})$. Then, there exists a path P' in G satisfying that $\sum_{i \in N(P^*)} b_i^* < \sum_{i \in N(P')} b_i^*$. Assume that P' is a path satisfying the inequality $\sum_{i \in N(P^*)} b_i^* < \sum_{i \in N(P')} b_i^*$ which minimizes the cardinality of $N' = N(P') \cap \mathrm{P}(\boldsymbol{B}, \boldsymbol{v})$. If N' is an interval of passed bidders, then $\sum_{i \in N(P')} b_i^* \le \sum_{i \in N(P(N'))} b_i^* \le \sum_{i \in N(P^*)} b_i^*$ and it is a contradiction. We only need to consider the case that N' is not an interval of passed bidders. Put $N' = \{p_{i_1}, p_{i_2}, \ldots, p_{i_{s'}}\}$ where $i_1 < i_2 < \cdots < i_{s'}$. Since N' is not an interval of passed bidders, there exists a passed bidder $p_{i^*} \notin N'$ satisfying that $i_1 < i^* < i_{s'}$. We denote the arc in E_2 corresponding to the bidder p_{i^*} by $(\ell^* - 1, h^*)$. We partition the path P' to two paths P'_1 and P'_2 satisfying that P'_1 is a subpath of P' from 0 to h^* and P'_2 is a subpath of P' from h^* to m. We also partition the path P^* at vertex h^* and denote the path from 0 to h^* by P^*_1 and the path from h^* to m by P^*_2. Then, either of the following inequalities holds;

$$\sum_{i \in N(P^*)} b^*_i < \sum_{i \in P'_1} b^*_i + \sum_{i \in P^*_2} b^*_i, \quad \sum_{i \in N(P^*)} b^*_i < \sum_{i \in P^*_1} b^*_i + \sum_{i \in P'_2} b^*_i.$$

Thus, either (P^*_1, P'_2) or (P'_1, P^*_2) is longer than P^* and it contradicts with the minimality of the cardinality of $N' = N(P') \cap \mathrm{P}(\boldsymbol{B}, \boldsymbol{v})$ of P'.

The above lemma implies that we can characterize the set of Nash equilibria as a set of minimal interior points in the polyhedral set defined by a system of linear inequalities consists of $\mathrm{O}(\min\{n^2, m^2\} + n + m)$ inequalities.

5   Conclusion

In this paper, we consider multi-object auctions in which each bidder has a positive reservation value for only one special subset of objects, called a necessary bundle. We showed that it leads to an efficient allocation through Nash equilibria under complete information. We also discussed the spectrum auctions analyzed in Krishna and Rosenthal [10] and Rosenthal and Wang [16]. In that auction, necessary bundles are intervals of discretized radio spectrum. We showed that the related bundle assignment problem (BAP) is polynomially solvable by using critical path method for PERT. We also discuss a method to choose an optimal solution randomly, when BAP has multiple optimal solutions. Lastly, we describe a polynomial size linear inequality system which includes the set of Nash equilibria as the set of feasible minimal interior vectors.

Appendix

Proof of Lemma 1.

We have $P(\boldsymbol{B}, \boldsymbol{v}) = P(\boldsymbol{B}, \boldsymbol{b}^*)$, $Q(\boldsymbol{B}, \boldsymbol{v}) = Q(\boldsymbol{B}, \boldsymbol{b}^*)$, and $R(\boldsymbol{B}, \boldsymbol{v}) = R(\boldsymbol{B}, \boldsymbol{b}^*)$ from the definition of a minimal vector. We also remark that any feasible solution x of $\mathrm{BAP}(\boldsymbol{B}, \boldsymbol{b}^*)$ is also feasible to $\mathrm{BAP}(\boldsymbol{B}, \boldsymbol{b})$ for any $\boldsymbol{b}$, so we denote that it is feasible for $\mathrm{BAP}(\boldsymbol{B})$.

(**case 1**) First, we consider the case that i is a rejected bidder of $\mathrm{BAP}(\boldsymbol{B}, \boldsymbol{v})$, i.e., $i \in \mathrm{R}(\boldsymbol{B}, \boldsymbol{v})$. From the definition of $\mathcal{F}_\varepsilon(\boldsymbol{B}, \boldsymbol{v})$, $b^*_i = v_i$. If the bidder $i \in \mathrm{R}(\boldsymbol{B}, \boldsymbol{v})$ submit a bid price b_i satisfying $b_i < b^*_i = v_i$ instead of b^*_i, the bidder i will not be accepted and so the payoff $U_i(\boldsymbol{B}, (b_i, \boldsymbol{b}^*_{-i}))$ is equal to 0. Let us consider the case that the bidder $i \in \mathrm{R}(\boldsymbol{B}, \boldsymbol{v})$ submit a bid price b_i satisfying $b_i > b^*_i = v_i$. If $i \in \mathrm{R}(\boldsymbol{B}, (b_i, \boldsymbol{b}^*_{-i}))$, $U_i(\boldsymbol{B}, (b_i, \boldsymbol{b}^*_{-i}))$ is also equal to zero. If $i \in \mathrm{P}(\boldsymbol{B}, (b_i, \boldsymbol{b}^*_{-i})) \cup Q(\boldsymbol{B}, (b_i, \boldsymbol{b}^*_{-i}))$, then $U_i(\boldsymbol{B}, (b_i, \boldsymbol{b}^*_{-i})) = (v_i - b_i)|\{\boldsymbol{x} \in \Omega(\boldsymbol{B}, (b_i, \boldsymbol{b}^*_{-i})) \mid x_i =$

$1\}|/|\Omega(\boldsymbol{B},(b_i,\boldsymbol{b}^*_{-i}))| < 0 = U_i(\boldsymbol{B},\boldsymbol{b}^*)$. From the above, if i is rejected bidder, then we have $U_i(\boldsymbol{B},\boldsymbol{b}^*) \geq U_i(\boldsymbol{B},(b_i,\boldsymbol{b}^*_{-i}))$.

(case 2) Next, we consider a questionable bidder $i \in Q(\boldsymbol{B},\boldsymbol{v})$. From the definition of $\mathcal{F}_\varepsilon(\boldsymbol{B},\boldsymbol{v})$, $b^*_i = v_i$. If $b_i > v_i$, then $\Omega(\boldsymbol{B},(b_i,\boldsymbol{b}^*_{-i})) = \{\boldsymbol{x} \in \Omega(\boldsymbol{B},\boldsymbol{b}^*) \mid x_i = 1\}$ and $i \in P(\boldsymbol{B},(b_i,\boldsymbol{b}^*_{-i}))$. Hence, we have $U_i(\boldsymbol{B},(b_i,\boldsymbol{b}^*_{-i})) = v_i - b_i < 0 \leq U_i(\boldsymbol{B},\boldsymbol{b}^*)$. Now consider the case that $b_i < v_i$, then $\Omega(\boldsymbol{B},(b_i,\boldsymbol{b}^*_{-i})) = \{\boldsymbol{x} \in \Omega(\boldsymbol{B},\boldsymbol{b}^*) \mid x_i = 0\}$ and $i \in R(\boldsymbol{B},(b_i,\boldsymbol{b}^*_{-i}))$. Hence, we have $U_i(\boldsymbol{B},(b_i,\boldsymbol{b}^*_{-i})) = 0 \leq U_i(\boldsymbol{B},\boldsymbol{b}^*)$. From the above, if i is a questionable bidder, $U_i(\boldsymbol{B},\boldsymbol{b}^*) \geq U_i(\boldsymbol{B},(b_i,\boldsymbol{b}^*_{-i}))$.

(case 3) Lastly, we consider the case that $i \in P(\boldsymbol{B},\boldsymbol{v})$. If $b_i > b^*_i$, then $\Omega(\boldsymbol{B},(b_i,\boldsymbol{b}^*_{-i})) = \Omega(\boldsymbol{B},\boldsymbol{b}^*)$. This implies $i \in P(\boldsymbol{B},(b_i,\boldsymbol{b}^*_{-i}))$ and so $U_i(\boldsymbol{B},(b_i,\boldsymbol{b}^*_{-i}))_i = v_i - b_i < v_i - b^*_i = U_i(\boldsymbol{B},\boldsymbol{b}^*)$. Now consider the case that $b_i < b^*_i$. The minimality of $\boldsymbol{b}^*$ and the definition of $\mathcal{F}_\varepsilon(\boldsymbol{B},\boldsymbol{v})$ implies that $\Omega(\boldsymbol{B},\boldsymbol{b}^*) \neq \Omega(\boldsymbol{B},(b_i,\boldsymbol{b}^*_{-i}))$. If $i \in R(\boldsymbol{B},(b_i,\boldsymbol{b}^*_{-i}))$, then $U_i(\boldsymbol{B},(b_i,\boldsymbol{b}^*_{-i})) = 0 \leq U_i(\boldsymbol{B},\boldsymbol{b}^*)$. In the rest of this proof, we consider the remained case that $i \in P(\boldsymbol{B},\boldsymbol{v}) = P(\boldsymbol{B},\boldsymbol{b}^*)$, $b_i < b^*_i$, and $i \in P(\boldsymbol{B},(b_i,\boldsymbol{b}^*_{-i})) \cup Q(\boldsymbol{B},(b_i,\boldsymbol{b}^*_{-i}))$.

(3-1) First, we show that $\Omega(\boldsymbol{B},\boldsymbol{b}^*) = \{\boldsymbol{x} \in \Omega(\boldsymbol{B},(b_i,\boldsymbol{b}^*_{-i})) \mid x_i = 1\}$. Since $i \in P(\boldsymbol{B},(b_i,\boldsymbol{b}^*_{-i})) \cup Q(\boldsymbol{B},(b_i,\boldsymbol{b}^*_{-i}))$, there exists an optimal solution $\boldsymbol{x}' \in \Omega(\boldsymbol{B},(b_i,\boldsymbol{b}^*_{-i}))$ satisfying that $x'_i = 1$. For any optimal solution $\boldsymbol{x}^* \in \Omega(\boldsymbol{B},\boldsymbol{b}^*)$,

$$(b_i,\boldsymbol{b}^*_{-i})\boldsymbol{x}^* = \boldsymbol{b}^*\boldsymbol{x}^* - (b^*_i - b_i) \geq \boldsymbol{b}^*\boldsymbol{x}' - (b^*_i - b_i) = (b_i,\boldsymbol{b}^*_{-i})\boldsymbol{x}',$$

and so $\boldsymbol{x}^*$ is optimal to $\mathrm{BAP}(\boldsymbol{B},(b_i,\boldsymbol{b}^*_{-i}))$. Since $i \in P(\boldsymbol{B},\boldsymbol{b}^*)$, $\boldsymbol{x}^* \in \Omega(\boldsymbol{B},(b_i,\boldsymbol{b}^*_{-i}))$ implies that $\Omega(\boldsymbol{B},\boldsymbol{b}^*) \subseteq \{\boldsymbol{x} \in \Omega(\boldsymbol{B},(b_i,\boldsymbol{b}^*_{-i})) \mid x_i = 1\}$. Conversely, for any $\boldsymbol{x}' \in \{\boldsymbol{x} \in \Omega(\boldsymbol{B},(b_i,\boldsymbol{b}^*_{-i})) \mid x_i = 1\}$,

$$\boldsymbol{b}^*\boldsymbol{x}' = (b_i,\boldsymbol{b}^*_{-i})\boldsymbol{x}' + (b^*_i - b_i) \geq (b_i,\boldsymbol{b}^*_{-i})\boldsymbol{x}^* + (b^*_i - b_i) = \boldsymbol{b}^*\boldsymbol{x}^*,$$

and so $\boldsymbol{x}'$ is also optimal to $\mathrm{BAP}(\boldsymbol{B},\boldsymbol{b}^*)$. It implies $\Omega(\boldsymbol{B},\boldsymbol{b}^*) \supseteq \{\boldsymbol{x} \in \Omega(\boldsymbol{B},(b_i,\boldsymbol{b}^*_{-i})) \mid x_i = 1\}$ and consequently, $\Omega(\boldsymbol{B},\boldsymbol{b}^*) = \{\boldsymbol{x} \in \Omega(\boldsymbol{B},(b_i,\boldsymbol{b}^*_{-i})) \mid x_i = 1\}$. The property $\Omega(\boldsymbol{B},\boldsymbol{b}^*) = \{\boldsymbol{x} \in \Omega(\boldsymbol{B},(b_i,\boldsymbol{b}^*_{-i})) \mid x_i = 1\}$ implies $i \notin P(\boldsymbol{B},(b_i,\boldsymbol{b}^*_{-i}))$. It is because, if $i \in P(\boldsymbol{B},(b_i,\boldsymbol{b}^*_{-i}))$, then $\Omega(\boldsymbol{B},(b_i,\boldsymbol{b}^*_{-i})) = \{\boldsymbol{x} \in \Omega(\boldsymbol{B},(b_i,\boldsymbol{b}^*_{-i})) \mid x_i = 1\}$ and so $\Omega(\boldsymbol{B},(b_i,\boldsymbol{b}^*_{-i})) = \Omega(\boldsymbol{B},\boldsymbol{b}^*)$. It is contradicts with the minimality of $\boldsymbol{b}^*$. Thus, we only need to consider the case that $i \in Q(\boldsymbol{B},(b_i,\boldsymbol{b}^*_{-i}))$.

(3-2) We show that $b_i = b^*_i - \varepsilon$. Let $\overline{\boldsymbol{b}}$ be the vector obtained from $\boldsymbol{b}^*$ by substituting b^*_i by $b^*_i - \varepsilon$. The definition of $\mathcal{F}_\varepsilon(\boldsymbol{B},\boldsymbol{v})$ and the minimality of $\boldsymbol{b}^*$ implies that $\Omega(\boldsymbol{B},\overline{\boldsymbol{b}}) \neq \Omega(\boldsymbol{B},\boldsymbol{b}^*)$. In the following, we show that the assumption that $b_i < b^*_i - \varepsilon$ implies $\Omega(\boldsymbol{B},\overline{\boldsymbol{b}}) = \Omega(\boldsymbol{B},\boldsymbol{b}^*)$. Let $\boldsymbol{x}^*$ be a solution in $\Omega(\boldsymbol{B},\boldsymbol{b}^*)$ and $\boldsymbol{x}$ be any feasible solution of $\mathrm{BAP}(\boldsymbol{B})$. If $x_i = 0$, then the property $\boldsymbol{x}^* \in \Omega(\boldsymbol{B},\boldsymbol{b}^*) \subseteq \Omega(\boldsymbol{B},(b_i,\boldsymbol{b}^*_{-i}))$ implies that

$$\overline{\boldsymbol{b}}\boldsymbol{x} = (b_i,\boldsymbol{b}^*_{-i})\boldsymbol{x} \leq (b_i,\boldsymbol{b}^*_{-i})\boldsymbol{x}^* \leq \overline{\boldsymbol{b}}\boldsymbol{x}^*.$$

If $x_i = 1$, then

$$\overline{\boldsymbol{b}}\boldsymbol{x} = \boldsymbol{b}^*\boldsymbol{x} - \varepsilon \leq \boldsymbol{b}^*\boldsymbol{x}^* - \varepsilon = \overline{\boldsymbol{b}}\boldsymbol{x}^*.$$

From the above inequalities, x^* is optimal to $\mathrm{BAP}(B, \bar{b})$ and so $\Omega(B, b^*) \subseteq \Omega(B, \bar{b})$. Next, we prove that $\Omega(B, b^*) \supseteq \Omega(B, \bar{b})$ by showing that for any feasible solution x of $\mathrm{BAP}(B)$, $x \notin \Omega(B, b^*)$ implies $x \notin \Omega(B, \bar{b})$. When $x_i = 0$, x satisfies that

$$\bar{b}x = (b_i, b^*_{-i})x \le (b_i, b^*_{-i})x^* = \bar{b}x^* - \varepsilon < \bar{b}x^*$$

and so x is not optimal to $\mathrm{BAP}(B, \bar{b})$. If x satisfies that $x_i = 1$,

$$\bar{b}x = b^*x - \varepsilon < b^*x^* - \varepsilon = \bar{b}x^*,$$

and so x is not optimal to $\mathrm{BAP}(B, \bar{b})$. It implies that $\Omega(B, b^*) \supseteq \Omega(B, \bar{b})$. From the above $\Omega(B, b^*) = \Omega(B, \bar{b})$ and it is a contradiction.

(3-3) From the above discussions, we have that $b_i = b^*_i - \varepsilon$ and $i \in Q(B, b)$. Then,

$$
\begin{aligned}
U_i(B, (b_i, b^*_{-i})) &= (v_i - b_i) \frac{\left| \{ x \in \Omega(B, (b_i, b^*_{-i})) \mid x_i = 1 \} \right|}{\left| \Omega(B, (b_i, b^*_{-i})) \right|} \\
&= (v_i - b_i) \frac{|\Omega(B, b^*)|}{\left| \Omega(B, (b_i, b^*_{-i})) \right|} = (v_i - (b^*_i - \varepsilon)) \frac{|\Omega(B, b^*)|}{\left| \Omega(B, (b_i, b^*_{-i})) \right|} \\
&= (v_i - b^*_i) - (v_i - b^*_i) \frac{\left| \Omega(B, (b_i, b^*_{-i})) \right| - |\Omega(B, b^*)|}{\left| \Omega(B, (b_i, b^*_{-i})) \right|} + \varepsilon \frac{|\Omega(B, b^*)|}{\left| \Omega(B, (b_i, b^*_{-i})) \right|} \\
&\le U_i(B, b^*) - (v_i - b^*_i)/2^n + \varepsilon \le U_i(B, b^*) - \varepsilon + \varepsilon = U_i(B, b^*),
\end{aligned}
$$

since the definition of $\mathcal{F}_\varepsilon$ implies that $b^*_i \le v_i - 2^n \varepsilon$.

From the above, b^*_i is a best reply with respect to b^* and so we have that for each bidder i, $U_i(B, b^*) \ge U_i(B, (b_i, b^*_{-i}))$. $\parallel$

Proof of Lemma 2.

Clearly, $U_i((T_i, B_{-i}), b)$ is nonnegative. If $T_i \setminus B_i \ne \emptyset$, then $U_i(B, b) \le 0 \le U_i((T_i, B_{-i}), b)$. Thus, we only need to consider the case $T_i \subseteq B_i$. In this case, each feasible solution for $\mathrm{BAP}(B, b)$ is also feasible to $\mathrm{BAP}((T_i, B_{-i}), b)$.

If $i \in P((T_i, B_{-i}), b)$, we have $U_i((T_i, B_{-i}), b) = v_i - b_i$ and it is always greater than or equal to $U_i(B, b)$. Hence, in the rest of the proof, we consider the case that $T_i \subseteq B_i$ and $i \in Q((T_i, B_{-i}), b) \cup R((T_i, B_{-i}), b)$. In this case, there exists an optimal solution $x^* \in \Omega((T_i, B_{-i}), b)$ satisfying $x^*_i = 0$. Let $\bar{x}$ be an optimal solution of $\mathrm{BAP}(B, b)$. Since $T_i \subseteq B_i$, $\bar{x}$ is also feasible for $\mathrm{BAP}((T_i, B_{-i}), b)$ and so $b x^* \ge b \bar{x}$. Conversely, since $x^*_i = 0$, x^* is also feasible for $\mathrm{BAP}(B, b)$. Hence, we have $b \bar{x} \ge b x^*$ and so $b \bar{x} = b x^*$. From the above discussion, we find that the following three properties hold:

(i) $\Omega(B, b) \subseteq \Omega((T_i, B_{-i}), b)$,
(ii) $\{ x \in \Omega(B, b) \mid x_i = 1 \} \subseteq \{ x \in \Omega((T_i, B_{-i}), b) \mid x_i = 1 \}$,
(iii) $\{ x \in \Omega(B, b) \mid x_i = 0 \} = \{ x \in \Omega((T_i, B_{-i}), b) \mid x_i = 0 \}$.

Assume that $i \in \mathrm{R}((T_i, \boldsymbol{B}_{-i}), \boldsymbol{b})$. Then, we can assert that $i \in \mathrm{R}(\boldsymbol{B}, \boldsymbol{b})$. Otherwise, there exists $\overline{\boldsymbol{x}} \in \Omega(\boldsymbol{B}, \boldsymbol{b})$ such that $\overline{x}_i = 1$. From (i), $\overline{\boldsymbol{x}}$ is also an optimal solution for $\mathrm{BAP}((T_i, \boldsymbol{B}_{-i}), \boldsymbol{b})$. However, it contradicts from $i \in \mathrm{R}((T_i, \boldsymbol{B}_{-i}), \boldsymbol{b})$. Hence, we have $i \in \mathrm{R}(\boldsymbol{B}, \boldsymbol{b})$, and so we have $U_i((T_i, \boldsymbol{B}_{-i}), \boldsymbol{b}) = U_i(\boldsymbol{B}, \boldsymbol{b}) = 0$.

Lastly, suppose that $i \in \mathrm{Q}((T_i, \boldsymbol{B}_{-i}), \boldsymbol{b})$. From (ii) and (iii), we have

$$U_i((T_i, \boldsymbol{B}_{-i}), \boldsymbol{b}) = (v_i - b_i) \frac{|\{\boldsymbol{x} \in \Omega((T_i, \boldsymbol{B}_{-i}), \boldsymbol{b}) \mid x_i = 1\}|}{|\Omega((T_i, \boldsymbol{B}_{-i}), \boldsymbol{b})|}$$

$$= (v_i - b_i) \frac{|\{\boldsymbol{x} \in \Omega((T_i, \boldsymbol{B}_{-i}), \boldsymbol{b}) \mid x_i = 1\}|}{|\{\boldsymbol{x} \in \Omega((T_i, \boldsymbol{B}_{-i}), \boldsymbol{b}) \mid x_i = 1\}| + |\{\boldsymbol{x} \in \Omega((T_i, \boldsymbol{B}_{-i}), \boldsymbol{b}) \mid x_i = 0\}|}$$

$$\geq (v_i - b_i) \frac{|\{\boldsymbol{x} \in \Omega(\boldsymbol{B}, \boldsymbol{b}) \mid x_i = 1\}|}{|\{\boldsymbol{x} \in \Omega(\boldsymbol{B}, \boldsymbol{b}) \mid x_i = 1\}| + |\{\boldsymbol{x} \in \Omega(\boldsymbol{B}, \boldsymbol{b}) \mid x_i = 0\}|}$$

$$= (v_i - b_i) \frac{|\{\boldsymbol{x} \in \Omega(\boldsymbol{B}, \boldsymbol{b}) \mid x_i = 1\}|}{|\Omega(\boldsymbol{B}, \boldsymbol{b})|}$$

$$= U_i(\boldsymbol{B}, \boldsymbol{b}).$$

Hence, we can conclude that $U_i((T_i, \boldsymbol{B}_{-i}), \boldsymbol{b}) \geq U_i(\boldsymbol{B}, \boldsymbol{b})$ for any B_i. $\qquad \|$

Proof of Lemma 3.

When $\mathrm{P}(\boldsymbol{B}, \boldsymbol{v}) = \emptyset$, both $\mathcal{F}_\varepsilon(\boldsymbol{B}, \boldsymbol{v})$ and $\overline{\mathcal{F}}(\boldsymbol{B}, \boldsymbol{v})$ are singleton, and so it is obvious. In the rest of this proof, we assume that $\mathrm{P}(\boldsymbol{B}, \boldsymbol{v}) \neq \emptyset$.

In this proof, we define the affine subspace H by

$$H = \{\boldsymbol{b} \in \mathrm{R}^N \mid b_i = v_i \ (\forall i \in \mathrm{R}(\boldsymbol{B}, \boldsymbol{v}) \cup \mathrm{Q}(\boldsymbol{B}, \boldsymbol{v}))\}.$$

First, we show that the minimum affine subspace including $\overline{\mathcal{F}}(\boldsymbol{B}, \boldsymbol{v})$ is H. Clearly, $\overline{\mathcal{F}}(\boldsymbol{B}, \boldsymbol{v}) \subseteq H$. For any passed bidder $i \in \mathrm{P}(\boldsymbol{B}, \boldsymbol{v})$, if η is a sufficiently small positive number, then $\boldsymbol{v} - \eta \boldsymbol{u}_i \in \overline{\mathcal{F}}(\boldsymbol{B}, \boldsymbol{v})$ where $\boldsymbol{u}_i$ is the ith unit vector. Since the minimum affine subspace including $\{\boldsymbol{v}\} \cup \{\boldsymbol{v} - \eta \boldsymbol{u}_i \mid i \in \mathrm{P}(\boldsymbol{B}, \boldsymbol{v})\}$ is H, the minimum affine subspace including $\overline{\mathcal{F}}(\boldsymbol{B}, \boldsymbol{v})$ is also H.

We define the set $\mathcal{F}'$ by

$$\mathcal{F}' \stackrel{\text{def.}}{=} \left\{ \boldsymbol{b} \in \mathrm{R}^N \,\middle|\, \begin{array}{l} b_i = v_i \ (\forall i \in \mathrm{R}(\boldsymbol{B}, \boldsymbol{v}) \cup \mathrm{Q}(\boldsymbol{B}, \boldsymbol{v})), \\ b_i < v_i \ (\forall i \in \mathrm{P}(\boldsymbol{B}, \boldsymbol{v})), \\ \Omega(\boldsymbol{B}, \boldsymbol{b}) = \Omega(\boldsymbol{B}, \boldsymbol{v}) \end{array} \right\}.$$

Then, we only need to show that $\mathcal{F}' = \mathrm{int}\overline{\mathcal{F}}(\boldsymbol{B}, \boldsymbol{v})$. For any point $\boldsymbol{b}_1 \in \mathcal{F}'$, we consider the open ball $\mathrm{Ball}(\boldsymbol{b}_1, \eta_1)$ with center $\boldsymbol{b}_1$ and radius η_1. Assume that η_1 is a sufficiently small positive number. Then, for any vector $\boldsymbol{b}' \in \mathrm{Ball}(\boldsymbol{b}_1, \eta_1) \cap H$, $\boldsymbol{b}' \in \mathcal{F}' \subseteq \overline{\mathcal{F}}(\boldsymbol{B}, \boldsymbol{v})$ and so $\mathrm{Ball}(\boldsymbol{b}_1, \eta_1) \cap H \subseteq \overline{\mathcal{F}}(\boldsymbol{B}, \boldsymbol{v})$. It implies that $\mathcal{F}' \subseteq \mathrm{int}\overline{\mathcal{F}}(\boldsymbol{B}, \boldsymbol{v})$. Let $\boldsymbol{b}_2$ be a point in $\mathrm{int}\overline{\mathcal{F}}(\boldsymbol{B}, \boldsymbol{v})$. Then there exists an open ball $\mathrm{Ball}(\boldsymbol{b}_2, \eta_2)$ satisfying that $\mathrm{Ball}(\boldsymbol{b}_2, \eta_2) \cap H \subseteq \overline{\mathcal{F}}(\boldsymbol{B}, \boldsymbol{v})$. Then, it is clear that for any passed bidder $i \in \mathrm{P}(\boldsymbol{B}, \boldsymbol{v})$, ith element of $\boldsymbol{b}_2$ is strictly less than v_i. Lastly, we show that $\Omega(\boldsymbol{B}, \boldsymbol{b}_2) = \Omega(\boldsymbol{B}, \boldsymbol{v})$. Assume on the contrary that $\exists \boldsymbol{x}^* \in \Omega(\boldsymbol{B}, \boldsymbol{b}_2) \setminus \Omega(\boldsymbol{B}, \boldsymbol{v})$. If $x_i^* = 1$ for all $i \in \mathrm{P}(\boldsymbol{B}, \boldsymbol{v})$, then $\boldsymbol{x}^* \in \Omega(\boldsymbol{B}, \boldsymbol{v})$

and it is a contradiction. Thus, $\exists i' \in P(\boldsymbol{B}, \boldsymbol{v})$, $x_{i'}^* = 0$. Let us consider the vector $\boldsymbol{b}_2 - (1/2)\eta_2\boldsymbol{u}_{i'}$. Since $\boldsymbol{b}_2 - (1/2)\eta_2\boldsymbol{u}_{i'} \in \mathrm{Ball}(\boldsymbol{b}_2, \eta_2) \cap H$, it is clear that $\Omega(\boldsymbol{B}, \boldsymbol{b}_2 - (1/2)\eta_2\boldsymbol{u}_{i'}) \supseteq \Omega(\boldsymbol{B}.\boldsymbol{v})$. Denote a solution in $\Omega(\boldsymbol{B}, \boldsymbol{v})$ by $\boldsymbol{x}'$. Then, $\boldsymbol{x}^* \in \Omega(\boldsymbol{B}, \boldsymbol{b}_2) \supseteq \Omega(\boldsymbol{B}, \boldsymbol{v}) \ni \boldsymbol{x}'$ implies the inequality

$$(\boldsymbol{b}_2 - (1/2)\eta_2\boldsymbol{u}_{i'}) \cdot \boldsymbol{x}' < \boldsymbol{b}_2 \cdot \boldsymbol{x}' = \boldsymbol{b}_2 \cdot \boldsymbol{x}^* = (\boldsymbol{b}_2 - (1/2)\eta_2\boldsymbol{u}_{i'}) \cdot \boldsymbol{x}^*$$

and so $\Omega(\boldsymbol{b}_2 - (1/2)\eta_2\boldsymbol{u}_{i'}) \not\ni \boldsymbol{x}' \in \Omega(\boldsymbol{B}, \boldsymbol{v})$. Contradiction. $\|$

References

1. Ahuja, R. K., Magnanti, T. L., and Orlin, J. B. (1993), *Network Flows, Theory Algorithms and Applications,* Princeton Hall.
2. A. Andersson, A., Tenhunen, M., and Ygge, F. (2000), "Integer Programming for Combinatorial Auction Winner Determination," *Proc. of the Fourth International Conference on Multiagent Systems* (ICMAS-00).
3. Bikhchandani, S. (1999), "Auctions of heterogeneous objects," *Games and Economic Behavior*, vol. 26, 193–220.
4. Bikhchandani, S. and Mamer, J. W. (1997), "Competitive equilibrium in an exchange economy with indivisibilities," *Journal of Economic Theory*, vol. 74, 385–413.
5. de Vries, S. and Vohra, R. "Combinatorial auctions; a survey," *Kellog School of Management, technical report.*
6. Elmaghraby, S. E. (1979), *Activity Networks*, John Wiley and Sons.
7. Engelbrecht-Wiggans, R. and Kahn, C. M. (1998), "Multi-unit auctions with uniform prices," *Economic Theory*, vol. 12, 227–258.
8. Gale, I. (1990), "A multiple-object auction with superadditive values," *Economic Letters*, vol. 34, 323–328.
9. Kashima, H. and Kajiwara, Y. (2000), "Optimal winner determination algorithms for E-procurement auction," *Technical Report of IEICE*, COMP, vol. 59, 17–23.
10. Krishna, V. and Rosenthal, R. W. (1996), "Simultaneous auctions with synergies," *Games and Economic Behavior*, vol. 17, 1–31.
11. Lawler, E. L. (1976), *Combinatorial Optimization: Networks and Matroids*, Holt, Rinehart and Winston, New York.
12. Levin, J. (1997), "An optimal auction for complements," *Games and Economic Behavior*, vol. 18, 176–192.
13. MacMillan, J. (1994), "Selling spectrum rights," *Journal of Economic Perspectives*, vol. 8, 145–162.
14. Noussair, C. (1995), "Equilibria in a multi-object uniform price sealed bid auction with multi-unit demands," *Economic Theory*, vol. 5, 337–351.
15. Rassenti, S. J., Smith, V. L., and Bulfin, R. L. (1982), "A combinatorial auction mechanism for airport time slot allocation," *Bell Journal of Economics*, vol. 13, 402–417.
16. Rosenthal, R. W. and Wang R. (1996), "Simultaneous auctions with synergies and common values," *Games and economic Behavior*, vol. 17, 32–55.
17. Rothkopf, M. H., Pekeć, A. and Harstad, R. M. (1998), "Computationally manageable combinatorial auctions", *Management Science*, vol. 44, 1131–1147.
18. Schrijver, A. (1986), *Theory of Linear and Integer Programming*, John Wiley and Sons, New York.

19. Tarjan, R. (1972), "Depth-first search and linear graph algorithms", *SIAM Journal on Computing*, vol. 1, 146–160.
20. Weber, R. J. (1983), "Multi-object auctions," in *Auctions, Bidding and Contracting*, Engelbrecht-Wiggans, R., Shubik, M. and Stark R. eds., New York University Press.

Strategic Multi-Personal-Agent Interaction

Aizhong (Alan) Lin

Faculty of Information Technology
University of Technology, Sydney
POBox 123, Broadway
NSW 2007, AUSTRALIA
alin@it.uts.edu.au

Abstract. A multi-personal-agent system --- EPMPAS (Emergent Process Multi-Personal-Agent System) --- is built for emergent process management in a university faculty environment. Personal agents' interaction performance plays important role in process performance. Applying different interaction strategy to interact with different individual agents by understanding their behavior so that to obtain higher interaction performance is our research goal. Understanding an agent's behavior is to understand an agent's APR, i.e. **A**bilities, **P**ersonalities and **R**elationships. An agent's APR can be observed and assessed from agents' interaction history. After several months of works as the assistants of process performers, the interaction performances of EPMPAS are measured according to a defined interaction performance scale.

1. Introduction

When CSCW (Computer Support Cooperative Work) is applied to business and market areas such as Networked Enterprise, eCommence and B2B, traditional human to human interaction model is changed to human-with-computer to computer-with-human interaction model. Because of their autonomous, communicate and adaptive properties [11], software personal agents are built to assist human process performers. They work on the behalf of their human principals and interact with other agents with their principals [9]. Such agents can also support human interactions such as process delegation [2], negotiation [8], or coordination [3].

Interactions are very common phenomena in human society. An interaction is a mutual or reciprocal action or influence that one depends upon another, so it is time-consume process because more than one person is involved in it. To achieve a process goal, working with different partner may result in different process performance. To find a suitable partner and cooperate with the partner, interactions are extremely necessary. A process performance is significantly based on its interactions' performance. An interaction performance can be evaluated with its *result*, *benefit*, and *time* dimensions [9]. Human beings usually pursue the higher interaction performance with its knowledge.

The level of one's interaction performance depends on the extent of one's understanding of its interaction objects. An ancient Chinese strategist's words --- "Knowing yourself and knowing your adversary, you could not be lost in a fight" --- is a vivid description. Understanding its interaction objects and trying "best" or "good" strategies to interact with different individuals result in a higher performance. Humans can percept and assess their interaction objects (cooperative or competitive) by numbers of means. Analyzing their interaction histories and forming the impression of others is one of the most important.

S.-T. Yuan and M. Yokoo (Eds.): PRIMA 2001, LNAI 2132, pp. 93-107, 2001.

Interaction history can be analyzed and applied in future interaction, unfortunately no model shows how to use them.

In EPMPAS [10], according to [11, pp299-330], individual agents have knowledge, culture, memories, history, and capabilities distinct from any single agent. They work on the behalf of individual human process performers. They could use different knowledge and different methods to solve same problems but get different result. They could be cooperative or competitive [1], selfless or selfish [7], and could cooperate with some agents but compete with others in the same society. To obtain higher interaction performance, agents should understand the behavior of their interaction objects.

We provide a method to understand agents' interaction behaviors and use different interaction strategy to interact with different agents so that to pursue a higher interaction performance. Understanding agents' behavior is to understand agents' *APR*, i.e. **A**bilities, **P**ersonalities and **R**elationships with different others. First of all, agent interaction history is recorded according to the definition of specific parameters used later. Based on the interaction history, three computational models are built and applied. A computational agent ability model (CAAM) is firstly built to measure an agent's problem-solving abilities that include the agent productivity, efficiency and quality. A computational agent personality model (CAPM) is then built to measure an agent's personalities including "cooperative", "selfish", "trust", "reliable" and so on. A computational agent relationship model (CARM) is finally built to measure an agent's in-depth relationships (such as "friends") with different other agents. Based on the understanding and managing of other agents' behavior, one agent could make suitable choice of interaction strategy to interact with different other agents to substantially improve the interaction performance.

The method has been used in our EPMPAS to support emergent process management in a university faculty and the performances are measured according to a defined scale.

2.   Backgrounds

The multi-personal-agent system is introduced briefly and agents' interaction concepts are described in this section.

2.1   EPMPAS --- Emergent Process Multi-Personal-Agent System

An emergent process multi-personal-agent system has been built and worked in a university faculty. All individual agents in EPMPAS are generated from a generic cooperative process agent based on a three-layered BDI hybrid agent conceptual architecture [2].

2.1.1   Multi-Personal-Agent System Architecture

The architecture of EPMPAS is in the middle level of Figure 1. It works as a "middle ware" which assists process performers (at the bottom level) to perform process tasks (on the top level). In this architecture, every performer is supported with one and only one personal agent.

The features of this architecture are:
- It is a pure distributed process management system that works as a real human society
- Individual agents are generated from a generic process agent
- Individual agents provide individual abilities that consists of not public services but also private services
- Process interactions are implemented via their personal agents so that memorizing interaction history is not a problem.

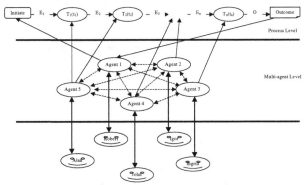

Figure 1: The architecture of EPMPAS

2.1.2   Generic Process Agent

The generic process agent is built with detecting mechanism, reasoning mechanism, decision-making mechanism and interacting mechanism (Figure 2) [10]. The detecting mechanism percepts specific events based on the events' settings in the events' library. The reasoning mechanism derives plan options or action options according to the logical path from beliefs to goals to plans and then to actions based on the triggers library, goals library, plan library and actions library (the goals, plans and actions library are combined and called agent's capability library). The decision-making mechanism decides which one should be instantiated from the options. And the interaction mechanism provides agent's interaction layered protocols.

Before a generic agent is instantiated to a personal agent for a process performer, all its libraries (including events library, trigger library, goal library, plan library and action library) are empty. Generating a personal agent from it is to setup capabilities and knowledge to correspond library. Both agent designers and process performers can do it. Individual agents own different capabilities and knowledge for different implementers. For supporting performers more convenient, visualized managers are provided such as:

- Process manager: process modeling, process instantiating and process advancing

- Capability manager: goal, plan and action library management
- Reasoning manager: message, belief, goal, plan, action and its commitment management
- Decision manager: local and social decision
- Interaction manager: delegation, negotiation and coordination protocols management

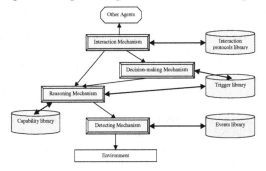

Figure 2: The components of generic process agent

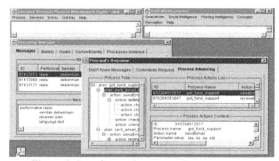

Figure 3: Interfaces of a personal process agent

In addition, we provides some common services in the framework:

- Send message: Send a KQML message to other agent/agents
- Find who is who: Find an agent's responsibilities
- Find where is who: Find an agent's address
- Upload documents: Upload documents to specific sites strategically
- Download documents: Download documents based on time table
- Diary manager: Manage the activities for an agent
- Performance manager: Process performance and interaction performance analysis

Figure 3 is a personal agent generated from the generic agent.

2.2 Interaction Protocols

Agents' interactions are supported by layered protocols described in figure 4. Interaction layer is agent-oriented and is directly supported by message layer. Content layer is embedded in message layer and works above a network layer.

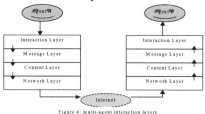

Figure 4 : multi-agent interaction layers

2.2.1 Network Layer

Network layer is in the bottom of all agents' interaction layers. It is implemented by high-level layer services of seven-layer model of ISO OSI such as socket (TCP/IP), SMTP&POP, and FTP. In EPMPAS, such protocols are used to support messages transformation.

2.2.2 Content Layer

FIPA [5] recommended several content layer protocols such as SL, RDF (Resources Description Framework), CSP (Constraint Satisfaction Problem) and KIF that can be used as agent semantics carriers. RDF is selected as content protocol of EPMPAS because it is XML (eXtensible Markup Language) based so it can be understood widely.

2.2.3   Message Layer

Message layer protocols define the wrapper of exchanging contents. KQML (Knowledge Query and Manipulation Language) [4] and ACL (Agent Communication Language) [6] are currently accepted widely. ACL is selected in EPMPAS due to it is more suitable to support interaction level protocols.

2.2.4   Interaction Layer

Agent interaction layer protocols can be identified with four types: (1) CC (casual conversation); (2) DE (delegation); (3) NE (negotiation); and (4) CO (coordination). Any of them could include many specific protocols. Negotiation, for example, includes Brokering Protocol, Recruiting Protocol, Auction Protocol, and Contract Net Protocol. EPMPAS picks up some of them from four types of protocols (Table 1).

Table 1. EPMPAS interaction protocols

Type	Protocol	Adapted from
CC	Casual-Conversation	10
DE	Delegation	2
NE	Contract-Net	6
CO	Distributed-Coordination	RFC, 2000

2.3 Primitives

Standard ACL primitives [6] are supported by EPMPAS, but more primitives are extended for process interaction protocols [2]:
- *initial*:   command, delegation, offer, invitation, assertion, request, appeal
- *middle*:   declaration, instruction, propose
- *terminal*:   commitment, agreement, acknowledgement, assent, declination, refusal, reject, deny, accept, confirm

The brief explanations of the initial primitives are:
- A *command* message is usually sent from an agent group leader to the group members for an important event. Normally, the receiver should do as the sender asked.
- A *delegation* message is usually sent any agent to another agent for a casual event during a complicate process. The sender wants the receiver to be responsible for its sub process.
- An *invitation* message is usually sent from any agent to another agent for a casual event. Then sender invites the receiver to be involved in an activity.
- ...

2.4 Strategic Interaction Model

An emergent process could normally cause a series of interaction processes that are formed with a number of messages exchanging. An interaction process is initiated by a message with an initial primitive and terminated by a message with a terminal primitive. All primitives from initial to terminal form an interaction pattern used as the basis of agent interaction analysis.

When initiating an interaction, agents could be involved in a delegation, a negotiation or coordination and the interaction is not finished until the negotiation or coordination is completed. Whether how complicated the interaction is, the interaction patterns are only important to us rather than the details of negotiation or coordination.

Figure 5 is a strategic interaction model. First, primitives are mined with time stamped. By using a FSM (Finite-States-Machine), all primitives are formed to correspondent interaction patterns that can be adjusted with additional factors (reply time, semantics and intensity). By patterns' analysis, one agent can assess other individual agents' APR with which next interaction could be driven strategically so that higher interaction performance could be obtained.

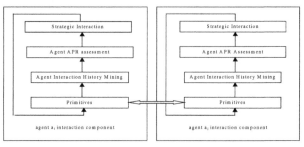

Figure 5. Obtainable path of friendship

2.5 IPES --- Interaction Performance Evaluation Scale

An interaction performance can be measured from three dimensions: (1) success (*successful to failure*); (2) profit (*benefits vs. costs*); and (3) time (*time from initiation to termination*).

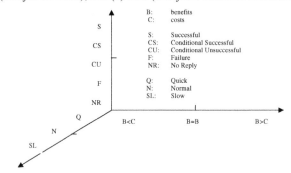

Figure 6. Interaction performance measurement scales

From the success dimension, it is categorized to (Figure 6):

- Success (S):   achieve the goal without additional interactions
- Conditional success (CS):   achieve the goal with additional interactions
- Conditional un-success (CU):   fail to achieve the goal with additional interactions
- Failure (F):   fail to achieve the goal with no reason
- No reply (NR):   no reply message

From the profit dimension, it is identified with:

- Benefits are larger than costs (B > C):   benefits are larger than costs
- Benefits equal costs (B = C):   benefits equal costs
- Benefits are less than costs (B < C):   benefits are less than costs

And from the time from initiation to termination dimension, it is identified with:

- Quick (Q):   reply time and fewer messages exchanging
- Normal (N):   suitable reply time and suitable messages exchanging
- Slow (SL):   long reply time and many messages exchanging

3.　Agent Interaction Pattern Mining

3.1　Message Data

Suppose n agents A_1, A_2, ..., and A_n live in an agent society, following matrix structure (Table 2) is a description of agent interaction database that any agent Ai could have about any others $(A_1, A_2, ..., A_{i-1}, A_{i+1}, ..., A_n)$. In EPMPAS, the most important interaction element is message data.

Table 2 --- Agent interaction database description

	A_1	A_2	...	A_j	...	A_n
A_1						
A_2						
...						
A_I				1. Process records 2. Task records 3. Message records 4.		
...						
A_n						

A message record is defined with two sections, one is for message description and another is for its meta-information:

- Message description:
  - ID:　　　　　　　message identifier such as m_3365788
  - Primitive:　　　　key words such as "ask", "command", "request", "reply",...
  - Content:　　　　　message contents such as "Could you help me to do..."
  - Language:　　　　message content language such as "Text"
  - Ontology:　　　　message ontology that define the terms of message contents
  - Sender:　　　　　who sends the message
  - Receiver:　　　　who receive the message
  - Reply with:　　　documents should attached with the reply
  - In reply to:　　　message that this message replies to
  - Comment:　　　　any other relevant information
- Meta-information:
  - Send time:　　　　message send time
  - Receive time:　　　message reply time
  - Type:　　　　　　message type
  - State:　　　　　　message current state
  - Interaction name:　which interaction process that message belongs to
  - Task name:　　　　which task process that message belongs to
  - Process name:　　　which process that message belongs to
  - Description:　　　　any other meta-information

3.2　Interaction Pattern

From the message data, we can mine all interaction patterns by using a FSM (Finite State Machine) algorithm. An interaction pattern, denoted by P, is a sequence of ACL messages beginning with an initial primitive and terminating with a terminal primitive. A message with initial primitive could cause different sequence of messages exchanging, but it can be arranged as the same group, denoted by G. G 1, for example, begins with the message with the command primitive.

　　　　G 1:
　　　　　　p 1:　　　command / commitment

p 2:   command / negotiation / commitment
p 3:   command / coordination / commitment
p 4:   command / negotiation / refuse
p 5:   command / coordination / refuse
p 6:   command / refuse
p 7:   command / no reply

G 2:

p 1:   delegation / accept

......

G 3:

p 1:   offer / accept

......

......

An interaction could be very simple with only two messages that one is the initial and another is the terminal. However, some of them could be very complex with a negotiation process or coordination process in the middle. A negotiation or coordination process is recognized during the interaction because it obeys its protocol.

3.3 Adjusting Factors

Besides the mining of interaction pattern, several other parameters such as reply time, semantics and intensity can be obtained from agents' message data. They are applied to adjust interaction patterns.

3.3.1   Reply Time

The time interval (t) in an interaction pattern is defined with the difference between initial primitive send time (t_i) and terminal primitive (t_t). It is an important adjusting factor of interaction pattern because normally it is a reflection of the behavior of the people.

The patterns described above are adjusted in terms of the reply time. Considering the group 1, for example:

G 1:

p 1 (t):   command (t_i) / commitment (t_t)
p 2 (t):   command (t_i) / negotiation (t_{m1}) / commitment (t_t)
p 3 (t):   command (t_i) / coordination (t_{m1}) / commitment (t_t)
p 4 (t):   command(t_i) / negotiation (t_{m1}) / refuse (t_t)
p 5 (t):   command (t_i) / coordination (t_{m1}) / refuse (t_t)
p 6 (t):   command (t_i) / refuse (t_t)
p 7 (t):   command (t_i) / no reply (t_t)

3.3.2   Semantics of Messages

From the semantics of messages, we may be able to obtain an agent's profit (denoted by $\delta = b-c$, it is the difference between benefit and cost of an interaction). The patterns described above are adjusted in terms of δ. Still considering the group 1, for example:

G 1:

p 1 (t) (δ):   command (t_i) / commitment (t_t)
p 2 (t) (δ):   command (t_i) / negotiation (t_{m1}) / commitment (t_t)
p 3 (t) (δ):   command (t_i) / coordination (t_{m1}) / commitment (t_t)
p 4 (t) (δ):   command(t_i) / negotiation (t_{m1}) / refuse (t_t)

p 5 (t) (δ):   command (t_i) / coordination (t_{m1}) / refuse (t_t)
p 6 (t) (δ):   command (t_i) / refuse (t_t)
p 7 (t) (δ):   command (t_i) / no reply (t_t)

3.3.3   Interaction Intensity

Interaction intensity is the amount of interaction times from the first interaction between agent a_i and a_j to current interaction. The time interval from their first interaction to current interaction is important in calculation of interaction intensity. A briefly calculation considers only the average number, i.e. $ii = \dfrac{N}{t}$, N is the times of the interaction during the time interval t, but an exactly calculation considers its changing rate, i.e. $ii = \dfrac{dN(t)}{dt}$. Considering the group 1 once more, for example:

    G 1:

       p 1 (t) (δ) (ii):   command (t_i) / commitment (t_t)
       p 2 (t) (δ) (ii):   command (t_i) / coordination (t_{m1}) / commitment (t_t)
       p 3 (t) (δ) (ii):   command(t_i) / negotiation (t_{m1}) / refuse (t_t)
       p 4 (t) (δ) (ii):   command(t_i) / negotiation (t_{m1}) / refuse (t_t)
       p 5 (t) (δ) (ii):   command (t_i) / coordination (t_{m1}) / refuse (t_t)
       p 6 (t) (δ) (ii):   command (t_i) / refuse (t_t)
       p 7 (t) (δ) (ii):   command (t_i) / no reply (t_t)

4.   Agent APR Assessment

Assessing individual agents APR is the basis of strategy selection before interacting with such agents.

4.1   Ability Assessment

4.1.1   CAAM --- Computational Agent Ability Model

Formally, an agent a_j's ability assessed by an agent a_i is $ABI_{i,j} = p_{i,j} * P_{i,j} + e_{i,j} * E_{i,j} + q_{i,j} * Q_{i,j}$, and in which:

- $p_{i,j}$:   the a_i's subjective weight about a_j's synthesized productivity of tasks completion
- $e_{i,j}$:   the a_i's subjective weight about a_j's synthesized efficiency of tasks completion
- $q_{i,j}$:   the a_i's subjective weight about a_j's synthesized quality of tasks completion
- $P_{i,j}$:   the a_i's assessment about a_j's synthesized productivity of tasks completion
- $E_{i,j}$:   the a_i's assessment about a_j's synthesized efficiency of tasks completion
- $Q_{i,j}$:   the a_i's assessment about a_j's synthesized quality of tasks completion

4.1.2   Productivity

Suppose agent a_i has interacted with a_j about k tasks t_1, t_2, ..., t_k. Agent A_j's objective productivity calculation in A_i is based on the formula $P_{i,j} = \sum_{m=1}^{k} r_{tm} * c_{tm} \Big/ k$, and in which:

-     r_{tm}: the success rate of task tm.
-     c_{tm}: the complexity of task tm.

Productivity is the success rate of a task.

4.1.3   Efficiency

Suppose agent a_i has interacted with a_j about k tasks $t_1, t_2, \ldots, t_k$. Agent A_j's objective efficiency calculation in A_i is based on the formula $E_{i,j} = \sum_{m=1}^{k} (ct_{tm} - st_{tm}) \Big/ \sum_{m=1}^{k} r_{tm} * c_{tm}$, and in which ct_{tm} and st_{tm} are the task tm finish time and start time respectively, and r_{tm} and c_{tm} are defined above. Efficiency is the average time consuming for one task.

4.1.4   Quality

Task quality $Q_{i,j}$ is directly assigned by agent's human principal.

4.2 Personality Assessment

4.2.1   CAPM --- Computational Agent Personality Model

An agent a_j's personality assessed by an agent a_i is a set of attributes, denoted by $ATT_{i,j}$ in which:

- $ATT_{i,j}$: the virtual objective personal attributes set in agent a_i about agent a_j. ATT_j = *{TRU_j, SUP_j, COM_j, LOY_j, UND_j, EMP_j, INT_j}*, denoted by *{att_1, att_2, att_3, att_4, att_5, att_6, att_7}*, and there:
- *TRU*:   trust
- *SUP*:   support
- *COM*:   communication
- *LOY*:   loyalty
- *UND*:   understanding
- *EMP*:   empathy
- *INT*:   intimacy

The elements in *ATT* is virtual objective because they are calculated from lower objective factors and subjective judgements. For example, a "trust" value is one's subjective probability based on the interaction history that is objective. For getting the elements in *ATT*, we define $att_m = < P, WEI_{i,att_m}, f_{att} >$ in which:

- *P*:   a set of interaction patterns;
- WEI_{i,att_m} :   the weights set that agent ai set up for interaction quality.

- f_{att} :   a function used to map P and WEI_{i,att_m} to an att_m, denoted by att_m

$$= \sum_{k=1}^{n} p_k * w_{k,att_m}$$

Therefore, agents' personalities can be obtained from the of interaction patterns.

4.2.2   Frequency of Patterns

The frequency of interaction patterns is defined by following method. Suppose during the interaction history, agent a_p has initialed n times of interaction to agent a_q, we have got n interaction patterns that distributed as $N_1, N_2, \ldots, N_n$ times with pattern 1, pattern 2, ..., pattern n, where $N = N_1 + N_2 + \ldots + N_n$. We define the frequency of pattern j in group I as:

$$f_{g_i,p_j}(a_p,a_q) = \frac{N_j}{N}, j = 1,2,...,n$$

Similarly, we can define the frequency of the adjusted patterns. Suppose during the interaction history, agent a_p has initialed n times of interaction to agent a_q, we have got n interaction patterns with micro-adjustment factors (t, δ, ii) and this patterns are distributed as $N_1, N_2, ..., N_n$ times with pattern 1, pattern 2, ..., pattern n, where $N = N_1 + N_2 + ... + N_n$. We define the frequency of pattern j in group i as:

$$a\_f_{g_i,p_j}(a_p,a_q,t,\delta) = \frac{\sum\limits_{m=1}^{N_j}(r_1 * t^{-1} + r_2 * \delta + r_3 * ii)}{N}; j = 1,2,...,n; r_1 * t + r_2 * \delta + r_3 * ii \le 1$$

4.2.3   Formal Assessment of Personalities

An agent's personal attribute is described with a mathematical formula, in there, $att_k(a_p, a_q)$ is the agent a_p's subjective judgement about a_q on personal attribute k.

$$att_k(a_p,a_q) = \sum_{i=1}^{m}\sum_{j=1}^{n_m} w_{g_i,p_j} * f_{g_i,p_j}(a_p,a_q)$$

or $att_k(a_p,a_q) = \sum\limits_{i=1}^{m}\sum\limits_{j=1}^{n_m} w_{g_i,p_j} * a\_f_{g_i,p_j}(a_p,a_q)$

here: w_{g_i,p_j} is the weight, its value could be taken from -1 to 1.

f_{g_i,p_j} is the frequency, and

(1). $\sum\limits_{i=1}^{m}\sum\limits_{j=1}^{n_m} w_{g_i,p_j} = 1$ (2). $\sum\limits_{i=1}^{m}\sum\limits_{j=1}^{n_m} f_{g_i,p_j} = 1$

In this model, frequencies are objective but weights are subjective. Different series of weights will define different personal attribute. The weights used to calculate an attribute are expressed with a matrix. In a multi-agent system, one agent serves for one and only one actor (the agent's principal), so the settings of w_{g_i,p_j} is decided absolutely by agent's principal and different principal assigns his/her own agent with different w_{g_i,p_j}. The designer of the agent framework could not provide standard subjective parameters. A method to obtain one's w_{g_i,p_j} is to design a set of questions for the agent and request its principal to answer, after the principal answers the questions, the agent will statistics the answers and his/her subjective judgements can be derived from the statistics. For example, my agent indicates my subjective judgement about *support* is:

0.01	0.007	0.003	0.001	0.001	−0.01	−0.02	0	0	0
0.05	0.02	0.01	0.005	0.005	0.003	0.002	0.001	−0.01	−0.02
0.1	0.05	−0.02	−0.02	0	0	0	0	0	0

......

4.3   Relationship Assessment

The relationship between A_i and A_j depends strongly on their personalities. If there is a good relationship between A_i and A_j, they like to cooperate with each other, otherwise, they may compete with each other.

4.3.1   CARM --- Computational Agent Relationship Model

An in-depth relationship such as friendship between a_i and a_j is modeled in $REL_{i,\,j} = <ATT_j,$ $WEI_i, f>$ in which:

- ATT_j: same as defined in CAPM
- $WEIi$:   the weights that agent a_i set for the virtual objective attributes. According to the definition of ATT, we have $WEI_i = \{wt_i, ws_i, wc_i, wl_i, wu_i, we_i, wi_i\}$, denoted by $\{w_1, w_2, w_3, w_4, w_5, w_6, w_7\}$

- f: a function used to map ATT_j and WEI_i, to $REL_{i,\,j}$, in here, f is $\displaystyle\sum_{k=1}^{7} att_{k,i} * w_k$

4.3.2   Relationship Assessment

In terms of the assessment of other agents' personalities, one agent can evaluate the relationships between itself and others. When an agent's principal configures its agent, he has to provide his subjective parameters about how important an individual personality in his relationship assessment. For example, table 3 is my subjective parameters.

Table 3:   A principal's subjective parameters

Personality No. (k)	Personality name	Percentage in relationship (0-1) ($perc_k$)
1	Trust	1
2	Support	1
3	Communication	0.7
4	Loyalty	0.9
5	Understanding,	0.9
6	Empathy	0.6
7	Intimacy	0.8

The calculation of relationship is defined on the formula in which $REL_{p,\,q}$ means the a_p's subjective judgement about a_q on relationship:

$$REL_{p,q} = \sum_{k=1}^{7} \lambda_k * att_{k,p} \quad \text{and} \quad \lambda_k = perc_k \Big/ \sum_{i=1}^{7} perc_i$$

5.   Interaction Strategy

An agent interaction strategy is to tell how an agent interacts with others. Formally, it is represented with a set of rules. Traditionally, once an agent is generated, its interaction strategies are fixed and those strategies are used for all other agents. It is irrational for different agent has different interaction strategy and tends to be that an individual agent uses different interaction strategy when interacting with different agents. Figure 8 is the illustration.

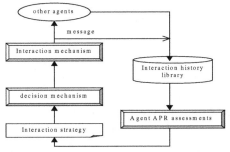

Figure 8: Interaction and adaptivity mechanisms

As agents' social personality definitions, agents' interaction strategy is independent from different individuals. We could not provide a standard strategy for all agents but we suggest an interaction strategy library for all agents so that individual agent can select one strategy from the library randomly or manually when it interacts with others firstly. Example strategy in the library could be:

Strategy 1:

```
rule 1:  when (comes(message))
         {
            if (message.primitive.is("borrow"))
            {
              //BeliefSpace bels = R_BELS(message event);
              //Goal g = D_GOAL(G_GOAL(bels), bels);
              //Plan p = D_PLAN(G_PLAN(g), bels);
              //Action a = D_ACTION(G_ACTION(p), bels);
              ......
              if(message.sender.is("aⱼ")&& TRU("me","aⱼ") > 0.8))
                 reply ("commitment");
              else
                 reply ("refuse");
            }
            else
            {
               ......
            }
         }
         ......
```

Strategy 2:

```
rule 1: when (comes(message))
         {
            if (next_action.is("delegation"))
            {
              ......

              if(ABI("aⱼ") > 0.8))
                  initiate ("delegation");
              else
```

```
                         repeat;
                 }
                 else
                 {
                     ......
                 }
         }
rule 2: ......
......
```

Strategy 3:
```
rule 1: when (comes(message))
         {
             if (message.performative.is("cfp"))
             {
                 ......

                 if(message.sender.is("aⱼ") && REL("aⱼ") > 0.8))
                     reply ("commitment");
                 else
                     reply ("refuse");
             }
             else
             {
                     ......
             }
         }
rule 2: ......
......
```

6.   Performance Measurement

Interaction performance is measured after six months of EPMPAS running from 26th Nov. 2000 to 24th May 2001 [Figure 9]. It is analyzed with two periods of time based on with or without strategies in interactions. In first period, we did not put strategic interaction component in any agent. In latter period, however, strategic interaction component has been added to all agents. The statistics figure shows that after the strategic interaction component has been added to all agents, even the number of processes is increased and the number of their decomposed tasks is increased, the number of interactions has been decreased obviously and the average time one process is reduced as well. In detail, The success rate is also got increased [Table 4].

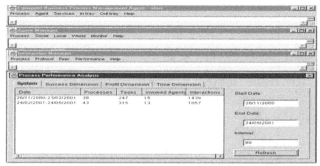

Figure 9: Measurement of Process Performance

Table 4 --- Success Dimension

	Interaction without strategic interaction component	Interaction with strategic interaction component
Success	28%	44%
Conditional Success	21%	18%
Conditional un-Success	23%	13%
Failure	24%	21%
No Reply	4%	4%

7. Conclusions and Future Works

From agent interaction history to drive agent future interactions by computational methods is a big challenge. From the description of this paper, the author provides systematic methods of understanding other agents APR and use these assessments to select "best" or "good" interaction strategies to respond different individual agents. The experiments' result shows us that higher-level interaction performance can be obtained by these methods.

The start point that formally discusses agent interaction is suggested. More theories and tools are to be explored to verify the hypothesis. In next step, process complexity and task complexity will be added to the model to make the measurement more exact.

References

[1] Walter Brenner, Rudiger Zarnekow, Hartmut Wittig, "Intelligent Software Agents: Foundations and Applications", Springer, 1998, ISBN 3-540-63411-8
[2] J.K. Debenham, "Delegation of responsibility in an agent-based process management system", in proceedings 3rd Pacific Rim International Workshop on Multi-Agents PRIMA2000, Melbourne, 28-29 August 2000.
[3] Keith S. Decker. "Environment Centered Analysis and Design of coordination Mechanism". Ph.D thesis. UMass CMPSCI Technical Report. May 1995.
[4] T. Finin, Y. Labrou and J. Mayfield. "KQML as an agent communication language". In Jeff Bradshaw (Ed.) *Software Agents*. MIT Press, 1997.
[5] FIPA (1998). FIPA Content Language Library. *http://www.fipa.org*.
[6] FIPA (1997). Agent Communication Language. *http://www.fipa.org*.
[7] L. M. Hogg and N. R. Jennings (1999) "Variable Sociability in Agent-Based Decision Making" Proc. 6th Int. Workshop on Agent Theories Architectures and Languages (ATAL-99), Orlando, FL, 305-318.
[8] N. R. Jennings, P. Faratin, T. J. Norman, P. O'Brien and B. Odgers (2000) "Autonomous Agents for Business Process Management" Int. Journal of Applied Artificial Intelligence 14 (2) 145-189.
[9] Aizhong Lin and John Debenham. (2001). "Interaction Adaptivity in Multi-agent Interaction". Proceedings of The Third International Symposium on Cooperative Database Systems for Advanced Applications (CODAS'2001), April 23-24, 2001Beijing, China.
[10] Aizhong Lin. "Multi-agent Business Process Management". Proceedings of ISA'2000, International ICSC Congress on INTELLIGENT SYSTEMS AND APPLICATIONS on December 11-15, 2000, University of Wollongong , NSW, Australia
[11] Gerhard Weiss (Ed.) "Multiagent System: A Modern Approach to Distributed Artificial Intelligence" MIT Press (1999).

Market Performance of Adaptive Trading Agents in Synchronous Double Auctions

Wei-Tek Hsu and Von-Wun Soo

Department of Computer Science, National Tsing-Hua University
TEL: (03)571-5131
{vichsu,soo}@cs.nthu.edu.tw

Abstract. We are concerned with the issues on designing adaptive trading agents to learn bidding strategies in electronic market places. The synchronous double auction is used as a simulation testbed. We implemented agents with neural-network-based reinforcement learning called Q-learning agents (QLA) to learn bidding strategies in the double auctions. In order to compare the performances of QLAs in the electronic market places, we also implemented many kinds of non-adaptive trading agents such as simple random bidding agents (SRBA), gradient-based greedy agent (GBGA), and truth telling agent (TTA). Instead of learning to model other trading agents that is computational intractable, we designed learning agents to model the market environment as a whole instead. Our experimental results showed that in terms of global market efficiency, QLAs could outperform TTAs and GBGAs but could not outperform SRBAs in the market of homogeneous type of agents. In terms of individual performance, QLAs could outperform all three non-adaptive trading agents when the opponents they are dealing with in the market place are a purely homogeneous type of non-adaptive trading agents. However, QLAs could only outperform TTAs and GBGAs and could not outperform SRBAs in the market of heterogeneous types of agents.

1 Introduction

Agent mediated e-commerce has recently raised much attention in agent community. Using agents in representing human traders to trade in many different auctions has nowadays become more and more feasible [1,5,7,13,14,23]. In double auction environment agents could both buy and sell goods in the market places and exchange their resources through a competitive bidding process with respect to their own preferences. In this paper, we study the issues of how autonomous agents learn appropriate bidding strategies in agent-based synchronous double auctions. Instead of modeling or learning other trading agents' behavior [6,22,25] which is too complicated to be computationally tractable in a large electronic market place, we allow each trading agent to model the market as a whole external environment, and to determine its strategies by observing the outcomes from the trading environment and to learn an appropriate policy function by trial and errors during trading process.

The main issues we concern with by involving learning agents in the market are two folds:

S.-T. Yuan and M. Yokoo (Eds.): PRIMA 2001, LNAI 2132, pp. 108-121, 2001.
© Springer-Verlag Berlin Heidelberg 2001

Can learning really help a trading agent? Can adaptive trading agents outperform other fixed (non-adaptive) strategy agents in the market places?

Can learning improve the market efficiency? Namely, can adaptive trading agents speed up as well as enhance the global satisfaction of resource allocation in terms of agents' utilities?

The learning skill that we adopt for an adaptive agent is a model-free reinforcement learning method called Q- learning and therefore an adaptive trading agent is called a Q-learning agent (QLA). This is in contrast to previous work of p-strategy by Sunju Park et. al. [25] that maintained a Markov Chain (MC) model of all transition probabilities of buying and selling history. The memory space cost of MC can be overwhelming, not to mention the effort needed to establish the correct transition probabilities of the MC model. We show QLAs could satisfy our expectations to some extent: to get better individual performance and to speed up the market efficiency in terms of overall (global) utilities of trading agents.

2   Auctions and Synchronous Double Auctions

McAfee and McMillan [12] define an auction as follows: An auction is a market institution with an explicit set of rules determining resource allocation and prices on the basis of bids from the market participants. The common types of auctions are English (Ascending-Bid) auction, Dutch (Descending-Bid) auction, first-price sealed-bid auction, second-price sealed-bid auction (Vickrey auction), and double auctions [20,21].

In a double auction [2, 3, 17], there are multiple buyers and sellers. A trader may submit both buying and selling bids in this market. Commodities are traded through the competitive market. A commodity is a collection of homogeneous goods. The basic clearing rule is to find the highest buying bid and lowest selling offer, and a transaction is made if the buying bid quote is higher than the selling ask quote. The clearing price is determined in the range of bid-ask difference with specific institution setting. The application of double auctions can be seen in the common stock market.

In the literature of experimental economics, double auctions could be viewed as two kinds of implementations, synchronous double auction (SDA) and asynchronous double auction (ASDA). The main difference between SDA and ASDA is whether the time of trading process is discrete or continuous [15, 16]. That is whether we can submit our bid just in a limited period of time in a trading tournament that consists of several periods, or on any point of time series in a trading process. The trading protocol of SDA is shown as the procedures in Table 2.1.

The characteristics of SDA are summarized as follows:
- In each round, agents could submit bids with information about the price that they want to pay (offer) for one unit of the traded commodity.
- Agents submit their bid sealed, that is, their bids are not seen by other agents in the trading process.
- The clearing price is uniform that is the transaction price of successful transactions in the same round is the same.

Table 2.1 The SDA Trading Protocol

1. Start a new round.
2. The trading agents prepare their bids with respect to their valuation on the good and the information provided by the auctioneer in the previous round. If no information is provided (at the beginning of the game) use stochastic method to generate these factors. Then agents submit their bids sealed to the auctioneer.
3. The auctioneer collects bids submitted from the trading agents and uses a matching rule to determine the clearing price and posts the bid- quote, ask-quote and transaction status to the trading agents.
4. If terminating condition (the preset number of rounds) is reached, go to step 5, else go to step 1.
5. End of game.

The information from the trading process includes bid quote (the highest unsuccessful buying bid), ask quote (the lowest unsuccessful selling offer), clearing price and transaction status (either transacted or rejected) in the previous round.

After the general description about the SDA mechanisms, we specify a SDA game descriptor to clarify the parameters used in this protocol as in Table 2.2.

Table 2.2 The SDA descriptors

A SDA game descriptor D as a tuple
$<B, S, r, M>$ such that:
- $B = \{b_i \mid i = 1 .. m\}$ is a set of identifiers of buyer agents.
- $S = \{s_j \mid j = 1 .. n\}$ is a set of identifiers of seller agents.
- r is the number of maximum allowable rounds.
- M is the matching rule defined as a tuple
  $< C_f, I_{info}, S, B, P_{clearing}, P_{bid}, P_{ask}>$ such that: $P_{clearing}$ is the clearing price; P_{bid} is the bid quote; P_{ask} is the ask quote; and
  $C_f : (\mathfrak{R}^m, \mathfrak{R}^n) \to \mathfrak{R}^3$ is defined as $C_f(P(B), P(S)) = (P_{clearing}, P_{bid}, P_{ask})$
  where $P(B)$ is a vector $(p(b_1), p(b_2), ..., p(b_m))$ of the bidding prices of buyers and $P(S)$ is a vector $(p(s_1), p(s_2), ..., p(s_n))$ of the asking prices of sellers.
  $I_{info} : (\mathfrak{R}, \mathfrak{R}^m, \mathfrak{R}^n) \to \mathcal{B}^{n+n}$ is defined as $I_{info}(P_{clearing}, P(B), P(S)) = S_{status}$
  where: $\mathcal{B} = \{0, 1\}$ indicating the transaction status and $S_{status} \in \mathcal{B}^{m+n}$ represents a vector of transaction status.

2.1   The Matching Rules

After the auctioneer collects bids from the buyer and the seller agents, it rearranges $P(B)$ and $P(S)$ in a single vector V in descending order. Then it applies a so called Mth-price and $(M+1)st$-price rules [18, 19] to determine the bid quote, ask quote and clearing price, where M means the number of sellers. The clearing price is the M-th highest price in V, the ask quote is the M-th price and the bid quote is the $(M+1)st$ price in V.

And the transaction status is provided as: All buy bids at prices equal to or greater than the clearing price can be matched to all selling asking prices that are less than the clearing price and the order of matching is arbitrary. Tie breakings are treated by assigning a uniform distribution of probabilities to the tied agents and by selecting the successful transactions accordingly.

And the transaction status is provided as: All buy bids at prices equal to or greater than the clearing price can be matched to all selling asking prices that are less than the clearing price and the order of matching is arbitrary. Tie breakings are treated by assigning a uniform distribution of probabilities to the tied agents and by selecting the successful transactions accordingly.

3   The Reinforcement Learning

In the double auction market problem, a trading agent could evaluate its performance by receiving reward from trading process. There is no explicit guidance for the agent to choose correct action in any specific situation. Therefore, it is potentially suitable for the agent to adopt a reinforcement learning strategy [9] to accomplish the learning task. In this paper we focus on a reinforcement learning algorithm called Q-learning that can acquire optimal control strategies from delayed rewards, even when the agent have no prior knowledge of the effect of its action on the environment. In this section we introduce an algorithm for updating the Q-value.

The learning rule is adopted from Sutton's *TD(0)* algorithm [24] that uses the following update rule:

$$V(s)=V(s)+\alpha(r+\gamma V(s')-V(s)),$$

where r is the immediate reward, α the learning rate, γ the discount rate. Thus we could define the learning rule to update Q- value as below:

$$Q(s,a)=Q(s,a)+\alpha(r+\gamma \max_{a'} Q(s',a')-Q(s,a))$$

And we employ an artificial neural network called Q-net [8] to accomplish the training process. The algorithm is summarized in Table3.1.

Table 3.1 The Q-learning algorithm

1. Observe the current state s.
2. Select an action a by a stochastic procedure
3. For the selected action a, use Q-net to compute $U_a \leftarrow Q(s,a)$
4. Execute action a
5. Observe the resulting new state s' and reward r
6. Use Q-net to compute $Q(s',a')$, $a' \in A$
7. $U_a \leftarrow r + max_{a' \in A}Q(s',a')$
8. Adjust the Q-net by backpropagating the error $\Delta U = U_{a'} - U_a$

An obvious strategy for the agent in state s to select the action a would be that maximizes $Q(s,a)$. That is based on the exploitation of the current best estimation of Q-value. But this strategy will have a risk of over-commitment to the action that has higher Q-value at the earlier training stage while failing to explore other actions that could have even higher values. Thus it is common to use a stochastic approach to select an action in Q-learning. And the strategy we will adopt is based on a Boltzmann distribution described as below.

$$P(a_i \mid s) = \frac{\exp\left[\dfrac{Q(s,a_i)}{T}\right]}{\sum_j \exp\left[\dfrac{Q(s,a_j)}{T}\right]}$$

where T is a temperature parameter for the annealing process.

When T is high, the fluctuation of actions becomes large, and when T is low, the fluctuation of actions becomes small. That is, as the learning progresses the agent tends to behave more exploitative than explorative in selecting actions.

4   The Adaptive Trading Agents

The adaptive trading agent consists of three components: the learning component, the action selection component, and the bidding component. The fundamental architecture is depicted in the Figure 4.1. The functions that work within the components are described as follows:

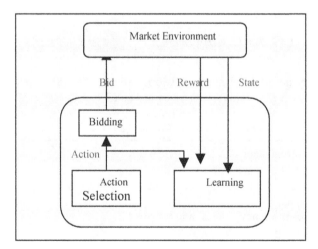

Figure 4.1 The adaptive trading agent architecture in auction market environment

1. Learning component: The function within learning component is implemented as a Q-net described in the previous section. The Q-net provides a data structure that represents the generalized policy function for the agent to follow.
2. Action selection component: The action selection component makes stochastic decision based on the Boltzmann probabilistic distribution as mentioned in section 3.
3. Bidding component: This component provides the bid that the agent is willing to submit to the auctioneer based on the action parameter provided by the action selection component.

4.1   Designing of Bidding Action Space

When considering the proper representation of bidding action space, we must assure that the actions are discrete and finite in order to be selected by the action selection element of the adaptive trading agents. The normalized way of representing bidding actions is desirable in the learning element for an adaptive trading agent. That is, we must provide a finite, unified and normalized representation of bidding actions. In a SDA, the price for an agent to bid can be defined as a real value that is bounded by the budge constraint. But to provide a unifying and normalized representation for bidding actions one must take into account the reservation prices and profit for both buying and selling agents.

4.1.1   The Profit Ratio

First, we define the profit as the value of difference between target transaction price and reservation price. The target transaction price is the price the agent expects to pay or ask at the transaction, and the reservation price is the lowest (highest) price for a buyer (seller) agent to accept the deal. The K-profit ratio is then defined as the ratio between the profit and K times of the reservation price, namely, (profit/K*reservation price). Finally we define the K-profit ratio space from -1.0 to 1.0 and partition the K-profit ratio into $2N+1$ levels with the values of at a step of $1/N$. If $N=10$, then we get 21 levels, namely, -1.0, -0.9, ..., 0.0, 0.1, 0.2, ..., 1.0. If the value of profit ratio is positive, it means the action is selling, and if the value is negative, the action is buying. The zero value means the action is not willing to bid. Thus we get a less general but a uniform and discrete representation for bidding action space. In this paper, we made a simplifying assumption by assuming that $K=1$, namely, the maximal profit for a selling agent to ask is one time of his reservation price and similarly for a buying agent. But with the increase of the parameter K and the partition granularity of the discrete intervals of the profit ratio, one can easily extend to approximate more general bidding action space.

4.1.2   The Bidding Price

With the bidding action space defined in terms of profit ratio, we can determine the actual bidding price in each bidding action in the following formula:.

$$\text{Bid price} = (\text{Reservation price}) * (1 + K * (\text{Profit ratio}))$$

4.2   The Design of State Space

The state space is defined as the collection of feasible state vectors that an agent could reach. A feasible state vector is composed of the following elements: the endowment status of commodities, and the information provided in the trading process. The information provided in the trading process includes the clearing price, the bid quote, the ask quote, and the transaction status in the previous round. And the transaction status includes the bid processing state (active or removed) and the role (seller or buyer).On using the state vectors as inputs of the Q-net, we normalize the input parameters in the range of [0, 1] for a concise and uniform presentation.

4.3   The Performance Evaluation Criteria

The most important problem in the designing of the autonomous agent in this trading game is how to evaluate the performance and the rewards of the agent that participate in the trading process. The most common way that has been used is the profit an agent gains in the trading process. The one that we adopted is the utility an agent could get in the trading process. By using utility function, we could assess the subjective preference attitude of an agent in a more general view [10,11]. Thus the question is how to properly define a utility function to represent an agent's preference.

4.3.1   The Utility Function

To fit our requirement, we introduce a utility function called CES (Constant Elasticity Substitute) utility function [20] to represent the preference of the autonomous agent. The utility function is described as below:

$$U(\mathbf{x})= (\Sigma \alpha_g x_g^{\rho})^{1/\rho}, g=1..m ,$$

where $\mathbf{x}=(x_1,x_2, ..., x_m)$ is a vector of the quantities of all commodities, α_g is the preference weight of specific good g, and ρ is the substitution parameter.

4.3.2   The Reward

With the utility function above, we could thus define the reward an agent should get in each transaction as:

$$r_t = U(\mathbf{x}_t) - U(\mathbf{x}_{t-1})$$

That is, the reward an agent gains is the utility of current endowed commodities minus the utility of the previous endowed commodities.

4.3.3   The Reservation Price

With the utility function given, we could derive the reservation price of an agent with a specific commodity to be traded. The concept is shown as below:

$$U(x_i -1, x_n + p_s, x_{-i,-n}) = U(x_i, x_n, x_{-i,-n})$$
$$U(x_i +1, x_n - p_b, x_{-i,-n}) = U(x_i, x_n, x_{-i,-n})$$

Where x_i means the quantity of the commodity that the agent wants to trade, x_n means the quantity of the commodity of money, p_s means the selling reservation price, and p_b means the buying reservation price. That is we define the reservation prices as the prices such that its utility keeps constant when buying or selling one unit of the commodity.

5   The Design of Experiments and Markets

For the purpose of comparing and training of our learning agents, we define three types of non-adaptive agents called Simple Random Bidding Agent (SRBA), Gradient-Based Greedy Agent (GBGA), and Truthful-Telling Agent (TTA). The characteristics and parameters of these non-adaptive agents are briefly described as below:

♦   **The Simple Random Bidding Agent (SRBA)**

The bidding strategy of a SRBA is to always randomly select an action from the action space and bid accordingly. By introducing this agent, we could thus provide the essential property of randomness in the dynamic market environment.

♦   **The Gradient-Based Greedy Agent (GBGA)**

The GBGA's submit their bids according to the information of the gradient of the utility function. By the direction derived from the gradient, a GBGA always chooses the action that immediately maximizes the utility. And thus the agent follows a greedy strategy to submit a bid.

♦   **The Truthful-Telling Agent (TTA)**

The strategy of a TTA always submits the bid as her reservation price to the auctioneer at each round in the SDA. That is, TTA always truthfully reveal the reservation price information about the good they want. The TTA provides the pure exchanging information in SDA, and serves as the basis for comparison of performance.

5.1   The Setting of Experiments

We conducted a series of experiments to investigate the performance of our adaptive trading agents as well as the market efficiency that they lead to. The commodities been traded in our experiments are food and gold. At the beginning of each game, each agent is endowed with both commodities according to a uniform distribution of probability. And the maximum quantity of each good is 100 units.

5.1.1   Markets with Homogeneous Agents

The performance is determined by total utilities owned by agents in each game. And we investigate the performance by average the total utilities in each game. The four settings of the experiment are:

♦ **Setting 1 (2,3,4): All QLAs (SRBAs, GRBAs, TTAs)**

10 QLAs (SRBAs, GRBAs, TTAs) participated in a SDA game. Each game ran 500 rounds of trading, and we conducted 10 games. We measured the market efficiency by observing total utilities gained by the learning agents in the trading process.

5.1.2   The Performance of QLA against Different Non-adaptive Agents

We conducted experiments to compare the performances of QLA with SRBA, GBGA and TTA respectively. The performance of each type of agents is investigated by averaging the utilities gained by all agents in the game. And we compare the performance between agents by averaging the utility gained in each game. And the three settings of experiments are:

♦ **Setting 1 (2,3): QLA vs. SRBA (GRBAs,TTAs)**

5 QLAs and 5 SRBAs participated in SDA games. Each game ran 500 rounds of trading, and we conducted 10 games. The performance of individual agent is measured by the average utilities gained in the games.

5.1.3   Heterogeneous Agents in SDA

5 QLAs, 5 SRPAs, 5 GBGAs, and 5 TTAs participated in SDA games. Each game ran 500 rounds of trading, and we conducted 10 games. The performance of individual agent is measured by the average utilities gained in the games. And we investigate the performance by averaging the utility gained for each type of agents in each game.

6   Experimental Results

6.1   Market Efficiencies in the Markets with Different Homogeneous Agents

With the setting of experiments described in section 5.1.1, we obtained the following results as in Figure 6.1 and Figure 6.2. Figure 6.1 shows the total utilities gained in different market settings of homogeneous agents participating in SDA. And Figure 6.2 shows in particular results yielded by TTA and GBGA.

In Figure 6.1, we observed that the markets of all QLAs and all SRPAs reached the saturation of market efficiency much slower than those of all TTAs, and all GBGAs. On the other hand, the markets of all TTAs and all GBGAs, although reached the saturation faster, could not gain any further market efficiency after about 50 rounds as shown in Figures 6.1 and 6.2. The reason is that at the early stage TTAs and GBGAs both have fixed bidding strategies can behave more "goal-oriented" to gain utilities for each individual agent. On the other hand, QLAs and SRPAs must either use "trial-

and-error" strategy or randomly behave at the early stage. This explains why in the early stage the market efficiencies in terms of total utilities grow faster for TTAs and GBGAs.

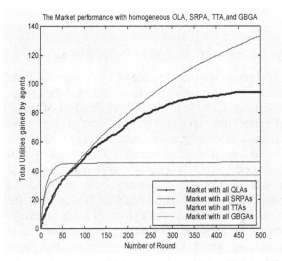

Figure 6.1 Market performances with homogeneous QLAs, SRPAs, TTAs, and GBGAs

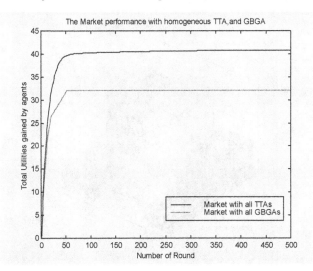

Figure 6.2 The market performance with homogeneous TTAs and GBGAs

However, at the later stage after 50 rounds, TTAs and GRBAs ceased to gain their utilities any further via trading. This is because the fixed strategies of TTAs and GRBAs had reached their best performance but could not gain any more utilities through trading. QLAs and SRBAs, on the other hand, could still explore the strategy space to find better reallocation of goods that led to higher utilities. It is interesting to see that the market of QLAs still could not outperform that of SRBAs in market efficiency. This implies that Pareto-efficiency of a market requires more freedom or "randomness" in search for a optimal satisfaction for all utilities of traders. When traders insist on their on strategies, it will be hard for the market to reach the global optimal of market efficiency.

6.2   The Performances of QLAs against Different Non-adaptive Agents

In this section, we investigate the performance of QLA against different non-adaptive agents using the settings 1-3 described in section 5.1.2. And the results of experiments are summarized in Figure 6.3. In Figure 6.3, QLA's (the row of learning agents in the back of the figure) outperform other agents in different settings. And the significant advantage in performance of learning agents could be seen in QLA vs. TTA and QLA vs. GBGA. This is because that when learning agents deal with the traders with simple and consistent strategy they will easily capture the appropriate reaction to get better rewards, and thus get benefit from learning ability. In QLA vs. SRPA, although learning agents could also benefit from learning ability, but the advantageous performance is not so significant, because of there is noisy information provided by the opponent. By the evidence provided by our experimental results, we can generally say that when a learning agent faces with opponents that have homogeneous behaviors it will easily capture some patterns of actions that that would be beneficial to it.

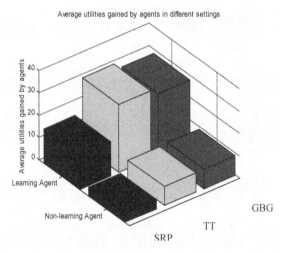

Figure 6.3 Average utilities gained by agents in different market settings

6.3   The Performance of Agents in Markets with Heterogeneous Agents

Finally, we investigate the SDA with heterogeneous trading agents. This is an experiment that is more likely to act as a real market, because the real market is usually full of heterogeneous traders.

We conducted the experiments with the settings in section 5.1.3. The experimental results are summarized in Figure 6.4. In Figure 6.4, we measured the trading agents in terms of the average utility gain over the same type of agents. All fixed strategy trading agents performed significantly worse than a random trader in the mixed heterogeneous market. We found that although QLAs could still outperform TTAs and GBGAs, they could not outperform SRPAs. This is also a very interesting finding. It seems to imply that due to the complexity and noise in the heterogeneous market, it is almost hopeless to have any obvious advantageous bidding strategy in the market even with learning capability.

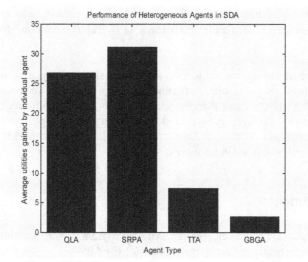

Figure 6.4 Performances of heterogeneous agents in SDA

7   Conclusions and Future Work

In this paper, we discussed issues of simulating and analyzing a synchronous double auction by introducing autonomous adaptive trading agents. We propose a learning agent who uses a reinforcement learning method to improve its ability of trading by learning to select an appropriate trading policy function during trading with other agents in a market. We conducted several experiments to investigate the performance of learning agents and the impacts on market efficiency in different market settings. Our experimental results showed that in terms of global market efficiency, QLAs could outperform TTAs and GBGAs but could not outperform SRBAs in the market of homogeneous type of agents. In terms of individual performance, QLAs could outperform all three non-adaptive trading agents when the opponents they are dealing with in the market place are a purely homogeneous type of non-adaptive trading agents. However, QLAs could only outperform TTAs and GBGAs and could not outperform SRBAs in the market of heterogeneous types of agents.

Based on the results from above experiments, we conclude that agents with learning skills cannot always gain benefit from the market places. The adaptive trading agents can only outperform TTAs and GBGAs when the market consists of only homogeneous types of agents. A trader with naïve fixed strategy may not outperform traders with random strategy in potentially random markets. Therefore neither "honest", "greedy",nor even "adaptive" traders could outperform random strategy traders as seen in cases in section 6.3. This conclusion seems to be compatible with the finding of Gode and Sunder on "zero intelligence" traders where the market equilibrium price is determined more by the market structure rather than the intelligence of the traders if traders act randomly [26]. But if the environment consistently reveals its information with less ambiguity as seen in cases in section 6.2, trading agents could really benefit from learning by rapidly adapting to the market environment.

The behavior of our agents could be viewed as risk-averse type according to the utility function setting in our experiments. For objective assessment of the performance of agents, we could adjust the parameter settings in utility function and control agents' risk preference. We could implement other types of sophisticated agents for comparison of trading agent performances in electronic market places. And these issues would be left as future works.

Acknowledgments

This research is supported in part by MOE Program for Promoting Academic Excellence of Universities under grant number 89-E-FA04-1-4.

References

1. David Cliff and Janet Bruten. Zero is not Enough: On The Lower Limit of Agent Intelligence for Continuous Double Auction Markets. HP Labs technical report HPL-97-141, Hewlett Packard Research Laboratories, Bristol England, 1997.
2. Daniel Friedman and John Rust. The Double Auction Market: Institutions, Theories and Evidence. Addison-Wesley, 1993.
3. Daniel Friedman. The Double Auction Market Institution: A Survey. In [2] , pp.3-25.
4. John H. Gagel and Alvin E. Roth. The Handbook of Experimental Economics. Princeton University Press, 1995.
5. E.G. Gimenez-Funes, L. Godo, J. A. Rodriguez-Aguilar, and P.Garcia-Calves. Design Bidding Strategies for Trading Agents in Electronic Auctions. In Proceedings of International Conference on Multi Agents System, 1998, Page(s): 136 -143
6. Jining Hu and Michael P. Wellman. Online Learning about Other Agents in a Dynamic Multiagent System. In Proceeding of the Second International Conference on Autonomous Agents. (Agents-98)
7. Junling Hu, Daniel Reeves, and Hock-Shan Wong. Agent Service for Online Auctions. In Proceedings of the AAAI-99 Workshop on AI for Electronic Commerce.
8. J-S. R. Jang, C.-T. Sun and E. Mizutani. Neuro-Fuzzy and Soft Computing: A Computational Approach to Learning and Machine Intelligence. Prentice-Hall, 1997.

9. Leslie Pack Kaelbling, Michael L Littman, and Andrew W. Moore. Reinforcement Learning: A Survey, Journal of Artificial Intelligence Research (1996), 4:237-285.
10. Ralph L. Keeney and Howard Raiffa. Decisions with Multiple Objectives: Preferences and Value Tradeoffs. Cambridge University Press 1993.
11. Andreu Mas-Colell, Michael D. Whiston and Jerry R. Green. Microeconomic Theory. Oxford University Press 1995.
12. R. Peterson McAfee and John McMillan. Auctions and Bidding. Journal of Economic Literature, Vol XXV, June 1987, pp. 699-738.
13. Sandip Sen and Karina Hernandez, A Buyer's Agents, In Proceedings of Autonomous Agents 2000.
14. Chris Preist. Commodity trading using an agent-based iterated double auction. Proceedings of the third annual conference on Autonomous Agents, 1999, Pages 131 – 138
15. John Rust, John H. Miller, and Richard Palmer. Behavior of Trading Automata in a Computerized Double Auction Market. In [2]. pp. 155-198.
16. Abdolkarim Sadrieh. The Alternating Double Auction Market: A Game Theoretic and Experimental Investigation. Lecture Notes in Economics and Mathematics System 466. Springer, 1998.
17. Robert Wilson. Incentive Efficiency of Double Auctions. Econometrica, Sept. 1985, 53(5), pp. 1101-115.
18. Peter R. Wurman, Michael P. Wellman, and William E. Walsh. A Parameterization of The Auction Design Space.
    http://www.csc.ncsu.edu/faculty/wurman/Papers/auction_parameters.ps.
19. Peter R. Wurman, William E. Walsh, and Michael P. Wellman. Flexible Double Auctions for Electronic Commerce: Theory and Implementation. Decision Support Systems 24, 1998, pp. 17-27.
20. Hal R. Varian. Microeconomics Analysis 3rd Edition . W. W. Norton & Company, 1992.
21. William Vickrey. Counterspeculation, Auctions, and Competitive Sealed Tenders. Journal of Finance, March 1961. 16(1). pp. 8-37.
22. J.M. Vidal and E.H. Durfee. The Impact of Nested Agent Models in an Information Economy. In Proceeding of the Second International Conference on Multiagent Systems, pp. 377-384, Menlo Park, CA, 1996. AAAI Press.
23. The Michigan AuctionBot. http://auction.eecs.umich.edu/
24. Sutton, R. S. (1988). Learning to Predict by the Methods of Temporal Differences. *Machine Learning* 3: 9-44.
25. Sunju Park, Edmund Durfee, William Birmingham, An Adaptive Agent Bidding Strategy based on Stochastic Modeling, In Proceedings of Autonomous Agents, 1999.
26. Gode, D. K., & Sunder, S. Allocative efficiency of markets with zero-intelligence traders: Market as a partial substitute for individual rationality. Journal of Political Economy, 101 (1), 119—137, 1993.

Negotiation-Credit Driven Coalition Formation in E-Markets

Yu-Hsin Lin and Soe-Tsyr Yuan

Information Management Department, Fu-Jen University
Taipei, Taiwan, R.O.C.
eric0724@im.fju.edu.tw
yuans@tpts1.seed.net.tw

Abstract: Consumers can obtain cheaper goods through collaboration. However, it's very difficult to find a certain group of people with the same demand in traditional markets. Internet makes this dream come true. Customers with mutual interests can get together easily and bargain with manufacturers by using the power of group. This paper presents a coalition formation mechanism which is based on Negotiation-Credit Based Negotiation. Buyers and sellers can bargain with different strategies, which also founding on Negotiation Credit, and close deals more efficiency. The concept of group buy could be extended to group sell and enhance the market function.

Keywords: software agents, coalition formation, negotiation, group buy, group sell

1 Introduction

Through Internet, virtual communities were created as well as the global village, in which individuals gathered by mutual interests, share information and resources. More and more business firms and consumers are driven to the possible profits from the virtual communities.

In traditional markets, consumers are constrained by geographic limitation and lack of detailed information about products, possibly ending up with the purchasing of the products that are not of the best deals. In contrary, Internet shopping provides sufficient information and options for consumers before purchasing made (i.e., the move toward a consumer-oriented market). Therefore, merchants require the provision of good quality, lower price, or better service in order to maintain their competitive advantages.

Negotiation has been used for the decision of the transaction terms in markets (such as ebay.com and onsale.com). However, due to the difference between personal recognition and the market environment, to a specific seller, the negotiation strategies used by different buyers with the same product demand may be different and thus result in different deal prices. In addition, the leverage of negotiation counts on resources at hand.

For example, from the viewpoint of a seller, the price under negotiation might be easily to get reduced in order to retain a frequent buyer who is of good reputation and purchases in large quantity with cash. Vise versa, service and quality are essential to customers who are willing to pay proper price.

S.-T. Yuan and M. Yokoo (Eds.): PRIMA 2001, LNAI 2132, pp. 122-138, 2001.

Cost of marketing for single customer is significantly lower than multiple, which motivate sellers (such as Makro and Costco) to take the wholesale pattern (i.e., reduced price for large quantity of purchase). However, the incentive of wholesaling might be eliminated whenever the costs (the total amount of price reduced) exceed the required profit [5]. Accordingly, individuals are driven by the incentive mentioned above and grouping on Internet to pursue specific product of lower price, in spite of the single demand is few. A group of allied individuals endows this group an aggregated bargaining power, i.e. *the power of group negotiation.*

Group Negotiation exchanges time for price. That is, more discounts in price go with higher quantities accumulated in time that customers buy. In real life, an individual is often unable to reach the minimum for discounting by certain product but might be tolerant to the time spent in grouping for favorable price.

Accompany.com and Mercata.com are famous examples regarding buyer grouping overseas. The Collective Buying Service and PowerBuy, the patent-pending demand coordination engine utilized by Mobshop.com, is able to group buyers with same demands for price biding. The Cool Bid and Bid.com.tw are also known in domestic.

Group negotiation is becoming essential in electronic business. However, most of activities of group negotiation are either side tracked or with intractable complexity although the heat is continuing up. The rational is two-fold:

- **Imperfect results:** Commonly, manufacturers or intermediate firms offer products within time frame and marked price on the website, and level-down discounts are provided when buyers scaling up. No communication has been brought up, as well as negotiation, and even the price may far beyond customers' expectation.

- **Intractable complexity:** The efficiency of pure negotiation play will drop off when participants scaling up. When we adopt a complex algorithm in the negotiation mechanism, they need not only a lot of time to compute the results but also have to wait for the response from the counter part. Communication costs increase with the size of group. When buyers and sellers are represented by software agents doing business transactions in an e-market, the communication operations reach $O(n^2)$.

With the problems associated with the current status of group negotiation, naturally arises a question: *how to devise a group negotiation mechanism that enables (near) perfect results with tractable complexity?* In this paper, we present such a mechanism called *Negotiation-Credit Based Negotiation* that facilitates the grouping of buyers and sellers and reaches the favorable prices for buyers and sellers eventually, i.e., *Negotiation-Credit Driven Coalition Formation.*

The envisioned contributions of the proposed mechanism are four-fold:

- **Devise a group negotiation mechanism:**
In traditional marketplaces, the value of goods is hard to determine without spending a lot of time, by sellers and buyers, to reach the balance point. In electronic marketplaces, the process can be expedited through negotiation. In this paper, we devise a group negotiation mechanism that empowers an electronic marketplace to allow group buy and group sell in behalf of buyers and sellers, which are represented by software agents [2].

- **Enable marketplace efficiency:**

The cost of time will be extremely high to reach the final results by agents without restraining the process of negotiation. Only bilateral communication is required between two individuals on the market, but negotiation become crucial and complicate as participants increase.

Inefficiency of time commonly is caused by refusal of concession in profit on both sides that ignore the cost of time, that is, in order to get the maximum profit agents would only make a little concession, taking a lot of time to finish the negotiation and cause inefficiency. However, when under the rule of 0-gain or single shot game plan, both sides with different strategies are willing to offer more attractive terms (instead of sustaining considerable profit by scarifying time), in order to reach the agreement.

This paper aims to achieve quality trades in e-markets by utilizing the proposed Negotiation–Credit Base negotiation, with limited time and process. Its essence is that both sides of the trading must finish the negotiation within an indicated number of times (we call such a number *Negotiation Credit*), keeping both of them from sustaining profit by scarifying time. They would propose more attractive terms with their strategies to form coalition under consideration. In other words, constrain the number of negotiation times in order to achieve high quality transaction.

- **Provide a proper strategy:**

Strategies between agents vary with different factors as well as human nature. Different strategies have been developed but complexity doesn't stand for outstanding [3]. An agent may change its strategy upon an external factor or imitate those agents which succeed in markets. The paper provides a Negotiation-Credit driven strategy that can close deals between agents with reasonable profit under time constraints.

- **Enforce healthy market:**

Within an e-market, an agent who has capable ability, reputation and credibility will be selected as a manager and represent a group for negotiation. The higher profit with better performance is expected to secure a sound cycle of economic.

- **Extend group buy to group sell:**

In general, group negotiation simply represents the joint benefits between customers and merchants, i.e., B2C coalition formation. However, the Negotiation-Credit Based Negotiation can extend the scope of coalition formation by including B2B coalition formation to make the marketplace more efficient.

This paper is organized as follows: Section 2 describes the methodology of Negotiation-Credit driven coalition formation, of which the core component, Negotiation-Credit Based Negotiation, is presented in Section 3. The evaluation results are then shown in Section 4. Finally, a conclusion is made in Section 5.

2   Negotiation-Credit Driven Coalition Formation

In this section, the descriptions of Negotiation-Credit Driven Coalition Formation are detailed in three-fold: (1) the assumptions behind the methodology (Section 2.1) (2) the framework of the methodology (Section 2.2) (3) the algorithm of the methodology (Section 2.3-2.4).

2.1   The Assumptions

The assumptions carries by the methodology are as follows:

(1) When buyer agents participate in the market, they form coalitions according to their needs of goods. In other words, their needs to specific goods are known before they get into the marketplace.

(2) In the marketplace, buyer agents and seller agents make decisions according to the specific function we proposed. They alter their strategies simply by changing certain variables in these functions.

(3) When agents can reduce computation cost and communication cost in each negotiation round, we call the mechanism is close to efficiency.

(4) Agents are assumed to experience a super-additive environment [7]. In other words, the benefits of the participators won't go down by the increasing number of agents in the marketplace.

(5) Every agent, participating in the marketplace, pursues its own maximum profit (rational agent). All of the agents can get sufficient and accurate information provided by other agents.

2.2   The Framework

Buyers and sellers prefer wholesale since they both can get more profits from it. In this paper, we set up a group-shopping environment carrying the methodology (its framework is shown in Figure 1), and seller agents can bargain with buyer agents with their own resources to reach the deal in a more efficient way.

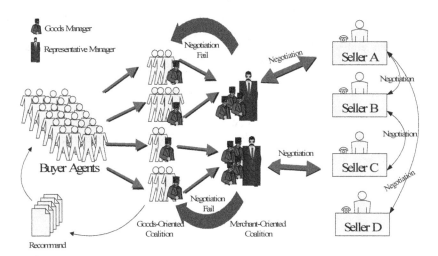

Figure 1. The framework for Negotiation-Credit Driven Coalition Formation

In this electronic shopping environment, the more the buyers with the same goods demand increase, the more bargaining power they have. However, does this reach the maximum payoff of buyers? Of course not, if buyer agents have different goods requirements but make the deal with the same merchant, they can form a larger coalition and get extra discount from the seller. The seller agent is willing to trade with the buyer coalition due to the volume of business is huge. Accordingly, before buyer agents and seller agents start to negotiate, buyer agents will run two rounds of coalition formation (*Goods-Oriented Coalition Formation* and *Merchant-Oriented Coalition Formation*) in order to group the buyer agents with the same seller together. For the purpose of performing coalition formation more efficiently, buyer agents with the same goods demand/with the same trading seller will choose one manager (*Goods Manager/Representative Manager*) to bargain on behalf of the coalitions they belong to in the process.

In other words, after buyer agents recognize their needs with the sufficient information provided by the system, the buyer agents with the same demand of goods will form a coalition and elect a Goods Manager[1] at the same time. The Goods Manager has the right to pick the seller agents. All the Goods Managers with same merchant will then form a larger coalition, in which they also elect a Representative Manager to represent the whole coalition and negotiate with the seller agents.

As the number of the agents at both sides increases, it may take a lot of time to form a coalition or elect the managers. In this paper, we limit the number of negotiation times (*Negotiation Credit*), i.e. the two parties will strike a bargain within a limited number of negotiation times. Agents may proceed with their negotiation more efficiently at the cost of paying higher price.

A Goods Manager may have more than one ideal merchant. While the Representative Manager fails to strike a bargain with the seller agent, the transaction does not terminate. The coalition does not break up but re-coalition on the basis of the second ideal merchant. Then the new Representative Manager will be elected again to negotiate with this seller agent.

From the viewpoint of the sellers, seller agents can form coalitions with other seller agents as well via negotiation to share their resources and become more competitive. In this paper, buyer agents and seller agents will form four different types of coalitions due to their interests. They are *Goods-Oriented Coalition, Merchant-Oriented Coalition, Buyer-Seller Coalition*, and S*eller-Oriented Coalition* (Figure. 2).

---

[1] It's very hard to have a common consensus between a great number of agents with different opinions. Therefore, a manager elected can represent a strong opinion body on behalf of its members and make further coalition formation much more efficiently.

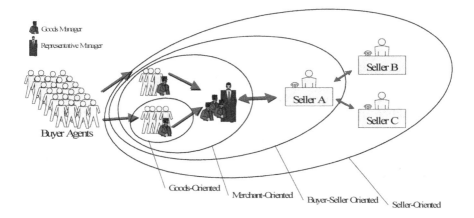

Figure 2. Coalition Architecture

2.3   Coalition Formation

Coalition Formation is the process of grouping together many agents to share resources and get the maximized interests. It is an important issue in a multi-agent system. Agents may work together for the reasons as follows: (1) The tasks associated with agents may be overlapped completely or partially. (2) Agents may share their tasks or resources in a bigger coalition because of their different abilities. (3) Various viewpoints about products or expected utilities at agents can be united and form a strong unified opinion body. Therefore, a group of agents can perform more efficiently than a single agent can [6,8,9,11,12].

There are four types of coalition formation in our system: Goods-Oriented Coalition Formation, Merchant-Oriented Coalition Formation, Buyer-Seller Coalition Formation, and Seller-Oriented Coalition Formation. Below are their descriptions:

- **Goods-Oriented Coalition Formation**

We presume buyer agents in the marketplace know what goods they're going to buy after needs identification. Buyer agents with the same goods demand in general will form one goods-oriented coalition in order to get lower price, higher quality and better service. Buyer agents in a coalition elect a Goods Manager based on their Negotiation Credits to represent the agents of the coalition. (There might be cases that buyer agents with the same goods demand are in different goods-oriented coalitions due to the reasons as the request of asking goods from a particular merchant or being unsatisfied with the existing coalition.) As follows are the steps to form goods-oriented coalitions:

(1) The marketplace waits for the admission of buyer agents in each time frame. (Without loss of generality, buyer agents are assumed to enter the marketplace in

sequence, and for each goods demand the first buyer is assigned as the Goods Manager of a goods-oriented coalition of size 1.)

(2) Each Goods Manager sends out its proposal[2] to incoming buyer agents of the same goods demand.

(3) Each buyer agent evaluates the proposals and ranks them into a preference list.

(4) The buyer agent negotiates with Goods Managers in an order according to this preference list. During a successful round of negotiation, terms agreements are made based on the method of Negotiation-Credit Based Negotiation, form a two-pair coalition [10], and then re-elect the Goods Manager. (That is, the coalition size is increased by 1 and the coalition's Goods Manager might be changed.)

(5) Repeat above steps until the end of the time frame.

- **Merchant-Oriented Coalition Formation**

In order to increase the bargaining power, Goods Managers with the same merchant under consideration for purchasing will seek for a larger coalition. This is called Merchant-oriented Coalition formation. The steps proceed as follows:

(1) Only Goods Managers are allowed to engage in Merchant-Oriented Coalition Formation. Goods Managers with the same merchant under consideration for purchasing send each other their proposals.

(2) Each Goods Managers evaluates the proposals and ranks them into a preference list.

(3) The Goods Manager negotiates with other Goods Managers in an order according to this preference list. During a successful round of negotiation, terms agreements are made using the method of Negotiation-Credit Based Negotiation and then form a two-pair coalition. At the same time, they elect a Goods Manager as the Representative Manager for their coalition.

(4) View the elected Representative Managers as a Goods Managers and repeat the above steps to them until they cannot form a coalition with a greater size.

- **Buyer-Seller Coalition Formation**

Every seller agent generally would like to strike a bargain with seller agents for the purpose of payoff generation. When a Representative Manager strikes a bargain with a seller agent based on Negotiation-Credit Based Negotiation, they form a Buyer-Seller Coalition. As follows are the steps required Buyer-Seller Coalitions:

(1) All of the Representative Managers have the rights to negotiate with seller agents base on Negotiation-Credit Based Negotiation. When they strike a bargain, all of the agents involved are formed into a coalition and are obligated to accomplish the engaged transaction.

(2) If the bargaining fails, the coalition will break and return to Merchant-Oriented Coalition Formation to seek for another round of coalition formation with new target of merchant under consideration.

---

[2] A proposal usually is composed of the following information: negotiation credit, volume of purchase, *etc.*

(3) Repeat above steps until striking a bargain or finish negotiation with all of sellers in the preference list.

Table 1. Preference list table

Seller1	Seller2	Seller3	Seller 4	....

Preference List	Manager 1	Manager 2	Manager 3	Manager 4
1	Seller 1	Seller 2	Seller 1	Seller 2
2	Seller 3	Seller 4	Seller 2	Seller 3
3	Seller 2	Seller 1	Seller 4	Seller 1
:				
:				

Table 1 gives a simple example as follows: We presume each Goods Manager lays different preference over the seller agents. In each round of Merchant-Oriented Coalition Formation, Goods Managers seek to form a greater coalition with the same target of merchant under consideration (based on their preference over the seller agents). For example, Goods Managers 1 and 3 (with seller agent 1 as their top priority consideration of merchant) successfully form a Merchant-Oriented Coalition and elect a Representative Manager. If the Representative Manager fails the bargaining with seller agent 1, the coalition breaks up and Goods Manager 1 and 4 start another round of Merchant-Oriented Coalition Formation with the merchant target being seller agent 3. Afterwards, Buyer-Seller Coalition Formation may take place between them.

- **Seller-Oriented Coalition Formation**

Because of group-buy, sellers may be not able to provide the huge volume of particular goods. However, seller agents may cooperate with other in order to get business opportunities by coalition. For instance, seller agents can share with each other the products, transportation, and services in order to increase their profits. The steps to form the coalition is shown as follows:

(1) A seller agent, who strikes a bargain, ranks other seller agents who have the desirable resources.
(2) This seller agent negotiates with other seller agents in an order according to its preference list base on the method of Negotiation-Credit Based Negotiation.
(3) Repeat above two steps until completing the bargain transaction or exhausting the seller agents in preference list.

Seller agents can ally with other seller agents before a transaction starts. Also they can rally with each other when buyer agents and seller agents are engaging their negotiation. Coalition formation applied to the trades between business and business (B2B) may reduce inventory costs, transportation costs and other purchasing costs.

3   Negotiation-Credit Based Negotiation

Agents can strike a bargain in a predictable period by restrict the number of negotiation times (Negotiation Credit). In this section, we address how Negotiation-Credit Based Negotiation makes agents with more experience as managers and to gain more profit for the coalition. This may also reduce cheating and incompetent agents to be managers.

The descriptions of Negotiation-Credit Based Negotiation are three-fold: (1) the value setting of Negotiation Credit in Section 3.1 (2) its method in Section 3.2 (3) a proper agent strategy based on Negotiation Credit in Section 3.3.

3.1   Negotiation Credit

Default value

When an agent enter the marketplace at the first time, the system will assign the agent a Negotiation Credit value (NC) according to its profile. NC includes base credit and reputation credit as shown in Formula (1). Reputation credits are computed simply by multiplying a weight to the reputation values[3].

$$NC = B_{credit} + R_{reputation} \bullet W_r \tag{1}$$

> NC : Negotiation Credit
> B_{credit} : agent's basic NC given by the designer
> $R_{reputation}$: agent's reputation
> W_r : Weight of Reputation

Before Manager Competition

In Goods-Oriented Coalition Formation and Merchant-Oriented Coalition Formation, each agent is assigned a NC by the system prior to manager competition. The percentage of the amount of money spent affects NC value. The intuition is that buying power usually is defined as the amount of money spent in transaction, which in tern is represented by the quantity of the product purchased multiplying the product's price.

$$NC \leftarrow NC + \frac{N_{product} \bullet P_{product}}{\sum_{1}^{n} N_{product} \bullet P_{product}} \bullet Wn \tag{2}$$

> $Nproduct$: Amount of goods the agent want to buy
> n : Number of agents in the coalition
> Wn : Weight of the adjust value
> $P_{product}$: the product price named by the merchant

---

[3] We assume each agent is associated with a reputation value. This value can be simply a social rank or computed by a complex reputation function.

After Manger Competition

After manager competition, if an agent is elected as a manager, it would represent the coalition to negotiate with other agents. That is, the capability of the coalition must be carried over to the agent. For simplicity, the carried-over NC is the sum of the original NC and the averaged NC of the coalition. We also give the average NC of the coalition a weight.

$$NC \leftarrow NC + \frac{\sum_{i=1}^{n} NC_i}{n} \bullet W_{group\_NC} \tag{3}$$

$W_{group\_NC:}$: *Weight of Average Group NC*

Negotiation fails

During Buyer-Seller Coalition Formation and Seller Coalition Formation, a manager' NC will be reduced when the manager does not strike a bargain for its coalition. This would make the chance of the agent being elected as a manager reduced in the next coalition formation round. The range to be reduced is agent's NC divided by the remaining agents (R) in the preference list (formula 4.1). Not only the manager but also the members of the coalition have to be punished (this is because the members elect the manager and hence need to share the responsibilities). However, the range of reduction should be less than the manager's. The weight W_{reduce} will be a constant between 0 and 1 (formula 4.2).

Managers:

$$NC \leftarrow NC - \frac{NC}{R} \tag{4.1}$$

Non-managers:

$$NC \leftarrow NC - \frac{NC}{R} \bullet W_{reduce} \tag{4.2}$$

R: *Remaining agents in the preference list*
W_{reduce}: *Weight of the adjust value*

Transaction finishes

After a transaction succeeds, the NC of the seller agents and the buyer agents involved will grow. For simplicity, the increment is an adjust value NC_{adj} for managers and NC_{adj} multiplied by a weight W_{adj} (ranging between 0 and 1) for non-manager members.

Manager:

$$NC \leftarrow NC \pm NC_{adj} \tag{5.1}$$

Non-manager:

$$NC \leftarrow NC \pm NC_{adj} \bullet W_{adj} \tag{5.2}$$

$NCadj$: adjust value for NC after transaction finishes
$Wadj$: Weight of NCadj

3.2   The Method

Negotiation-Credit Based Negotiation is used for agents to compete for manager's positions as addressed in Section 2. Therefore, the way we describe the method of Negotiation-Credit Based Negotiation is through the process of manager competition between two agents.

Each agent has different abilities according to its reputation, adoption of strategy, or personal utilities laid on goods. Due to the existence of NC, agents with higher NC will become a manager easily than ones with lower NC. The process of manager competition between two agents is described as follows:

(1) Both agents calculate the coalition utilities.
(2) Both agents send to each other their proposals.
(3) Both agents bargain with each other based on the mechanism of Negotiation-Credit Based Negotiation until striking a bargain or running out of Negotiation Credit.
(4) The agent with no Negotiation Credit available either accepts the contract or leave.

As follows is a simple example used to explain the mechanism:
- Agent A with NC=5 expects the coalition utility to be 9. Agent B with NC=3 expects the coalition utility to be 10. They compete with each other to be a manager.

Table 2. Manager competition.

NC	A	NC	B
5	6	3	6.01
4	6.02	2	7
3	7.01	1	8.5
2	8.9	0	Accept or leave
1			

- With the expected value by A being 9, A begins with an offer of 6. In other words, A promise to give 6 to B if B agrees that A takes the manager's position. Meanwhile B begins with a higher offer of 6.01   in a hope of becoming a manager. As the bargaining round goes, the NC will be reduced in order to strike a bargain more efficiently. For example, when the agent has no Negotiation Credit left (NC = 0), he has to either accept the contract or leave the coalition.
- In order to compete to be a manager within a limited number of negotiation rounds, an agent's bargain prices must progress quite attractively in order for surviving the competition. For instance, B will take the manager's position if B is

willing to give an offer of 9.1 at the third round. This is the risk the agent B should take on because of lower NC, but this also can avoid the lengthy bargaining process.

3.3   Negotiation Strategy

When agents start to bargain, they adopt different strategies. In other words, they adjust their price according their strategies. The negotiation strategy is represented as functions shown below:

$$Buyer\_price_{t+1} = Min(Upper\_bounds, Buyer\_price_t + \frac{Motivation \bullet Diff\_price}{NC})$$

$$\text{(6)}$$

t : negotiation round.
Buyer_price : bargain price of a buyer agent in the current round.
Upper_bounds : the highest price the buyer agent would pay.

Motivation : the motivation for the buyer to buy the product (between 0 and 1).
Diff_price : the price gap between the buyer agent and seller agent.

The motivation of a buyer agent is a parameter used in the negotiation strategy. The value of motivation ranges from 0 to 1. The motivation being 0 indicates the buyer agent has no motivation to strike a bargain, and hence the bargain price will be the same as the previous round's. The motivation being 1 indicates the buyer agent would try its best to strike a bargain under the allowable negotiation rounds.

The negotiation strategy for a seller agent is similar to a buyer agent's; however, the bargain price is adjusted in the opposite direction. A buyer agent and a seller agent can strike a bargain only on condition that either of their motivation is not equal to zero. With the NC increased, the price gap between the buyer and the seller will get smaller (formula 7).

$$Seller\_price_{t+1} = Max(Lower\_bounds, Seller\_price_t - \frac{Motivation \bullet Diff\_price}{NC})$$

$$\text{(7)}$$

Seller_price : bargain price of seller agent in the current round.
Lower_bounds : the lowest price the buyer agent would pay.

In each coalition, an agent will use Negotiation-Credit Based Negotiation to conduct manager competition. The bargain number of times also based on Negotiation Credit. When agent run out of NC, the agent has to agree the other party to be a manager or leave the coalition (formula 8).

$$Agent\_price = Agent\_price_{another} + (Motivation \bullet \frac{Upper\_bound - Agent\_price_{another}}{NC})$$

(8)

Agent_price : Bargain price to compete to be a manager.
Upper_bounds : the highest price the buyer agent would pay.

Bargain price between seller agent and buyer agent gets closer as negotiation round goes. However, during manager competition, bargain price increases as negotiation round increases. This price will be changed according another agent's bargain price and the range of the addition increases as the value of motivation increases.

As the NC decreases, agent may change its value of motivation to bargain. In other words, agents can adopt different strategy to bargain in order to gain more coalition utilities.

4   Evaluation and Discussion

The conduction of coalition formation in general has two schools of thought: decentralized coalition formation (i.e., coalitions are formed bottom-up by agents) and centralized coalition formation (i.e., coalitions are formed top-down by a centralized controller). This paper adopts the decentralized option. The rational is two-fold: (1) Due to lack of trust and varying behaviors between agents, agents often prefer their own participation in computation and communication. (2) With centralized coalition formation, individual profit may be sacrificed in order to maximize group profit.

Our evaluation was performed in a decentralized environment, which guarantee the coalitions can be formed in polynomial time. Furthermore, "no detachment policy" [4] is assumed and enforced in order to prevent coalition from being unstable. In other words, an agent is not allowed to detach from its coalition when the coalition is formed (that is, the agent should be responsible for its choices of goods demand and managers).

This decentralized environment can be examined with two views, agent view and coalition view:

- **Agent View:**

Agents representing buyers or sellers varies at their abilities and behavior: (1) Their Negotiation Credit (NC) may be different due to different experience and amount of purchasing. (2) Their utilities laid on goods may be different. (3) The highest and lowest price proposed may be different. All of the difference would influence the results of coalition formation and the deals between agents.

- **Coalition View:**

Through coalition formation, buyer agents and seller agents can acquire more profit by buying and selling in wholesale. Agents will elect a manager in each coalition in order to seek for a greater coalition efficiently. Moreover, the managers will bargain with each other based on Negotiation-Credit Based Negotiation according to the total amount of money of his members.

With these two views, the evaluations are conducted through two directions: the results of coalition formation from the agent view (in Section 4.1), and the results of coalition formation from the coalition view (in Section 4.2).

4.1   Quality from Agent View

Agents are independent entities and the results of coalition formation depend on their utilities, Negotiation Credit, and their strategies of pricing. It might be cases that certain agents with specific demands would rather trade solo than in coalition. However, *what we concern is if an agent in coalition obtains its maximized payoff.*

When a Representative Manager strikes a bargain with a seller agent, the payoff will be distributed to his Goods Managers, which further distribute its payoff to buyer agents. For simplicity, an agent's payoff is represented by the bargaining power achieved as shown in formula (9):

Payoff = (Upper price - Deal price) / (Upper price – Start price)   (9)

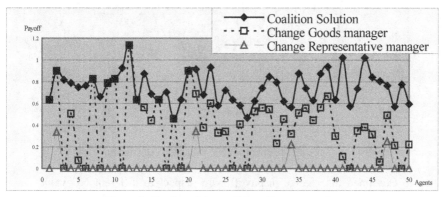

Figure 3. Quality of the coalitions from agent view

We designed an experiment environment in which there were fifty buyer agents. After the coalitions of the fifty buyer agents were formed, the payoffs at these agents were examined as shown in the solid line of Figure 3.

This solid line is the payoff results from our Negotiation-Credit Driven Coalition Formation. We believe that the elected Goods Managers and Representative Managers can acquire the highest payoff for their member agents. In order to justify this claim, we try all possible other manager combinations (i.e., we make each other member in a coalition be a Goods Manager/Representative Manager and average their results). The results shows that the payoffs obtained at agents with other manager combination are smaller than the payoffs acquired by our methodology. In other words, our system is able to achieve a Pareto Optimal (PE) allocation (i.e., agents' payoffs are maximized; no other allocations, the results obtained by all other manager combinations, would get one agent better off without hurting the others).

4.2   Efficiency from Coalition View

It is quite obvious that the efficiency of negotiation will drop off as the number of agents increases. However, Negotiation Credit can be used to control the efficiency in coalition formation. Nevertheless, what we concern is how this control affects the payoffs at agents and how to control Negotiation Credit.

Figure 4 shows the relations between NC and the payoff at 100 agents. Each line represents the payoff results at agents with an indicated NC. These results show the payoffs at agents increase with the increase at NC.

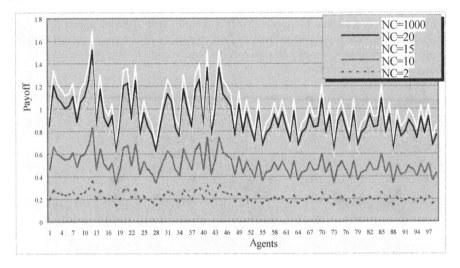

Figure 4. The effects of NC values on each agent

Figure 5 examined the change in payoff with respect to different NC values for 6 agents, Agent1, Agent2, ..., Agent6. The results are two-fold: (1) For each agent, its payoff increases obviously when the value of NC ranging from 5 to 20. (2) For each agent, its payoff changes slowly when the value of NC is greater than 20 as well as less than 5, especially when the value of NC is between 100 and 1000.

In other words, agents can acquire its (near) maximum payoff around 20 times of negotiation, and extra negotiation does not help much to raise its payoff and sometimes it even gets worsen off. Here is a tradeoff between quality in results and system resources exhausted. Therefore, NC allocation should depend on the scale of marketplace and the resources of the system.

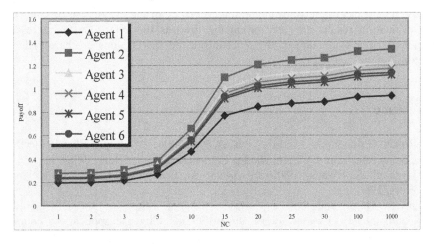

Figure 5. Change in payoff with respect to different NC values

4.3   Discussion

In addition to the results shown in Section 4.1 and 4.2, we summarize further results as follows: An agent's payoff grows with the increase in the value of NC. However, besides the factor of NC, agent's active and strategy of pricing affect an agent's payoff. For instance, the payoff of an agent would decline with the increase in the value of active because an agent would sacrifice its payoff to strike the bargain due to high interest in specific goods. As to strategy of pricing, a buyer agent's payoff would grow with the decrease in the agent's start price; however the agent would not close a deal when the start price is too low. The change of payoff is opposite at seller agents' side. In addition, the upper price or lower price set by seller agents or buyer agents would not affect the final payoff of an agent.

NC plays a very important role for facilitating the marketplace. With 50 agents implemented in the simulated marketplace, we found that an agent's payoff changes obviously for the NC values ranging from 5 to 20. That is, the saturated NC value is about 20 for the market size of 50. A saturated NC value is appreciated for bounding the process of negotiation between agents. However, the saturated NC value may change with the market size. We currently are investigating the relationship between saturated NC values and market sizes in a hope to strengthen the contribution of the method, Negotiation-Credit Driven Coalition Formation.

5   Conclusion

Group negotiation is becoming essential in electronic business. However, most of activities of group negotiation are either side tracked or with intractable complexity although the heat is continuing up. In this paper, we present a mechanism called Negotiation-Credit Based Negotiation that facilitates the grouping of buyers and sellers and reaches the favorable prices for buyers and sellers eventually, i.e., Negotiation-Credit Driven Coalition Formation. With this mechanism, we expect agents' payoff can be maximized and the efficiency of the market can be controlled. The evaluation results are very promising towards this end. Our future research includes further evaluation of the mechanism and fielding this mechanism in real domains.

Reference

[1] Robert Guttman, Alexandros Moukas, Pattie Maes, "Agent-mediated Electronic Commerce: A Survey", Knowledge Engineering Review,June 1998.

[2] Hyacinth S. Nwana, "Software Agent: An Overview", Cambridge University Press, 1996.

[3] Javier Bejar and Ulises Cortes ," Agent Strategies on DPB Auction Tournaments", a classwork for an artificial intelligence applications course at UPC.

[4] K.Lerman , O.Shehory, "Coalition Formation for Large-Scale Electronic Markets", supported in part by MURI contract N00014-96-1222.

[5] Maksim Tsvetovat, Katia Sycara, Yian Chen, James Ying, "Customer Coalitions in Electronic Markets",Robotics Institute, Carnegie Mellon University, Pittsburgh PA .

[6] Matthias Klusch, Onn Shehory, "A Polynomial Kernel-Oriented Coalition Algorithm for Rational Information Agents", supported in part bye the NSF, Grant IRI-9423967

[7] Onn Shehory ,Sarit Kraus, " Coalition formation among autonomous agents: Strategies and complexity", Proceedings of the Fourteenth International Joint Conference on Artificial Intelligence(IJCAI 95), Montréal, Québec, Canada, 1995.

[8] Onn Shehory, Katia Sycara, Somesh Jha, "Multi-agent Coordination through Coalition Formation ", supported in part by ARPA Grant #F33615-93-1-1330

[9] Steven Ketchpel, " Coalition Formation Among Autonomous Agents ". Proceedings of the Fourteenth International Joint Conference on Artificial Intelligence(IJCAI 95), Montréal, Québec, Canada, 1995.

[10] Steven Ketchpel. " Forming Coalitions in the Face of Uncertain Rewards ", Proceedings of the 12th National Conference on Artificial Intelligence, Seattle, WA, USA,1994,

[11] Sandholm Tuomas, Lesser Victor, "Coalition Formation among Bounded Rational Agents" , Proceedings of the Fourteenth International Joint Conference on Artificial Intelligence(IJCAI 95), Montréal, Québec, Canada,1995.

An Adaptive Agent Society for Environmental Scanning through the Internet

Rey-Long Liu

Department of Information Management, Chung Hua University
HsinChu, Taiwan, R.O.C.
rlliu@mi.chu.edu.tw

Abstract. Business managers need to promptly respond to environmental changes. Environmental scanners are thus important in discovering and monitoring the information of interest (IOI). In this paper, we explore *continuous* and *resource-bounded* environmental scanning (CRBES). The scanner continuously scans for new IOI without consuming too much resource (e.g. bandwidths of computer networks and services of information servers). In that case, new IOI may be discovered in a *complete* and *timely* manner without making the related networks and servers too exhausted to provide services. We develop a multiagent framework ACES to achieve CRBES. The agents form an *adaptive* society by adapting their population and specialty to information needs of individual users, resource limitation of environmental scanning, distribution of IOI in the environments, and update behaviors of the IOI. The delivery of ACES to businesses may constantly provide timelier IOI without causing serious problems to the Intranet and the Internet communities.

1   Introduction

Environmental scanning is a key activity for a business [8]. It aims to *discover* and *monitor* those external information pieces that are related to the operation and success of the business. Typical environmental information includes various kinds of information from the government, competitors, customers, and partners of the business. The business should respond to the newest status of the environment in a timely manner. To achieve that, it requires an environment scanner that may scan critical environmental information comprehensively. The scanner should also detect updates of the environment in a timely manner so that the business may have more time to respond to the environmental change.

In this paper, we introduce multiagent technology to environmental scanning. In particular, we focus on how a multiagent system may be developed to support Continuous and Resource-bounded Business Environmental Scanning (CRBES), whose two main requirements include: (1) continuously discovering and monitoring environmental information, and (2) properly controlling the amount of the resources consumed by the scanner. The resources include internal resources (e.g. Intranet

S.-T. Yuan and M. Yokoo (Eds.): PRIMA 2001, LNAI 2132, pp. 139-153, 2001.

bandwidth) and external resources (e.g. the Internet bandwidth and the web servers). Obviously, the resources are limited, and the uncontrolled consumption of the resources may make both the Intranet and the external servers too exhausted to provide normal services [12]. Simultaneously fulfilling the two requirements of CRBES is of great significance to business administration and multiagent technology.

In the next section, we precisely define the problems, requirements, and major challenges of CRBES. A multiagent framework ACES (adaptive Agents for Continuous and resource-bounded Environmental Scanning) for supporting CRBES is then outlined in section 3. In section 4, we investigate the performance of ACES in a simulated information space on the World-Wide-Web (WWW). Related work is discussed in section 5 to illustrate the theoretical impacts of the framework.

2   Continuous and Resource-Bounded Business Environmental Scanning

Given an upper bound of resource consumption and a set of information needs of the business, CRBES aims to continuously *discover* the information of interest (IOI) and *monitor* the IOI for possible updates. It needs to work in a *continuous* manner, since the environment is always dynamically changing. It also needs to work under a *resource-bounded* condition, since its delivery to the business should not cause serious performance problems to the Intranet, the Internet, and the related information servers. Once a new IOI is discovered or an update is detected, suitable actions (e.g. event logging and user notification) are triggered. In this paper, we focus on the information space on the Internet, which is currently a major source of environmental information for businesses.

Table 1. Major concerns of CRBES

Concern	Definition
Timeliness of Environmental Scanning (TES)	(A) Time Delay = Σ {Time of being found - Time of happening}, for all IOI items found (B) Average Time Delay = Time Delay / Total number of IOI items found (C) TES = 1 / Average Time Delay
Effectiveness of Environmental Scanning (EES)	Number of IOI items found / Times of checking the information space
Completeness of Environmental Scanning (CES)	Number of IOI items found / Total number of IOI items that happened

Table 1 defines three major concerns of CRBES. The definitions are based on the practical needs of environmental scanning in businesses. *Timeliness of Environmental Scanning* (TES) measures how timely the detection of IOI is. A timely scanner may help the managers to capture IOI in a timely manner so that they may have more time to respond to the IOI. *Effectiveness of Environmental Scanning* (EES) measures how effectively a scanner utilizes the limited amount of resources to find IOI. A scanner with a better performance in EES may utilize less resource to discover more IOI. It helps the managers to capture more IOI without incurring heavy overheads to the Intranet and Internet communities. *Completeness of Environmental Scanning* (CES) measures how completely a scanner finds IOI. A scanner with a better performance in CES may help the managers to capture a higher percentage of IOI from the dynamic information space. A scanner with better performances in TES, EES, and CES may helps the managers to promptly capture a higher percentage of new IOI without incurring heavy overheads to the Intranet and Internet communities.

Major challenges of CRBES lie on intelligent environmental scanning under the constraint of limiting the amount of the resource that may be consumed. In general, to promote the quality of environmental scanning (i.e. TES, EES, and CES), the system often needs to consume more resource (for crawling through the Internet and querying the related information servers). Since there may be a large number of businesses having to continuously scan various aspects of their environments, uncontrolled consumption of resource may make the Intranet, the Internet, and the information servers too exhausted to provide their normal services. That is, a scanner for CRBES should properly control the loading it incurs, while at the same time, maintain its quality of services in environmental scanning.

Previous studies closely related to CRBES are the studies of information gathering and monitoring. They often focused on satisfying users' "one-shot" needs (e.g. searching for IOI [4, 26] with consideration of time/cost/quality tradeoffs of the search [14]) and monitoring a predefined set of IOI (e.g. periodical monitoring [6, 17, 18] and adaptive monitoring [15, 16]). The integrative treatment of information discovery and monitoring in the context of limited resource consumption deserves more exploration. It is both essential and significant to business administration.

3   Adaptive Agents for CRBES through the Internet

Figure 1 outlines an adaptive multiagent model ACES for supporting CRBES. ACES consists of a controlling agent and a dynamic population of scanning agents. The system administrator may enter a resource limit to the controlling agent, which serves as a platform on which the scanning agents cooperate with each other for achieving CRBES. For the purposes of fault tolerance and load distribution, there may be multiple controlling agents.

A scanning is delegated to check a web site (i.e. a uniform resource locator, URL) for satisfying a set of information needs. An information need consists of a specification of IOI (e.g. a set of keywords) and its corresponding user. Each scanning agent learns to monitor IOI and spawn new agents for new IOI found. It also shares with other agents what it needs and finds through the coordination of the controlling agent. Upon receiving a resource limit from the system administrator, the controlling agent controls the amount of resource consumed for satisfying users' information needs. Thus the scanning agents, together with the controlling agent, form an *adaptive* agent society in the sense that they automatically adapt their population and specialty to (1) information needs of individual users, (2) resource limitation of environmental scanning, (3) distribution of IOI in the environments, and (4) update behaviors of the IOI.

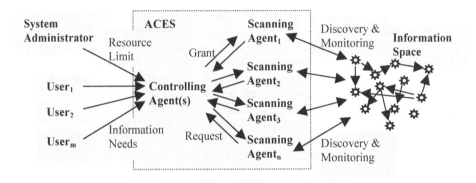

Figure 1. Overview of ACES

3.1   The Scanning Agents

Table 2 defines the behavior of each scanning agent. Given a set of information needs as the goals (i.e. *Goal*), a target web site (i.e. *Target*), and a resource consumption limit (i.e. *ResourceU*), the agent repeatedly checks the web site for new information that satisfies the associated information needs. Its resource consumption is governed by the resource consumption limit, which is transformed into a maximum frequency of checking the web site (ref. steps 5). The agent adaptively adjusts *ResourceU* based on the current update behavior of *Target*. When it succeeds (fails) in finding new information in two consecutive trials of checking *Target*, it requests the controlling agent for a higher (lower) level of *ResourceU* (ref. *Type-R-More* request in step 5.3 and *Type-R-Less* request in step 5.4). In this way, the agent society learns to maximize the utility of limited amount of resource that may be consumed by the system.

When the agent finds new information from *Target*, it issues a *Type-E* request to the controlling agent for *socially* evaluating what it finds. The social evaluation aims to identify which goals of the agent society are satisfied by the finding (i.e. *SatisfiedGoal* in step 5.2.1) and to what extent is the satisfaction (i.e. *SocialEvaluation* in step 5.2.1). The agent accordingly enlarges its *Goal* by additionally considering *SatisfiedGoal*. (ref. step 5.2.2), and adjusts its *Aliveness* value to reflect how well it has done (ref. step 5.2.3). When the aliveness value is higher than a predefined threshold α, it issues a request (to the controlling agent) to spawn new agents that are to be in charge of the web sites linked by the current web site (ref. *Type-S* request in step 5.2.5). When the aliveness value is below a predefined threshold β or the agent's *Goal* is empty, the agent terminates itself and issues a request to release its resource (ref. *Type-T* request in step 7).

When the agent is informed (by the controlling agent) that a user removes an information need, it removes the need from its *Goal* (if the need is in *Goal*, ref. step 6). Each time the agent finds new IOI corresponding to the information needs in *Goal*, the event is logged and corresponding users are notified (ref. step 5.2.4). Through the different types of requests, the agents may share what they find and need, and accordingly adapt their population and specialty to the environments.

Table 2. Behavior of each scanning agent

(1) *Goal* = Set of information needs to be satisfied by the agent;
(2) *Target* = the target site from which the agent is delegated to find IOI;
(3) *ResourceU* = Upper bound of resource consumption by the agent;
(4) *Aliveness* = 1.0;
Repeat
(5) If the agent is ready to retrieve information (according to *ResourceU*),
(5.1) Retrieve information from *Target*;
(5.2) If new information is found,
(5.2.1) Issue a *Type-E* request to get (*SocialEvaluation, SatisfiedGoal*);
(5.2.2) *Goal* = *Goal* ∪ *SatisfiedGoal*;
(5.2.3) *Aliveness* = *Aliveness* * ω + *SocialEvaluation*;
(5.2.4) If the new information satisfies any need in *Goal*, trigger suitable procedures, including event logging and user notification;
(5.2.5) If *Aliveness* ≥ α, for each target *d* found in the new information,
(5.2.5.1) Issue a *Type-S* request to get InitialResource;
(5.2.5.2) If InitialResource>0, spawn a new agent with its goal, target, and resource upper bound being set to *Goal, d,* and InitialResource, respectively;
(5.3) If two consecutive retrievals succeed in finding new information, issue a *Type-R-More* request for a higher *ResourceU*;
(5.4) If two consecutive retrievals fail in finding new information, issue a *Type-R-Less* request for a lower *ResourceU*;
(6) If an information need is no longer valid, remove the need from *Goal*;
Until *Aliveness* ≤ β or *Goal* is empty;
(7) Terminate the agent and issue a *Type-T* request to release resource.

3.2   The Controlling Agent

Table 3 defines the behavior of the controlling agent. The controlling agent receives from the system administrator a system-wide resource consumption limit μ, which is transformed into a system-wide maximum frequency of checking web sites (ref. step 1). That is, it maintains a resource pool that initially contains an amount μ of resource. Under the resource constraint, the controlling agent serves as a platform on which the scanning agents cooperate to satisfy the information needs of users.

The controlling agent accepts various kinds of requests from the scanning agents. Upon receiving a *Type-R-Less* request from an agent, it releases η_1 percents of the agent's resource (i.e. frequency) to the resource pool (ref. step 3). When there are multiple *Type-R-More* requests from scanning agents, the controlling agent sequentially allocates additional η_2 percents of resource to the agents according to their aliveness values (i.e. those agents with higher aliveness values get higher priorities, ref. step 4). The allocation process continues until the resource pool is empty or all the *Type-R-More* requests have been processed.

Table 3. Behavior of the controlling agent

(1) μ = Upper bound of the network bandwidth that the system may consume;
(2) SocialGoal = ϕ;
Repeat
(3) If there is a *Type-R-Less* request from agent k, release (from k) η_1 percents of resource;
(4) If there are *Type-R-More* requests, allocate (to the agents) η_2 percents of resource (those agents with higher *Aliveness* vales are preferred);
(5) If there is a *Type-E* request from agent k,
(5.1) *SocialEvaluation* = $\sum$ {degree of satisfaction for each goal in SocialGoal};
(5.2) *SatisfiedGoal* = Set of the satisfied goals;
(5.3) Reply k with (*SocialEvaluation, SatisfiedGoal*);
(6) If there is a *Type-S* request from agent k to spawn an agent for target d,
(6.1) If there is no agent being in charge of d and the system can allocate an initial amount δ of resource to the new agent, reply k with δ;
(6.2) Else reply k with 0;
(7) If a user enters a new information need e,
(7.1) Generate (if possible) a new agent for e;
(7.2) SocialGoal = SocialGoal $\cup$ {e};
(8) If a user removes his/her information need e,
(8.1) Inform all agents to remove e;
(8.2) SocialGoal = SocialGoal - {e};
(9) If there is a *Type-T* request from agent k, release all resource of k;
Until the system is terminated.

Upon receiving a *Type-E* request from an agent that finds new information, the controlling agent evaluates the information based on current goals of the agent society (i.e. social evaluation, ref. step 5.1). Technically, the degree of satisfaction (DOS) for a goal may be measured using domain-dependent metrics (e.g. if the goal is expressed using keywords, DOS may be defined as the density of the keywords in the new information found). On the other hand, upon receiving a *Type-S* request attempting to spawn an agent for target d, the controlling agent grants the request based on two considerations: (1) whether d is a new target for the agent society, and (2) whether the system has enough resource to support the new agent. If the answers to both questions are 'yes', it grants the request by allocating an initial amount δ of resource to the agent (ref. step 6.1); otherwise, the new agent cannot be generated (ref. step 6.2). When a user enters a new information need, the controlling agent generates a new agent based on similar considerations (ref. step 7). On the other hand, when a user removes one of his/her information needs, the controlling agent passes the information to all scanning agents (ref. step 8) to remove the need from their goals (ref. step 6 in Table 2). A *Type-T* request from a terminating agent releases the agent's resource to the resource pool (ref. step 9 in Table 3).

4   Experiment

A simulated information space on the WWW was designed to investigate performances of ACES in terms of *all* the criteria defined in Table 1 (note: some criteria such as TES and CES can be investigated only in a simulated environment, since we need to know *when* and *how many* IOI items are generated and updated).

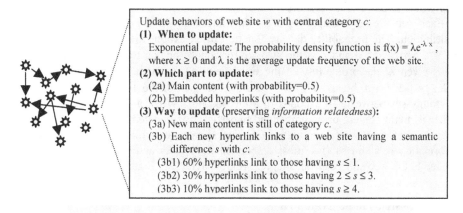

Update behaviors of web site *w* with central category *c*:
(1) When to update:
    Exponential update: The probability density function is $f(x) = \lambda e^{-\lambda x}$, where $x \geq 0$ and λ is the average update frequency of the web site.
(2) Which part to update:
    (2a) Main content (with probability=0.5)
    (2b) Embedded hyperlinks (with probability=0.5)
(3) Way to update (preserving *information relatedness*):
    (3a) New main content is still of category *c*.
    (3b) Each new hyperlink links to a web site having a semantic difference *s* with *c*:
        (3b1) 60% hyperlinks link to those having $s \leq 1$.
        (3b2) 30% hyperlinks link to those having $2 \leq s \leq 3$.
        (3b3) 10% hyperlinks link to those having $s \geq 4$.

Figure 2. Simulated update behaviors of each web site

4.1   Simulation of the Information Space

Figure 2 illustrates the simulation of the WWW information space. The simulation was based on a practical property of the information space: *information relatedness*. That is, at each moment, most information contained in a web site (including its main content and embedded hyperlinks) should be related. Based on the information relatedness property, without loss of generality, we assumed that there were 10000 web sites in the simulated information space and there were 100 information categories that could be of interest for a particular business. Each web site embedded 10 hyperlinks and was associated with a "central" category. The difference between the numbers of two categories reflected the *semantic difference* between the categories (e.g. the semantic difference between category 5 and category 7 is 2). To respect the information relatedness property, for a web site with a central category c ranging from category 1 to 100, its main content was of category c. Each of its embedded hyperlinks linked to a web site having a semantic difference s with c. There were 60% of the hyperlinks linked to those having $s \leq 1$, 30% to those having $2 \leq s \leq 3$, and 10% to those having $s \geq 4$. For example, if a web site's central category is 45, its main content should be of category 45, and 60% of its embedded hyperlinks linked to those web sites ranging from category 44 to 46.

In practice, most information on the WWW could not be IOI for a particular business (e.g. for a business that provides financial services, only finance-related information may be IOI). Therefore, there was an additional category *NonIOI* representing all the information that was impossible to be of interest for the business. Among the 10000 web sites, 95% were associated with *NonIOI* as their central categories (i.e. hosting the information of category *NonIOI*). Each of the remaining 5% web sites contained the information that was related to a central category ranging from category 1 to 100. Among the 100 categories, 10 categories were randomly selected as users' information needs to be satisfied. For a web site with *NonIOI* as its central category, all its main content and hyperlinks were of category *NonIOI* (i.e. impossible to be IOI for the users).

Each web site may be updated in the time intervals with the exponential probability distribution. The probability density function of an exponential distribution is $f(x) = \lambda e^{-\lambda x}$, where $x \geq 0$ and λ is the average (or rough) update frequency of a web site. Thus given λ, the probability of the web site being updated in time interval γ was $P(X \leq \gamma) = 1 - e^{-\lambda \gamma}$ (ref. behavior 1 in Figure 2). For each of the 10000 web sites, λ was randomly set between 10 seconds to 1000 seconds. When a web site was updated, either its main content or an embedded hyperlink was updated with equal probability (i.e. 0.5, ref. behavior 2 in Figure 2). The update also followed the principle of information relatedness (i.e. most embedded hyperlinks and the new content were related to the web site's central category, ref. behavior 3 in Figure 2).

4.2   Systems to be Evaluated

We experimented two versions of ACES: ACES-1 and ACES-2. Both versions shared the same settings for the controlling agent: $\eta_1 = \eta_2 = 20\%$, $\mu = 1$ request per second, and $\delta = 1$ request per 200 seconds. They differed from each other in the settings for each scanning agent. In ACES-1, $\alpha = 0.7$, $\omega = 0.7$, and $\beta = 0.3$; while in ACES-2, $\alpha = 0.9$, $\omega = 0.9$, and $\beta = 0.1$. These parameters were related to the strategies of agent cloning (i.e. α), agent aliveness evaluation (i.e. ω), and agent termination (i.e. β). We aimed to investigate their effects in the adaptive agent society.

In addition to ACES, there were two kinds of baseline systems for performance comparison: BestFirstD and BestDPeriodicalM. BestFirstD was for representing most state-of-the-art best-first information discovery systems, which selected a number of "best" hyperlinks to traverse [26]. Previous best-first discovery systems often relied on a predefined measuring scheme to select best hyperlinks for traversal. By representing information and users' interest using categories (as introduced above), BestFirstD could select hyperlinks in an "optimum" way (i.e. there was no error in judging the relevance of a hyperlink with respect to a user interest). Thus, by comparing ACES with the best-first discovery system that could perfectly determine which hyperlinks to traverse, we could focus our investigation on the contributions of integrating information discovery with information monitoring. As in many previous systems, BestFirstD was also designed to avoid duplicated traversals to a web site being traversed on for a user interest. There were two versions of BestFirstD: BestFirstD-1 and BestFirstD-2. They selected those hyperlinks whose semantic differences with the user interest were less than or equal to 1 and 2, respectively. Obviously BestFirstD-2 had a larger traversal space than BestFirstD-1. We aimed to investigate the effect of the size of the traversal space.

BestDPeriodicalM was a best-first discovery system (i.e. BestFirstD) with an additional functionality of periodical monitoring, which monitors the discovered web sites in random frequencies. The frequencies randomly ranged from 1/10 to 1/1000 query/seconds (i.e. they have a similar distribution with the update frequencies of the information items being scanned, ref. section 4.1). Since best-first discovery and periodical monitoring were the most popular techniques in information discovery [26] and monitoring [15, 16] respectively, BestDPeriodicalM could represent the naive way of building those environmental scanning systems with the functionalities of information discovery and monitoring. It facilitated the investigation of the contributions of integrating collaborative discovery with adaptive monitoring. There were two versions of BestDPeriodicalM: BestDPeriodicalM-1 and BestDPeriodicalM-2. They selected those hyperlinks whose semantic differences with the user interest were less than or equal to 1 and 2, respectively. The design was based on similar considerations for BestFirstD.

Table 4. Average performance (average of 30 runs)

	ACES-1	ACES-2	BestFirstD-1	BestFirstD-2	BestDPeriodicalM-1	BestDPeriodicalM-2
Timeliness (TES)	0.0083	0.0084	0.0053	0.0047	0.0025	0.0028
Effectiveness (EES)	0.0929	0.0737	0.0285	0.0251	0.0134	0.0118
Completeness (CES)	0.3993	0.4145	0.2453	0.2186	0.0552	0.0585

4.3   Result and Analysis

Table 4 lists the final average performances (in terms of the criteria defined in Table 1) of 30 runs. When taking their standard deviations into account, performances of ACES-1 were not significantly different from those of ACES-2, except for their performances in EES (i.e. 0.0929 vs. 0.0737). This was because the population of the agents in ACES-1 could be adjusted more flexibly (i.e. agents were more likely to spawn new agents and terminate themselves), reducing the amount of resource wasted by those agents with poor performances.

After performing a hypothesis test for verifying the significance of the performance differences, ACES-1 and ACES-2 were found to significantly outperform all the baseline systems in terms of all the criteria of CRBES. When comparing average performances of ACES-1 ACES-2 with average performances of the baseline systems, there was 118% improvement in TES, 323% improvement in EES, and 182% improvement in CES. As the baseline systems could represent most related state-of-the-art ways of approaching CRBES, the adaptive agent society in ACES demonstrated more promising performances to fulfill the practical requirements of CRBES

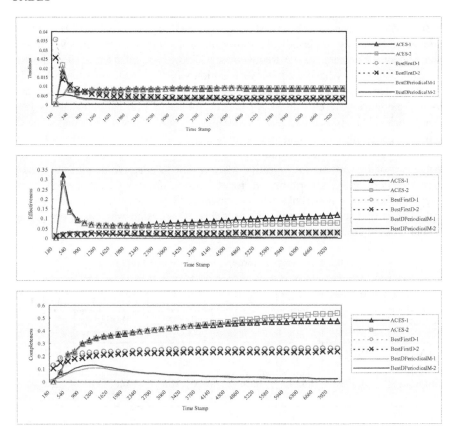

Figure 3. Experimental result (average of 30 runs)

Figure 3 illustrates the average cumulative performances of the systems. It shows that ACES-1 and ACES-2 performed better in most of the time. An interesting result to be noted is that BestDPeriodicalM had poorer performances than BestFirstD, even though it was endowed with the functionality of information monitoring. A detailed analysis shows that the functionality of periodical monitoring wasted a great amount of resource to monitor IOI (i.e. the random monitoring frequencies could not fit the actual update frequencies of IOI). On the other hand, although BestFirstD did not have the functionality of information monitoring, its continuous traversal through the most-related parts of the information space could re-visit a web site, and hence produced a similar functionality of monitoring. This indicates that the straightforward way of integrating information discovery and information monitoring could not be a good approach to support CRBES. Adaptability of the integrated framework is the key to success.

5   Related Work

The contributions of ACES lie on achieving CRBES by an adaptive agent society. In this section, we evaluate the framework from the viewpoints of its related work.

5.1   Intelligent Agents for Information Gathering

Information discovery is a fundamental mission of ACES. Comprehensive provision of information is an essential function of executive information systems (EIS) as well. To achieve that, EIS should gather information [8, 24] in a timely manner. Since executives often have difficulties in capturing useful information all the time by themselves, agent technology was introduced to the EIS community and facilitated more applications such as electronic commerce. However, most of the previous studies focused on the aspect of information gathering (rather than continuous environmental scanning). They aimed to satisfy users' "one-shot" needs (e.g. intelligently locating the information [4, 26] with consideration of time/cost/quality tradeoffs of the search [7, 14]). Continuous environmental scanning, which is also a fundamental function of EIS, deserves more exploration. It supports the acquisition of environmental information without issuing queries all the time by the managers. Once a change of IOI is detected, it is logged and the manager is notified. Thus both quality and productivity of the manager's job may be promoted.

5.2   Intelligent Agents for Information Monitoring

Information monitoring is an important mission of ACES as well. Previous information monitoring studies often predefined a set of information items to monitor [15, 16]. ACES integrates information discovery into information monitoring so that the information to be monitored may be *dynamically* located. This is of particular importance for environmental scanning, in which managers cannot have a complete idea of *where to find* IOI.

ACES also considers the issue of *how* to *monitor* the IOI. Previous information monitoring packages often required the information updating systems (e.g. spreadsheet editors such as Excel) to notify the monitoring system (e.g. using the Dynamic Data Exchange technique, DDE [19]). However, it is unrealistic to expect that the information systems currently running on the Internet may provide the service of update notification. Therefore, there were packages that actively checked for information updates in a periodical way [18], which was employed in previous studies of scanning systems as well [6, 17]. However, periodical monitoring could not be an effective strategy either [16]. ACES monitors the IOI by properly coordinating the agents, which adapt to the update behavior of the environmental IOI. This way of adaptive monitoring is essential for the managers to capture environmental changes from the Internet. The consideration of limiting the maximum level of resource consumption also makes the delivery of the system to businesses smoother. It is both essential and significant to business administration.

5.3   Decision Support Systems that are Adaptive to the Environments

Decision support systems (DSS) aim to provide the services of information retrieval, information validation, scenario playing, simulation, and decision suggestions. Since there may be many routine jobs of the above kinds, agent technology was introduced to the DSS community as well. To capture and then adapt to different users' preferences, adaptive DSS models were also developed to provide personalized information for decision support [7]. As to information monitoring, the identification of *what to monitor* was explored in previous studies [22].

ACES supports managers' needs in environmental scanning. As discussed above, it focuses on the aspects of *where to find* and *how to monitor* IOI (rather than what to monitor). Instead of adapting to different users' preferences, it adapts to (1) information needs of individual users, (2) resource limit of environmental scanning, (3) distribution of IOI in the environments, and (4) update behaviors of the IOI.

5.4   Multiagent Coordination and Negotiation

Coordination and negotiation are necessary for the agents to achieve their collective goal of continuous environmental scanning. Previous studies on multiagent coordination and negotiation aimed to effectively resolve conflicts among agents. Typical coordination techniques included planning, social knowledge encoding (e.g. [2, 5]), and task structuring (e.g. [11]). Previous negotiation techniques focused on how agreements may be built among agents. Their major concerns included *efficiency* of negotiation [13, 20] and *quality* of negotiation (e.g. maximizing the fulfillment of some quality criteria such as customer satisfaction [9]). The tradeoffs between the two concerns were noticed in previous studies as well [1]. Typical applications came from both cooperative domains and noncooperative domains, such as price offering [27], conflict resolution [28], on-line auction, constraint satisfaction, task distribution [1, 13], and data allocation [21].

We treat environmental scanning as a cooperative domain, due to two reasons: (1) the IOI often have an integrative effect to decision making of the manager, and (2) the cost incurred by the agents often has a global effect to both the businesses and the Internet community. Therefore, the controlling agent in ACES serves as the platform on which each agent negotiates with others for resource distribution. It dynamically controls the total amount of resource consumption (i.e. μ). No complex symbolic planning and task structuring are required in coordination.

The negotiation protocol in ACES is related to those market-based or auction-based techniques that allow agents to bid for resources based on their individual profiles or considerations. ACES extends the idea by considering the fact that each agent's profile may be initially unknown and dynamically changing. The resource need of an agent may be intensive at a certain time, but non-intensive at another time, since the update behaviors of the information items being monitored may change over time. Therefore, the agents learn to estimate their resource needs. Based on the estimations, the agents may be properly coordinated. The learning capability incrementally promotes the quality of negotiation.

5.5   Learning for Multiagent Coordination, Negotiation, and Organization

Machine learning for multiagent coordination, negotiation, and organization has been a focus of recent studies as well. On the coordination part, they focused on learning how agent actions affect each other (e.g. the enable and disable relationships [11]), what information is required for coordination (e.g. situation-specific coordination rules [23]), and when to trigger agent coordination (e.g. a confidence level of triggering coordination [10]). On the negotiation part, they focused on predicting how other agents behave (e.g. price offering in bargaining [27]) and prefer (e.g. time preferences in meeting scheduling [3]) so that consensus could be built in an efficient way. On the organization part, they focused on the automatic restructuring of organization for coordination and collaboration (e.g. reducing the coordination overheads by restructuring the organization [25]).

The agent society in ACES learns to discover and monitor IOI, and accordingly adapts (1) its population to the location of IOI, and (2) its specialty to the update behavior of the IOI. The adaptability promotes the quality of coordination. It facilitates the proper allocation of resource to suitable agents at suitable time. From the viewpoint of multiagent negotiation, each agent in ACES learns to effectively pursue its own goal (rather than learning to predict how other agents behave and prefer). When each agent knows its need and performance, both the quality and the simplicity of negotiation may be improved. From the viewpoint of adaptive multiagent organization, the adaptability facilitates the restructuring of the organization (including population and delegation) of the agent society. It is for properly directing the limited resource to maximally satisfy users' information needs (rather than for reducing coordination overheads).

6   Conclusion and Future Work

Environmental scanning through the Internet has been a must for many businesses. It serves as a fundamental step for the businesses to identify trends, problems, and opportunities from their environments. However, there exist several gaps between environmental scanning and information technology. In practice, environmental scanning should be continuous and resource-bounded. It calls for an intelligent scanner that may continuously discover and monitor information of interest under the constraint of limiting the maximum consumption of resource. This leads to several challenges that should be simultaneously tackled in an *adaptive* and *scalable* manner: (1) generation of scanning tasks, (2) resource allocation for each scanning task, (3) discovery of information, and (4) monitoring of information. The multiagent mechanism ACES presented in this paper successfully tackles the challenges and is shown to be able to provide a higher percentage of information of interest in a timelier manner using less system resource. Its delivery to businesses may bring significant contributions without incurring intolerable overheads.

We are integrating ACES to an environmental scanner eScanner running on the Internet. In addition to incorporating ACES as its front-end component, eScanner invokes an information classification module (for classifying the information found by ACES) and a data mining module (for identifying useful trends and patterns from the classified information). In the integration of ACES to eScanner, we aim to explore three main issues in real-world contexts: (1) interfaces between ACES and the managers, (2) impacts of ACES to managers (including the impacts of social evaluation, timely monitoring, continuous scanning, and resource-bounded scanning), and (3) contributions of ACES to information classification and mining. The answers to the issues may more precisely define the extent to which a business may expect information technology to support the identification of trends, problems, and opportunities from the environment.

Acknowledgement

The author would like to thank Yun-Ling Lu for her kindly support in conducting the experiments reported in this paper.

References

1. Andersson M. and Sandholm T.: Time-Quality Tradeoffs in Reallocative Negotiation with Combinatorial Contract Types, *Proc. of the 16th National Conference on Artificial Intelligence* (1999).
2. Barbuceanu M.: Coordinating Agents by Role-Based Social Constraints and Conversation Plans, *Proc. of AAAI-97* (1997).
3. Bui H. H., Kieronska D., and Venkatesh S.: Learning Other Agents' Preferences in Multiagent Negotiation, *Proc. of AAAI-96* (1996).
4. Chen H., Chung Y.-M., Marshall R., and Christopher C. Y.: An Intelligent Personal Spider (Agent) for Dynamic Internet/Intranet Searching, *Decision Support Systems* 23, 41-58 (1998).
5. Cuena J. and Ossowski S.: Distributed Models for Decision Support, in *Multiagent Systems -- A Modern Approach to Distributed Artificial Intelligence,* Weiss G. (ed.), The MIT Press (1999).
6. Decker K. S. and Sycara K.: Intelligent Adaptive Information Agents, *Journal of Intelligent Information Systems* (1997).

7. Fazlollahi B., Parikh M. A., and Verma S.: Adaptive Decision Support Systems, *Decision Support Systems*, Vol.20, No. 4, 297-315 (1997).
8. Frolick M. N., Parzinger M. J., Rainer R. K., and Ramarapu N. K.: Using EISs for Environmental Scanning, *Information System Management* (1997).
9. Guttman R. H. and Maes P.: Cooperative vs. Competitive Multiagent Negotiations in Retail Electronic Commerce, *Proc. of the 2nd International Workshop on Cooperative Information Agents* (1998).
10. Horling B. and Lesser V.: Using Diagnosis to Learn Contextual Coordination Rules, *UMass Computer Science Technical Report 99-15* (1999).
11. Jensen D., Atighetchi M., Vincent R., and Lesser V.: Learning Quantitative Knowledge for Multiagent Coordination, *Proc. of AAAI-99* (1999).
12. Koster M.: Guidelines for Robot Writers, http://info.webcrwaler.com/mak/papers/robots/guidelines.html.(1993).
13. Kraus S., Wilkenfeld J., and Zlotkin G.: Multiagent Negotiation under Time Constraints, *Artificial Intelligence* 75, 297-345 (1995).
14. Lesser V., Horling B., Klassner F., and Raja A.: BIG: A Resource-Bounded Information Gathering Agent, *UMass Computer Science Technical Report 1998-03* (1998).
15. Liu R.-L., Shih M.-J., and Kao Y.-F.: Adaptive Exception Monitoring Agents for Management by Exceptions, to appear in *Applied Artificial Intelligence (AAI)*.
16. Liu R.-L. and Lin S.-Y.: Adaptive Coordination of Agents for Timely and Resource-Bounded Information Monitoring, *Proc. of the 4th International Conference on MultiAgent Systems*, Boston, U.S.A, pp. 175-182 (2000).
17. Liu S.: Business Environment Scanner for Senior Managers: Towards Active Executive Support with Intelligent Agents, *Proc. of 31st Annual Hawaii International Conference on System Sciences*, pp. 18-27 (1998).
18. Openfind: Cyberspace Information Agent 2000 (CIA2000), http://www.openfind.com.tw/About_us/p-2-04.html (2000).
19. Pilot Software: Pilot Decision Support Suite, http://www.pilotsw.com (1999).
20. Sandholm T. and Vulkan N.: Bargaining with Deadlines, *Proc. of AAAI-99* (1999).
21. Schwartz R. and Kraus S.: Negotiation on Data Allocation in Multi-Agent Environments, *Proc. of AAAI-97* (1997).
22. Seligman L., Lehner P., Smith K., Elsaesser C., and Mattox D.: Decision-Centric Information Monitoring, *Journal of Intelligent Information Systems*, 14, 29-50 (2000).
23. Sugawara T. and Lesser V. R.: Learning to Improve Coordinated Actions in Cooperative Distributed Problem-Solving Environments, *Machine Learning* (1998).
24. Volonino L., Waston H. J. and Robinson S.: Using EIS to Respond to Dynamic Business Conditions, *Decision Support Systems*, Vol.14, pp.105-116 (1995).
25. Willmott S. and Faltings B.: The Benefits of Environment Adaptive Organizations for Agent Coordination and Network Routing Problems, *Proc. of the 4th International Conference on MultiAgent Systems*, Boston, U.S.A, pp. 333-340 (2000).
26. Yang C. C., Yen J., and Chen H.: Intelligent Internet Searching Agent Based on Hybrid Simulated Annealing, *Decision Support Systems* 28, pp. 269-277 (2000).
27. Zeng D. and Sycara K.: Benefits of Learning in Negotiation, *Proc. of AAAI-97* (1997).
28. Zlotkin G. and Rosenschein J. S.: Cooperation and Conflict Resolution via Negotiation among Autonomous Agents in Noncooperative Domains, *IEEE Transactions on System, Man, and Cybernetics*, Vol. 21, No. 6 (1991).

Gaz-Guide:
Agent-Mediated Information Retrieval
for Official Gazettes

Jyi-Shane Liu[1], Von-Won Soo[2],
Chia-Ning Chiang[3], Chen-Yu Lee[2], and Chun-Yu Lin[2]

[1] Department of Computer Science, National Chengchi University, Taipei
[2] Department of Computer Science, National Tsing Hua University, Hsinchu
[3] Section of Government Documents, National Central Library,
Taipei, Taiwan, R.O.C.
jsliu@cs.nccu.edu.tw
soo@cs.nthu.edu.tw

Abstract. Information retrieval tasks concerns with leading the user to those documents that best match his/her information needs. We consider missing concepts and wrong terms in user query as the fundamental problem of information retrieval. We propose a multiagent system that assists information retrieval by mediating the user's information needs and the semantic structure of the data domain. The multiagent system embeds both ontology and thesauri to traverse different cognitive spaces. During an interactive process, the user's query is transformed and led to appropriate semantic constructs that enable effective retrieval. We consider the data domain of government official gazettes. A prototype system, Gaz-Guide, has been developed and experiments are conducted by recording system response to real users with practical questions. The initial results show encouraging sign of the utility and effectiveness of Gaz-Guide in articulating domain resources on thesauri and ontology and guiding users with interactive assistance.

1 Introduction

Information retrieval concerns with leading the user to those documents that best match his/her information needs [1]. The most important tools of any information retrieval systems include indexing, clustering, and ranking algorithms. An index term "is a (document) word whose semantics helps in remembering the document's main themes" [2]; indexing is "the act of assigning index terms to documents which are the objects to be retrieved" [3]. Clustering involves grouping similar documents together to expedite information retrieval [4]. Two classes of similarity measures are considered: the similarity of a document and a query and the similarity of two documents in a database. The results are then used for retrieving and/or ranking a subset of documents. Ranking concerns with establishing a sequential order of retrieved documents that indicates descending likelihood of matching user information needs. Excellent reviews on information retrieval techniques can be found in [5][6].

S.-T. Yuan and M. Yokoo (Eds.): PRIMA 2001, LNAI 2132, pp. 154-167, 2001.
© Springer-Verlag Berlin Heidelberg 2001

As networked connectivity expands and computing power advances, information retrieval has become a day-to-day activity for many users, e.g., finding information on the web or accessing digital libraries. The most common experience comes from a keyword-based query interface of a search engine that retrieves documents based on full text matching. User queries are either too broad to filter out useless documents or too specialized to retrieve any documents. The user would need to think of alternative query terms and/or go through a large set of retrieved documents in order to find needed information. In other words, most information retrieval systems suffer from poor precision and recall.

The problems associated with keyword-based full text matching retrieval are well known [1]. The retrieved documents are often far from what the user is looking for. Alternative information retrieval models, such as vector space model and probabilistic model, have been proposed to better determine the relevance of a document to the user's information needs. However, the results have not been very satisfactory. It has been recognized that information retrieval is actually a cognitive communication process which involves such entities as document creators, information content in the document, text surrogates representing information contents, document users, user information need, and text surrogates representing information needs [7] [8]. Matching is only one step in the process that evaluates the relations between documents and user queries, and is only approximate transformation of relevance of information contents and user information needs (see Figure 1). In addition, text surrogates used by different persons may be inconsistent, inaccurate, and incompatible. A better information retrieval approach must consider these issues.

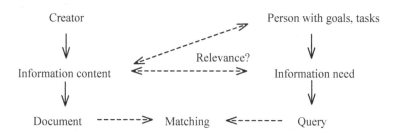

Fig. 1. A cognitive communication process in information retrieval

In a traditional library setting, users may be familiar with the experience of professional help from reference librarians for finding books/documents pertaining to their needs. The reference librarian works as a mediator who uses a searching system and finds the needed items for users. The search process is typically an interactive one during which the librarian adjusts and refines search strategies based on user feedbacks and his/her domain knowledge on the subject. Usually, users would enjoy an effective retrieval if the librarian has sufficient domain knowledge. This satisfactory result comes from the librarian's ability to transform user needs to appropriate search surrogates.

We propose a multiagent-based approach to construct an information retrieval system that interacts with users to reduce the conceptual distance between text surrogates of target documents and expression of user information needs, much like what a reference librarian does. An agent is a software component or system that is embedded in an environment and is capable of performing useful tasks for its users without direct manipulation [9]. Agent characteristics, such as autonomous, proactive, responsive, and adaptive [10], are well suited for our purpose of developing an "expert assistant" for information retrieval tasks. In particular, we consider a number of notions that may contribute to the improvement of information retrieval performance.

- An agent is designed to interact with its environment, including users as well as other agents. This interaction capability is important in information mediation [11] to assist user throughout the search process and obtain helps from other agents.
- By incorporating user models [12], an agent can assist users according to user preferences and user needs.
- An agent's inference capability allows context-dependent analysis, which leads to appropriate decision-making on how to assist users in different search situations.
- Multiagent systems provide an excellent metaphor to integrate and articulate heterogeneous functional modules and knowledge/data sources. This is especially convenient for a common situation in libraries where various resources (e.g., catalogues, thesauri, etc.) exist but are either isolated or unused.
- A multiagent architecture provides flexibility in future extension as functional modules can be improved and/or added to support more powerful services.

In this paper, we report research results on developing an agent-mediated information retrieval system for government official gazettes. Published periodically by different sections of both central and local governments, the official gazette serves as one of the most important and authoritative channels for dissemination as well as acquisition of government administrative information. Contents in the official gazettes include administrative announcement, statute, code, amendment, legal interpretation and case, decree, proclamation, public address, meeting record and minutes, treaty and agreement, administrative report, etc. In Taiwan, the national central library (NCL) is designated to collect and store the official gazettes of the R.O.C. government. Among all publications, 28 major gazettes are selected to convert to electronically accessible versions, which involves manually scanning and indexing these documents. The retrospective conversion has been continued to gazettes published in 1975 and will be continued back to their first publication. Currently, there are more than 280,000 documents in the NCL database of R.O.C. official gazettes. They are open to public use on the Internet with a traditional database indexing system using Chinese MARC.

The data domain is unique in the combination of official documents and general users. There exist potentially large gaps between the conceptual representation of the official documents and the user's cognitive space. As a result, user query expression is either out of focus or ill-posed to retrieve needed information. User attempts in query adjustment often fail to improve retrieval results due to the non-intersected cognitive boundaries. We propose a multiagent system that assists information retrieval by mediating the user's information needs and the semantic structure of the data domain. The multiagent system embeds both ontology and thesauri to traverse different cognitive spaces. During an interactive process, the user's query is transformed and led to appropriate semantic constructs. These derived semantic constructs represent joint cognitive spaces, thereby enabling effective retrieval. We have developed and implemented Gaz-Guide – an agent-mediated information retrieval system for government official gazettes. Experiments are conducted by recording system response to real users with practical questions. Initial results show that Gaz-Guide provides satisfactory performance.

The rest of the paper is organized as follows. In section 2, we present Gaz-Guide, explaining the design considerations and illustrating the structure and operation of each component. We provide a conceptualization of system operation and showcase system performance in section 3, followed by a report of initial evaluation results. In section 5, we discuss our experiences in developing the system as well as other related issues. A conclusion of the paper is given in the last section.

2   A Multiagent System for Mediating Information Retrieval

Gaz-Guide is composed of four types of agents: librarian agent, thesaurus agent, ontology agent, and information gathering agent. Each agent represents a specialized functional module or expertise in the domain of government official gazettes.

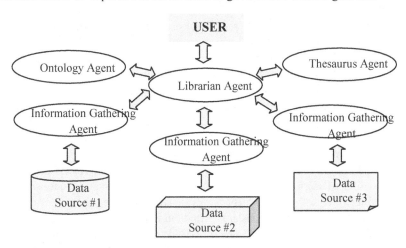

Fig. 2. Organization of Gaz-Guide

In particular, the librarian agent interacts with users to mediate information retrieval and allocates subtasks to other agents. The thesaurus agent performs term[1] (phrase) operations to produce better search surrogates (terms). The ontology agent provides domain knowledge to facilitate the librarian agent in making more efficient

---

[1] A term is a word or expression with a specific meaning, especially one that is used in relation to a particular subject. In Chinese language, a word is encoded in a single character. A sentence or a phrase is composed of a sequence of consecutive words with no space interval. In this paper, we prefer to use "term" for user query, instead of "keyword", to differentiate with each other.

search decisions. Finally, the information gathering agents are responsible for accessing certain data sources and retrieving documents based on specified constraints.

Gaz-Guide agents coordinate with a priori organizational structure, as shown in Figure 2. The librarian agent plays the role of master agent, while all other agents are slave agents. This simple master/slave relationship is adequate and useful for our purpose because of the convenience of a global view from a single contact point with users. The design of individual slave agents is also justified based on their functional complexity and independent enhancement. We adopted KQML [13] as the agent communication language, in which performatives, such as "ask", "reply", "inform", and "confirm", are used for current interactions in Gaz-Guide. We provide descriptions of each agent in the following sub-sections.

2.1   Librarian Agent

The librarian agent plays a major role in Gaz-Guide in that it is the interface between the system and users and coordinates the task requirements of other agents. The primary function of the librarian agent is to make context-dependent decisions in order to guide users throughout the information retrieval process with interactive suggestions and assistance. The librarian agent performs the following activities:

- Modeling user needs and preferences: User needs are characterized by a set of predefined service types, document types, and user queries. They can be either explicitly given by users or implicitly derived with user behaviors. User preferences are specified by a set of parameters for controlling search result presentation and assistance. In order to maintain this user information, the librarian agent creates a user profile for each new user and updates it during the interaction process with the user.
- Analyzing search contexts: This is the primary decision-making activity of the librarian agent. It concerns with assessing the degree of mismatch between user needs and current retrieval results, determining the types of assistance and suggestions to offer to users, considering user feedbacks, and deciding the most appropriate search strategies for subsequent retrieval. The inference process is structured as a finite state automaton. Actions are carried out in other related activities.
- Formulating subtasks for other agents: Based on the chosen search strategy, this activity formulates actual subtasks to be performed by slave agents and deliver them to designated ones. Possible subtasks include retrieving documents from specified sources with filtering constraints, finding other search surrogates based on term relationships, analyzing and summarizing document characteristics, etc.
- Coordinating task allocation and integrating task results from other agents: This activity is responsible for communicating with other slave agents in task delegation. Interactions are realized in message exchange with KQML performatives. Based on subtask formulation, task sequence is determined and followed. Task results from slave agents are examined and integrated for further processing.
- Presenting search results and suggesting assistance to users: Search results are organized according to different composite "views", such as issuing government unit, issuing time, document type, document relationship, estimated relevance with

user query, etc. Users can switch among these views and examine search results based on selective views. Assistance such as query adjustment, query expansion, search results pruning based on view constraints, etc., are offered to users.

• Getting user feedbacks: User inputs, such as user query and user response to suggestions, are received through pre-defined forms, itemized options, and action buttons.

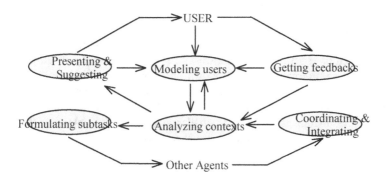

Fig. 3. High-level relationships among the librarian agent activities

2.2   Thesaurus Agent

We conjecture that the inefficiency of information retrieval can be attributed to two problems: missing concepts and wrong terms. Missing concepts refer to the situation when the user is not aware of the particular concepts that are most represented for his/her questions. Wrong terms occur when the user does not know the official terms and/or the most appropriate terms for particular concepts. These problems are especially severe in the domain of official gazettes due to its potential cognitive distance to general users. Therefore, the function of the thesaurus agent is to provide suitable terms that can be used by the librarian agent to improve search results or by the user to recognize missing concepts with respect to his/her questions in mind.

The thesaurus agent performs three types of term operation: (1) term extraction – extract index terms associated with a full-text document; (2) term tokenization – produce shorter but meaningful terms from a longer term by segmentation; and (3) term alteration – find other terms of particular relations to a term based on pre-defined structures in thesauri. Term extraction is useful in producing a characterization of a set of retrieved documents. Each document is associated with a few index terms, which were manually indexed by a NCL librarian as part of his/her professional work. The set of index terms extracted from these documents can be prioritized based on relevance and frequency, and can be useful for the user to recognize missing concepts.

Term alteration and term tokenization are used to find more suitable terms than the given term that would lead to retrieval of needed documents. Three methods are considered: generalization, specialization, and shift, each corresponding to moving up, moving down, and moving laterally to a new node in the term hierarchy. In particular, term generalization refers to finding a term having a more general concept than that of the given term. This can be done either by looking up the broader term of the given term in the thesaurus or by performing term tokenization on the given term. Likewise, term specialization refers to finding a term representing a more specific concept and is done by looking up its narrow term in the thesaurus. Term shift refers to finding a term that is of the same concept with the given term and is done by looking up its related term in the thesaurus.

The purpose of these term operations is to change the space of the retrieved documents such that needed documents are included and can be retrieved more effectively. In Figure 4, needed documents are represented by the cross mark, space of retrieved documents based on a given term is shown in a solid circle, space of retrieved documents based on an alternative term is shown in a dotted circle. Term generalization and term shift produce a new document space containing the needed document that was outside the document space of the given term. On the other hand, term specialization reduces the document space to a smaller size, yet still containing the needed documents, thereby facilitating a more focused retrieval.

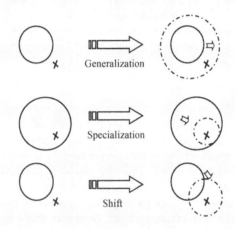

Fig. 4. Document space changes from term operations

We develop the lexical knowledge bases of the thesaurus agent by exploiting a set of resources in professional work and existing dictionaries. In particular, the thesaurus agent contains four types of knowledge bases:

- Document subject terms: Each official gazette is annotated by a professional librarian with a set of subject terms that represent the major theme of the document. A table records the document ID and its associated subject terms. This knowledge base is particularly useful in term extraction. Currently, we have about 7,500 subject terms in more than 280,000 documents.
- Legal index terms: A special thesaurus in legal domain is used to provide a basic term hierarchy. It consists of about 3,900 index terms and a total of 18,400 broader terms, narrow terms, and related terms.
- Chinese thesaurus: A particular Chinese thesaurus is selected and modified to provide a conceptual hierarchy of general terms. It consists of about 62,800 terms

in 12 major conceptual categories, 150 mid-level conceptual categories, and 1,720 low-level conceptual categories.

• Chinese dictionary: This is a list of common terms with no hierarchy. It contains more than 200,000 terms and is used in term tokenization.

Upon requests from the librarian agent, the thesaurus agent performs term operations based on its lexical knowledge bases. The primary task of the thesaurus agent is to find search terms that are useful for retrieving user needed documents. Inputs to the thesaurus agent are a task type and either a set of document IDs or a given term. Outputs of the thesaurus agents are a set of terms to be used as search surrogates.

2.3   Ontology Agent

Another aspect of mediation concerns with the role of domain knowledge in information retrieval tasks. Domain knowledge provides derived characteristics and relations of documents. These properties are potentially more powerful in indexing document contents with respect to user information needs. Similar ideas have been explored in citation relations of scientific papers [14] [15] and in structure and linking relation of web pages [16]. In our data domain, we consider subject knowledge on both information structures and information sources.

Information structure of official gazettes concerns with characterization and association of documents in some meaningful ways. For example, documents can be distinguished in different types such as administrative law, amendment, decree, advisory opinion, public address, meeting minutes, etc. A subset of documents is also linked to each other by certain relations, such as revise, nullify, support, explain, etc. This structural representation of documents enables grouping of documents based on certain criteria for different purposes, thereby allows more expressive power of user information needs and more effective retrieval. For example, a user may request documents concerning topic X of type Y with relation Z and constraint C (e.g., time, source, etc.). Knowledge on information structure is derived by consulting domain experts and by devising a schematic representation of documents. We believe this knowledge is useful for focusing search targets and pruning search results.

Information source refers to where the gazette comes from, e.g., sections or branches of government. Knowledge on information sources concerns with characterization of government institutions, including administrative functions, contact information, URL links, and their hierarchical relations. This knowledge is useful for two purposes. First, it is possible to determine which government institutions are most relevant to user queries, thereby allow prioritization or filtering of retrieval results. Second, web pages of relevant government institutions can be accessed and processed to provide complementary information as available and as needed.

Much like a reference librarian employs knowledge on subject domains to adjust search directions and search strategies, the ontology agent embeds domain knowledge of government official gazettes to assist the librarian agent in focusing on areas that are more relevant to user information needs. Upon requests from the librarian agent, the ontology agent performs characteristic grouping on documents or relevance analysis on government institutions. Inputs to the ontology agent are a task type and either a set of document IDs or a set of user queries. Outputs of the ontology agents are a set of groupings of documents or a set of relevant government institutions.

2.4   Information Gathering Agent

Information gathering agents are responsible for accessing data sources of different forms, such as HTML pages, CGI links, and databases, for needed information. Each of them is constructed with a particular access method and path for retrieving needed information from designated data source. Information gathering agents are also responsible for monitoring updates and new additions on designated data sources. In particular, one of the information gathering agents is developed to access the database of government official gazettes and retrieve documents based on specified constraints. Inputs to the information gathering agents are a set of constraints and a target URL. Outputs of the information gathering agents are a set of retrieved documents or information.

3   Guiding Users with Concepts and Terms

We consider concepts and terms as the primary vehicles for enabling effective retrieval of needed information. The structure of Gaz-Guide is to realize such an approach to assisting users in information retrieval tasks. The librarian agent interacts with users to determine the search context and to mediate upon concepts and terms such as to retrieve user needed information. The thesaurus agent provides term expertise so that the librarian agent can assist users in correcting wrong terms for user concepts and identifying missing concepts in user query. The ontology agent employs domain knowledge to provide a characteristic summarization of search results and to assist users in exploiting concepts in domain structure to conduct a more focused retrieval. The information gathering agents access data sources and perform filtering based on given constraints.

The interactive processes between users and Gaz-Guide and among the agents can be alternating as needed to conduct a particular information retrieval task. However, there are a few basic patterns of interaction that are skeletons to the mediated information retrieval. We illustrate one scenario to exemplify a typical process of information retrieval in Gaz-Guide.

In 1999, September 21, a major earthquake hit central Taiwan, causing considerable damages. Suffered from property loss, a user wants to find out information about a special loan program for earthquake victims, such as the duration, maximum amount, interest rate, return payment, etc. This user queries Gaz-Guide with the term "震災(earthquake disaster)重建(re-build)專案(program)貸款(loan)" that he picked up from newspaper. The scenario proceeds as followed:

1. *[Retrieving documents]* The librarian agent asks the information gathering agent to retrieve documents based on this particular term. The information gathering agent returns no document satisfying the constraints.

2. *[Fixing wrong terms]* The librarian agent asks the thesaurus agent to broaden the term. The thesaurus agent performs term tokenization and returns a set of terms – "重建(re-build)" "專案(program)" "貸款(loan)". The term "震災(earthquake disaster)" is not recorded in the dictionary as a common term, and therefore is not tokenized.

3. *[Retrieving documents]* The librarian agent tries different combinations of these broader terms for the information-gathering agent to retrieve documents. One of the combinations returns the smallest set of 73 documents.

4. *[Finding terms of relevant concepts]* The librarian agent asks the thesaurus agent to perform term extraction on this set of retrieved documents. The thesaurus agent returns a set of index terms associated with these documents.

5. *[User identifying missing concepts]* The librarian agent provides the set of index terms for the user to further specify his query. Among these index terms, the user selects "購屋(house buying)貸款(loan)" and "住宅(house)貸款(loan)" as most relevant. (See Figure 5.)

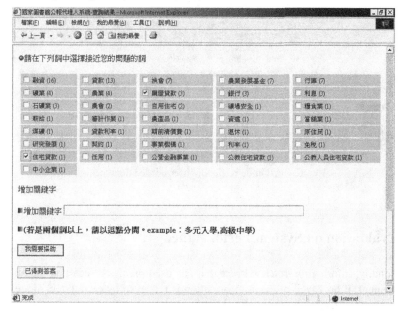

Fig. 5. Relevant concepts are presented by the system and selected by the user

6. *[Retrieving documents]* The librarian agent asks the information gathering agent to filter out documents based on these added terms. The information gathering agent returns 11 documents. (See Figure 6.)

7. *[User getting needed information]* The librarian agent presents these documents to the user, among which 4 documents are considered to be directly relevant to his question.

In this scenario, the ontology agent is not involved in the process. This is because the user begins with a very narrow term. By having the thesaurus agent to manipulate this term and its associated concepts, the librarian agent has been able to guide the user into a reasonably focused set of documents. In another scenario, a user may begins with a very broad term "☐☐(loan)". The information gathering agent will retrieve a set of 1,732 documents. Then the librarian agent will need the ontology agent to provide domain structure concepts in order to enable an effective search focus. We omit further elaboration due to space limitation.

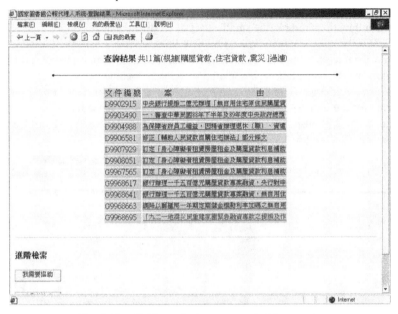

Fig. 6. Gaz-Guide retrieving user needed documents

4   Evaluation on System Performance

Traditionally, information retrieval research has used precision/recall as the objective measurement of how well relevant information is retrieved by certain technique. Let S denote the set of documents considered, U denote a user query, X denote a subset of S that is retrieved based on U, Y denote a subset of X that is determined to be relevant to U, Z denote a subset of S that is determined to be relevant to U. Then, precision refers to the ratio Y/X and recall is the ratio Y/Z. In fact, the measurement of precision and recall requires knowing the answers to questions in advance. This may not be possible for very large sets of data. Therefore, alternative evaluation methods are needed.

We consider an empirical evaluation of system performance based on user experiences. The NCL reference librarians collect more than 500 practical queries from real users to establish a set of test data. User query behaviors are simulated over Gaz-Guide and system response is recorded for evaluation. As an initial study, we have completed testing 64 use cases (using different terms) of 33 queries. The results are summarized in Table 1.

We compare Gaz-Guide with a simple keyword-matching retrieving method. In 54 use cases, Gaz-Guide is able to assist users finding needed information within a focused range (less than 20 documents). In 10 use cases where user needed information is not found, it is possible that the information does not exist in the official gazettes at all. Although the scale of the experiment is not large enough to provide conclusive evidence, the initial results show encouraging sign of the utility and effectiveness of Gaz-Guide in information retrieval tasks. We plan to conduct a more extensive experiment to establish the evaluation.

Table 1. Initial test results of Gaz-Guide performance

Results from simple keyword matching				Results from Gaz-Guide	
Answers NOT found			Answers FOUND	Answers NOT found	Answers FOUND
A	B	C			
18/64	6/64	21/64	19/64	10/64	54/64
70.32%			29.68%	15.62%	84.38%

A: Query terms do not result in any documents being retrieved.
B: Answers are not found in the set of retrieved documents.
C: The set of retrieved documents is too large (> 20 documents)[2] to find answers.

5   Discussions

Agent-based techniques have been applied to integrate distributed data sources and articulate information flow, as exemplified by the UMDL work [17], RETSINA architecture [18], and InfoSleuth [19]. Our research focuses on a more fundamental problem of getting what users really need in a very large database, especially when user concepts and query terms may not be oriented well with the data domain. We consider agent-mediated assistance, term operations based on thesauri, and knowledge of domain structure as the primary enablers for advancing information retrieval performance to the next level. Some of the views have been parallel to the literature, for instance, multiple channels of user interactions [20] [21], and conceptual indexing [22]. We emphasize an integrated approach based on the multiagent metaphor and show encouraging results based on initial experiments.

The development of Gaz-Guide has resulted in a working prototype and shown the interactive capability of guiding users with terms and concepts to facilitate effective information retrieval. However, some of the components are rather primitive and deserve further studies. For example, user modeling in the librarian agent relies on simple parametric setting of constraints and preferences. A better model of user behaviors and needs is preferred and required to provide more customized assistance.

---

[2] We consider the amount of 20 retrieved documents as a reasonable size for users to find needed information. Therefore, a retrieval system should be able to provide a focused search within the range.

Ontology is another area that we have not elaborated in adequate sophistication. Currently, only knowledge of document types and knowledge of government institutions are used. We believe that further investigation on domain knowledge will provide considerable sources of exploitation for accurate retrieval of user needed information, such as effective pruning of irrelevant documents, and schematic search/retrieval.

Building upon information retrieval, the system allows potential extension to an array of domain-related information services, for instance, subscription/notification services of related gazette publications, and knowledge portal of government administration. As the function of each component becomes more advanced and the system provides more services, interactions among agents will require more sophisticated coordination rather than simple master and slave relationship. All these issues will be addressed in our future research.

6   Conclusion

Information retrieval tasks are essential to the notion of digital libraries where distributed data sources are organized and can be accessed remotely. We consider missing concepts and wrong terms in user query as the fundamental problem of information retrieval. We propose to improve effectiveness of information retrieval by bridging the conceptual gap between users and document contents. An agent-mediated approach is taken to articulate domain resources on thesauri and ontology (e.g., traditional library resources) and guide users with interactive assistance. We developed Gaz-Guide as a prototype system to examine the ideas. Initial experiment has shown encouraging results. We see great potentials in extending Gaz-Guide to a practical government administration information service system. Our future goal is to further improve current system so as to provide online services for real users, and by doing such, verify our research results.

Acknowledgement

This research is partly supported by a project with the National Central Library of Taiwan and by the Ministry of Education in the Program for Promoting Academic Excellence of Universities under grant number 89-E-FA04-1-4 and by National Science Council under the grant number NSC 89-2750-P-007-002-4.

References

1. Salton, G. and McGill, M. J. *Introduction to Modern Information Retrieval.* McGraw-Hill, Inc., 1983.
2. Baeza-Yates, R. and Ribeiro-Neto, B. *Modern Information Retrieval.* Addison-Wesley, 1999.
3. Korfhage, R. R. *Information Storage and Retrieval.* John Wiely and Sons, Inc., 1997.

4. Anick, P. G. and Vaithyanathan, S. Exploiting clustering and phrases for context-based information retrieval. *SIGIR Forum 31, 1*, pp. 314-323, 1997.

5. Raghavan, P. Information retrieval algorithms: a survey. *Proceedings of the Eighth Annual ACM-SIAM Symposium on Discrete Algorithms*, Pages 11 – 18, 1997.

6. Kobayashi, M. and Takeda, K. Information retrieval on the web. *ACM Computing Surveys*, Vol. 32, No. 2, pp. 144-173, June 2000.

7. De Mey, M. The relevance of the cognitive paradigm for information science. In Harbro, O. et. al. (eds.) *Theory and Applications of Information Research*, pp. 48-61, 1980.

8. Belkin, N. J. Cognitive models and information transfer. *Soc. Sci. Inf. Stud. 4*, pp. 111-129, 1984.

9. Bradshaw, Jeffery. (ed.) *Software Agents*. AAAI Press/MIT Press, 1997.

10. Wooldridge, M. J., and Jennings, N. R. Intelligent Agents: Theory and Practice. *Knowledge Engineering Review* 10(2):115-152, 1995.

11. Wiederhold, G. Mediation in information systems. *ACM Computing Surveys*, Vol. 27, No. 2, pp. 265-267, June 1995.

12. Allen, R. B. User Models: Theory, Method, and Practice. *International Journal of Man-Machine Studies*, Vol. 32, pp. 511-543, 1990.

13. Finin, T., Labrou, Y., and Mayfield, J. KQML as an agent communication language. In *Software Agents*, ed. J. M. Bradshaw. AAAI Press, 1997.

14. Giles, C. L., Bollacker, K., and Lawrence, S. CiteSeer: an automatic citation indexing system. *Proceedings of the Third ACM Conference on Digital Libraries*, pp. 89-98, ACM Press, 1998.

15. Bradshaw, S., Scheinkman, A., and Hammond, K. Guiding people to information: providing a digital library using reference as a basis for indexing. *Proceedings of the 2000 International Conference on Intelligent User Interfaces*, pp. 37-43, 2000.

16. Brin, S. and Page, L. The anatomy of a large-scale hypertextual web search engine. *Proceedings of WWW '98*, 1998.

17. Durfee, E.H., Kiskis, D.L., and Birmingham, W.P. The Agent Architecture of the University of Michigan Digital Library. In *Readings in Agents*, Huhns & Singh, (Eds.) pp. 98-110, 1998.

18. Sycara, K., and Pannu, A. P. The RETSINA Multiagent System: Towards Integrating Planning, Execution, and Information Gathering, In *Proceedings of the Second International Conference on Autonomous Agents*, 1998, Pages 350 – 351.

19. Bayardo, R. J. et.al. InfoSleuth: agent-based semantic integration of information in open and dynamic environments. *Proceedings of the ACM SIGMOD international conference on Management of data*, pp. 195-206, 1997.

20. Hearst, M. Interfaces for searching the web. *Scientific American*, pp. 68-72, 1997.

21. Rao, R., Pedersen, J. O., Hearst, M. A., et. al., Rich interaction in the digital library, *Communications of the ACM*, Vol. 38, No. 4, pp. 29-39, April 1995.

22. Woods, W. A. Conceptual indexing: Practical large-scale AI for efficient information access. *Proceedings of Seventeenth National Conference on Artificial Intelligence*, invited talk, pp. 1180-1185, 2000.

Technological Innovation of High-tech Industry and patent policy
-Agent based Simulation with Double Loop Learning-

Hao Lee[1] and Hiroshi Deguchi[2]

[1] Graduate School of Economics, Kyoto University
Yoshida-honmachi, Sakyou-ku, Kyoto-city, Japan
`e60a0311@ip.media.kyoto-u.ac.jp`
[2] Graduate School of Economics, Kyoto University
Yoshida-honmachi, Sakyou-ku, Kyoto-city, Japan
`deguchi@econ.kyoto-u.ac.jp`

Abstract. In this paper, we formulate a multi-agent model of virtual high-tech industry by agent-based simulation. We introduce a classifier system as a decision-making tool of agent who makes its decision depending on the rules in the classifier system. Firm agent determines how much R&D investment and product investment it will spend. We assumed three different types of firm agents in our virtual societies, in which each different agent has a different goal. Agents of different types have different evaluation functions; also agents may change their goals (evaluation functions) when they have survival problem in industry. We verify the Schumpeter Hypothesis and effect of industrial policies in our virtual high-tech industry. We found that the difference in speed at which technology increases, when comparing imitation and innovation, affects the effectiveness of patent policy.

1   Introduction

Computer simulation is becoming popular in economical and organizational research. Many economists and organizational scientists use simulation for their research [1, 2, 3, 4, 5, 7, 12]. We formulate a simulated society of firms in a virtual industry and analyze the society by agent-based simulation. It is a useful method to generate new theories and also to verify effects of policies. Agent based simulation is one modern methods in computer simulation

In this paper, we formulate our model of high-tech industry as a multi-agent system. We use classifier system as an action and learning model of agents. We focus on learning process of agents. What kind of agent is most powerful in our virtual high-tech industry, this is our first concern. Our second concern is to verify Schumpeter Hypothesis. Our last concern is to analyze the effects of policies.

S.-T. Yuan and M. Yokoo (Eds.): PRIMA 2001, LNAI 2132, pp. 168-182, 2001.

The definition of a high-tech industry in our model is as follows:

1. Important technology innovation occurs easily.
2. New technology innovation occurs frequently.
3. Cost of production is much lower than the cost of R&D investment.
4. Different consumers purchase different products.

Our simulations are performed under the several types of initial and boundary conditions. First, we analyze the effect of numbers of firms in industry to verify Schumpeter Hypothesis. Second, we analyze the effect of tax-subsidy policy. Next, we analyze the effect of time delay patent policy. Finally, we analyze the effect of permission fee patent policy.

2   Assumptions of Model

In this paper, consumers are divided into three groups. The first consumer group prefers high-technological products; we call them PU (Power User). The second group buys average and normal products; they are called RU (Regular User). The last group is always interested in cheap products; they are called EU (Economical User). Thus the market is separated into three parts: UM (Upper Market), MM (Middle Market), and LM (Lower Market).

There are twelve firms in our basic model. Each firm agent has its own technological level. The level affects the quality of the product, but firms always provide the best product they can make. PUs purchase the products of higher technology firms, EUs purchase products of lower technology firms and RUs purchase the products of average technology firms.

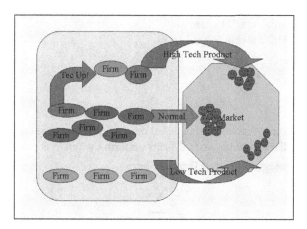

Fig. 1. Structure of the industry and the market

Firm agent evaluates its action rule, which is described in the classifier system. The learning process of the rules in an agent is performed by the classifier system. They have different evaluation functions when they have different goals. Firm agents also change their goals in period. The firms with low profit try to change their goals for survival.

Figure 1 show the structure of the industry and the market in our model. There are many firms in the industry and many consumers in the market. Firms compete with each other based on their respective technology. Firms having superior technology sell their products to consumers who prefer high-tech products at a higher price. Firms having lower technology sell their products to consumers who prefer cheap product at a lower price.

The price of products in each market is determined by the demand and supply in the market. n denotes the total number of firms. Q_u, Q_m and Q_l denote the supply quantity of each market respectively. The demand function is given as follows:
Demand function of the Upper market is:

$$P_u = 20 - Q_u / (n/2) \tag{1}$$

Demand function of the Middle market is:

$$P_m = 10 - (Q_m / (n*2)) \tag{2}$$

Demand function of the Lower market is:

$$P_l = 5 - (Q_l / (n*20)) \tag{3}$$

All firm agents have evaluation functions depending on their goals. The actions of agents are evaluated by their evaluation functions. The types of goals are classified as the types follows:

1. Type P, maximize profit
2. Type S, maximize market share
3. Type T, maximize technological level

3   Model

$\overline{T}_t$ denotes the average technological level on term t. The average technological level is determined by the technology of all firms on term t where n is the number of firms. $T_{i,t}$ denotes technological level of firm i on term t.

$$\overline{T}_t = \frac{\sum_{i=1}^{n} T_{i,t}}{n} \tag{4}$$

$I_{i,t}$ denotes the R&D investment of firm i on term t. $Q_{i,t}$ denotes the supply quantity of firm i on term t. The decisions for $I_{i,t}$ and $Q_{i,t}$ are determined by the action rule in the internal classifier system of firm i.

The conditions of action rules in the classifier system are the firms' cash and the difference between their technological level and average technological level. $K_{i,t}$ denotes the cash owned by firm i on term t. Firm agents select an action rule to be performed from their action rule sets in proportion to the weight of the action rule (Roulette Selection) . DM denotes the process of decision making in our model, which is shown as follows:

$$\{Q_{i,t}, I_{i,t}\} = \text{DM}[K_{i,t}, T_{i,t-1}, \overline{T}_{t-1}] \tag{5}$$

The action rule sets are shown in (6). A_x and B_x denote the conditional part of the rule. C_x and D_x denote the action part of the rule. Wp_x denotes the weight of profit maximization for rule x,; Ws_x denotes the weight of market share maximization for rule x; Wt_x denotes the weight of technological level maximization for rule x.

If $A_x = K_{i,t}$ and $B_x = T_{i,t-1} - \overline{T}_{t-1}$ then the firm may choose the rule x. The firm will choose one of the rules based on the rules by the weight of its goal. A higher weight means a higher probability of being chosen. The firm agent choose rule x and spend C_x as its R&D investment and D_x as budget of production.

□Rule 1□($A_1, B_1, C_1, D_1, Wp_1, Ws_1, Wt_1$)

…

Rule x□($A_x, B_x, C_x, D_x, Wp_x, Ws_x, Wt_x$) $\tag{6}$

…

Rule m□($A_m, B_m, C_m, D_m, Wp_m, Ws_m, Wt_m$)□

The R&D investment, the firm's past technological level and the average technological level in the industry prescribe the technological level the firm develops. Figure 2 shows how $T_{i,t}$ is determined. The Y-axis shows the R&D investment necessary to increase one technological level. The X-axis shows the difference between a firm's technological level and industry's average technological level.

The cost of imitation is lower than cost of innovation in our model. The firm having lower technological level is possible to imitate the firm having higher technological level. Therefore the lower the technological level a firm attains, the lower the R&D investment it must make to raise its technological level.

Innovation is the only method for the firm having superior technological level to improve its technological level. Innovation of higher technology is harder than lower technology. Thus the higher technological level a firm attains, the higher the R&D investment it must make to raise its technological level.

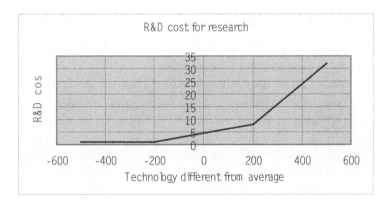

Fig. 2. Cost for technology level raise for R&D investment

$R_{i,t}$ denotes which market firm i will sells on term t. MS denotes the market selection algorithm for firm agents. The firms with technological levels higher then the average technological level of the top half of all firms will sell their products to the Upper Market. The firms with technological levels lower then the average of the bottom half of all firms will sell their products to the Lower Market. Other firms will sell their products to the Middle Market.

$$R_{i,t} = \text{MS}(T_{1,t} \dots T_{n,t})$$ (7)

$\overline{C}$ denotes the fixed production cost of firms. It is constant for all firms in all terms. Then the average production cost of firm i on term t is denoted by $C_{i,t}$ and defined in (8).

$$C_{i,t} = \overline{C} + \frac{I_{i,t}}{Q_{i,t}}$$ (8)

$Q_{r,t}$ is defined in (9) as the total supply of market r on term t.(r$\in$ {U, M, L})

$$Q_{r,t} = \sum \{Q_{i,t} \mid r = R_{i,t}, i = 1\dots n\}$$ (9)

D_r denotes the demand function of market r. Then $P_{r,t}$ is defined in (10) as the product price in market r on term t.

$$P_{r,t} = D_r(Q_{r,t})$$ (10)

$\pi_{i,t}$ is defined in (11) as the profit per unit product for firm i on term t.

$$\pi_{i,t} = P_{r,t} - C_{i,t}$$ (11)

Firm i has $K_{i,t}$ cash on term t. Then $K_{i,t+1}$ is defined in (12).

$$K_{i,t+1} = K_{i,t} + \pi_{i,t} * Q_{i,t} \tag{12}$$

4   Simulation and Process of Learning

We formulate our firm agents by using the classifier system with profit sharing evaluation [15] and reinforcement learning. Also, we introduce double-loop learning [6] in classifier system. The process of our agent-based simulation is shown as follows.

1. Each agent makes 4000 action rules (classifiers) randomly.
2. Agents choose a rule in their rule sets to be executed by pattern matching of the conditional part of the rule. Firm agents determine how much R&D investment and how much the investment of production they will spend.
3. Firm agents improve their technological level by spending R&D investments. Then firm agents use their new technology to make products.
4. Firm agents choose markets to sell their products by comparing their technology with others.
5. Firm agents compute their profits and market share.
6. Firm agents adjust the weights of the rules they choose. For profit sharing evaluation, they also adjust the weights of the rule they execute in recent four terms by profit sharing mechanism. This is because the past action also affects the outcome in this term. This is the process of single loop learning.
7. A firm agent that fails to survive will change its goal in this step every 10 terms. The firms with lower cash have a higher probability to change their goal. They will imitate the firms that gain better profits, as selected by roulette selection. This is the process of double loop learning.
8. Back to step 2

Agents create their action rules in step 1. There are 4000 action rules in the classifier system of each agent. The structure of classifier is given as (13).

{Technological information, Cash: R&D cost, production cost: weights}   (13)

Conditions of classifiers are technological information and cash. The technological information is the technological level of a firm agent and average technological level of industry. Cash held by a firm agent is also a condition. Actions of classifiers are R&D investment and production investment.

In step 2, firm agents choose a rule to be executed. They pick up all classifiers that match their current conditions, and then select one by roulette selection. Roulette selection means that the agents have more chance to select a rule with higher weight, but they still have some chance to select a rule with lower weight.

Firm agents spend their R&D investments to improve their technological level in step 3. They compete their technological level in market at step 4. If technological level of a firm is high enough, the firm sells its products to Upper Market. After firms sold their products, they compute their profits and market share in step 5.

Firm agents execute their learning process in step 6 and 7. Double loop learning is a modern learning method [6]. The first loop of learning is in step 6; the second loop of learning is in step 7. Firm agents evaluate their rules by adjusting the weight in the first loop of learning, and changing their evaluation function in second loop of learning.

The adjustments of weights are always between –1 and + 1. The adjustment process of weights is given as follows:

1. Profit maximization, weight adjustment of type P is based by cash on hand. The more cash is increasing, the more positive adjustment of weight.
2. Share maximization, weight adjustment of type S, is based on market share. The larger the market share, the more positive adjustment of weight.
3. Technological level maximization, weight adjustment of type T, is based on the difference between local technological level and global average technological level.   The higher the technological level of the firm, the more positive adjustment of weight.

5   Results of Simulations

There are two hundred terms in one time of simulation. The firm agents repeat twenty four times of simulation for learning before the formal simulation. Therefore a firm agent executes fifty hundred terms in a full-set of simulation. Under all initial and boundary conditions, we perform ten full-set of simulation to gather data.

In our first simulation, there is only one type of firm agent in an industry. The results are shown as Figures 3 and 4. Figure 3 shows technological levels of three types of industries. Figure 4 shows cash held by firm agents in different industries. In these industries, all firm agents in an industry have same goal.

When all firm agents are profit maximizers, the technological level of the industry is lowest and lots of cash held by the firm agents. The technological levels are almost same when all firm agents are market share maximizers and technology maximizers. In all situations, leader of a particular technological level takes in most profits in a given industry. Our simulation is Winner-take-all

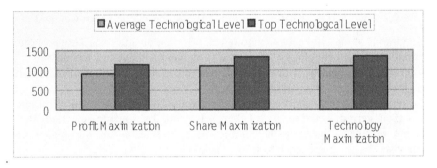

Fig. 3. Technological Level of different types of industries

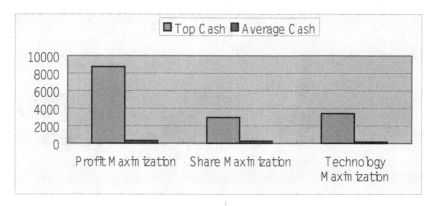

Fig. 4. Cash held by firms in different types of industries

In the first simulation, we assumed the agents in the industry have the same goals. In other words, there is no double loop learning in the first simulation. Now we assumed that firm agents have different goals in the industry. We analyze the effect of numbers of firms to verify Schumpeter hypothesis. In Schumpeter hypothesis, only large firms could induce technological innovation because small firms were incapable of expenditures on R&D. However, large firms will not have enough incentive to invest in R&D without short-run legal protection that will provide enough market power [14].

In Nelson & Winter 's research to verify Schumpeter hypothesis, they pointed out that the concentration of industry is important in technological innovation [12]. Technology innovation is quicker if the number of firms is smaller. We perform similar results in our model.

The result is shown as Figures 5-9. Figure 5 shows technological levels of industries with six firm agents, twelve firm agents and eighteen firm agents. Figure 6 shows cash held by firm agents of industries with six firm agents, twelve firm agents and eighteen firm agents.

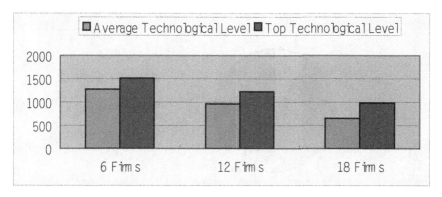

Fig. 5. Technological level under different numbers of firms

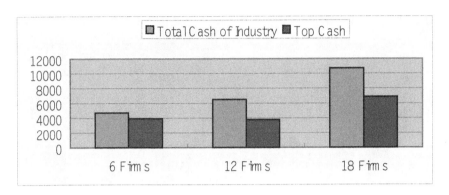

Fig. 6. Cash held under different numbers of firms

Figure 7 shows the rate of survival of firm types when there are six firms in industry. Figure 8 shows the rate of survival of firm types when there are twelve firms in industry. Figure 9 shows the rate of survival of firm types when there are eighteen firms in industry.

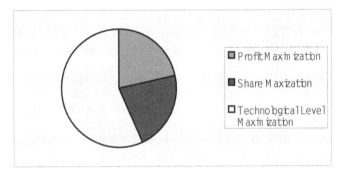

Fig. 7. Rate of survival of firm types: six firms

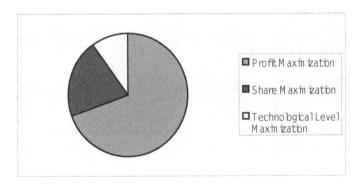

Fig. 8. Rate of Survival of firm types: twelve Firms

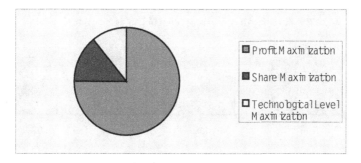

Fig. 9. Rate of Survival of firm types: eighteen Firms

Both top and average technological levels decrease when the number of firms increases. Firms seeking technological level maximization have a greater chance to survive when the number of firms is small. Firms seeking profit maximization have a greater chance of survival when the number of firms increases.

The competition in the upper market is weakest when the number of firms is small. So, once a firm seeking technological level maximization gains control of the upper market, it will not be defeated. Firm agents seeking technological level maximization take a more positive attitude toward R&D, so they have a greater chance to be the leader of their technological levels.

When there are more firms in the industry, there will also be more firms in the upper market. Firms seeking technological level maximization are unskillful at competition, so they will have a lower chance of survival. Finally, firms seeking profit maximization gain leadership of their technological level. They make lots of money, but are not interested in R&D investment. Therefore when there are many firms in the industry, firms seeking profit maximization survive more and the average technological level of the industry is lower.

Next, we verify the effect of industrial policies. We introduced three types of policies in our simulation. The first one is a tax and subsidy policy. The second one is a time delay patent policy. The last one is a permission fee patent policy.

There are three tax rates in the tax and subsidy system: 5%, 10% and 20%. Under this policy, firms have to pay the taxes to government when they have positive profit. Government also gives subsidy to the firms that invest in R&D. Taxes are always greater than subsidies.

The results are shown as Figures 10-11. Figure 10 shows technological level under a tax and subsidy policy. Figure 11 shows cash held by firms under the tax and subsidy policy.

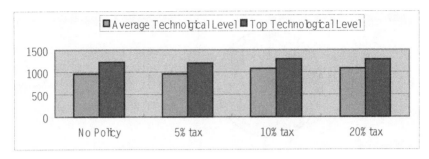

Fig. 10. Technological Level under the Tax and subsidy policy

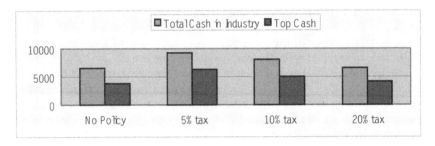

Fig. 11. Cash held by firms under the Tax and Subsidy policy

A tax and subsidy policy is slightly effective to increase the technological level of an industry. The technological level increases when the tax rate is 10% and 20%, it decreases when tax rate is 5%. We conclude that this is due to a negative effect from resource loss being stronger than a positive effect when the tax rate is too low.

We examine two kinds of patent policies in our simulation. The first one is a time delay patent policy. This means that firms can only imitate older technology. The results of patent of time delay are shown in Figures 12-13. Figure 12 shows technological levels under the time delay patent policy. Figure 13 shows cash held by firms under the time delay patent policy. In the figures, 5 terms, 10 terms and 20 terms mean the time delay until old technology can be imitated.

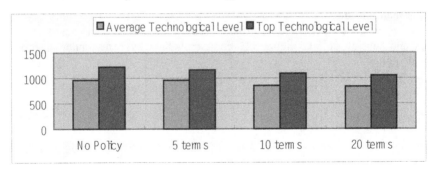

Fig. 12. Technological levels under the time delay patent policy

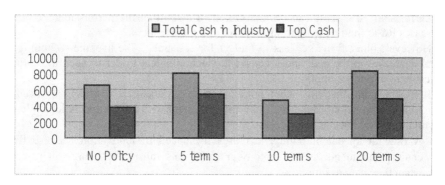

Fig. 13. Cash under the time delay patent policy

Next patent policy is the permission fee patent policy. Firms must pay a permission fee when they imitate the good technology. The results of permission fee patent policy are shown in Figures 14-15. Figure 14 shows technological level under a permission fee patent policy. Figure 15 shows cash held by firms under a permission fee patent policy. In the figures, 5%, 10% and 20% mean the permission fee to imitate the new technology.

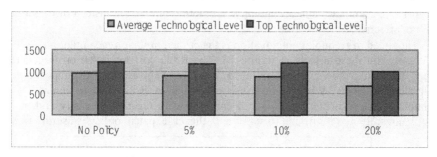

Fig. 14. Technological Level under Permission fee patent policy

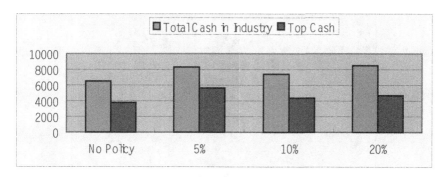

Fig. 15. Cash under the Permission fee patent policy

Both patent policies decrease technological levels in the industries. The only slight exception is that the case of top technological level increases under the patent policy of permission 10%. This can be interpreted to mean that the permission fee policy increases R&D funding availability for technological leaders.

However, other firms get less to budget for research. The average technological level decreases in the end, and it causes the technological leader to need more R&D investment in our assumption.

It is surprising that all patent policies cause an unexpected effect on speed of technology innovation. The result does not agreement with usual expectation. We can postulate several reasons, as follows:

1. A time delay patent policy decreases the speed of innovation because firms cannot imitate newest technology. Firm agents must invest more in research when they cannot imitate.

2. A policy of permission fees also decreases the speed of innovation. This is because the firms that imitate pay more for research, thus their technological levels increase slowly. Leaders of technology gain the permission fee, so they have more cash for R&D investment. But R&D spending for firms with high technological levels is expensive (see figure. 1). They can only improve their technological level a small amount by using their additional income. On the whole, the average technological level got worse.

3. Our model is a specific one. The technology is homogeneous in our model, so all firms research the same technology. Promoting innovation instead of imitation is not effective.

4. The speed of technology innovation is faster than imitation in simulation.

We explain these effects in Figure 16. The R&D cost for imitation is generally lower than innovation. Imitators need less R&D investment to improve their technological levels. When innovators spend lots of R&D cost to improve their technological levels, but imitators can catch up with technology easily and at low cost, innovators find it difficult to survive. In this case, patent policy is useful.

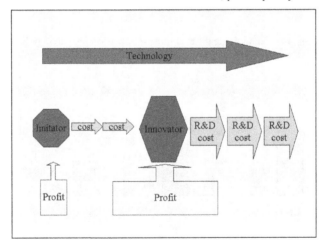

Fig. 16. Speed difference between innovator and imitator

However, innovators make higher profit if they become monopolists/oligopolists within the Upper Market. Even if R&D investment for innovation is higher than for imitation; innovators improve their technological more because they have a larger budget for R&D. The result is that patent policies are not effective in our model because incentive for innovation is high enough in our model.

In the simulations, we find out that profit maximization is the most powerful strategy in this virtual industry, and technological level maximization is disadvantages. But if there gexists a firm seeking technological level maximization, the average technological level of industry will be higher. The patent policy gives firms seeking technological level maximization a better chance to survive.

In all conditions, the technological leader gains most of the profit in industry. (See Figure.4, Figure.6, Figure.11, Figure.13 and Figure.15).

6   Conclusion

In our high-tech industry, winner takes all. The only method to become winner in the industry is to become a monopolist or an oligopolist in the Upper Market. After analyzing the winner's histories of strategies in the classifier system, we find that there are several patterns to success.

1. The successful firm agent invests lots in R&D when other firm agents do not or can not do so. Then successful firm agent becomes monopolist of upper market in early terms and gains huge benefits. Most winners seeking technological level maximization win in this pattern.

2. The successful firm agent doesn't invest in R&D in early terms when other firm agents are competing technology hardly. The successful firm agent makes lots of product in Middle Market and gains well profit when other firm agents gain small profits and compete hardly in the Upper Market. After the successful firm agent saves enough money and other firm agents in the Upper Market are out of cash, the successful firm agent spends its cash in imitation to increase its technological level rapidly. Then the successful firm agent becomes the monopolist of upper market. Most winners seeking market share maximization win in this pattern.

3. The successful firm agent spends minimum R&D investment to stay in the Upper Market and spend all rest money on production to gain profits. The successful firm gains better profit than other competitors in the Upper Market because it invests more on production than others. The successful firm agent makes a lot of products in the Upper Market, thus the price falls down. Then other competitors make few profits and cannot have enough money to invest in R&D. Then the successful firm agent monopolizes the Upper Market and become the winner. Most winners seeking profit maximization win in this pattern.

Profit maximization strategy is most effective one and technology maximization is most disadvantageous one in this simulation.

Schumpeter hypothesis is valid in our virtual industry. The speed of technology innovation becomes faster when the number of firms is smaller. In this virtual high-tech industry, innovators have enough incentive to invest in R&D because they gain enough profit in the Upper Market. The tax and subsidy policy is still effective to support innovation in this virtual industry. However the patent policy is not an effective policy to create enough incentive in R&D.

The tax and subsidy policies give support to increase technological level of industry. The patent policy is not an effective policy to increase the speed of technology innovation in our model. The patent policies of time delay decrease the speed of technological increasing in all cases. The patent policies of permission fee decrease the speed of technological innovation in most cases.

In future research, we will investigate more about the policy effects in technological innovation by simulations, and try to combine simulation results with theoretical approach and actual cases of industries.

References

1. Robert Alexrod, The Complexity of Cooperation, Agent-Based Models of Competition and Collaboration, Princeton University Press.1997
2. Esben Sloth Andersen, Evolutionary Economics, Post-Schumpeterian Contributions. A Cassel Imprint. 1996.
3. W.Brian Arthur. *Increasing Returns and Path Dependence in the Economy.* The University of Michigan Press.1994
4. W.Brian Arthus, Steven N. Durlauf, David A.Lane. *The Economy as an Evolving Complex System II.* Addison-Wesley 1997
5. Kathleen M. Carley, Michael J. Prietula. *Computational Organization Theory.* Lawrence Erlbaum Associates, Publishers.
6. M.D. Cohen and L.S. Sproull. *Organizational Learning,* SAGE Publications, 1995.
7. Hiroshi Deguchi, Agent Based Approach for Social Complex Systems - Management of Constructed Social World In Toru Ishida(Ed), Community Computing and Support Systems LNCS 1519, Springer, p.62-77, 1998.
8. Richard J. Gaylord, Louis J.D'Andria. Simulation Society: A Mathematica Toolkit for Modeling Socioeconomic Behavior. Springer-Verlag, 1998.
9. Hao Lee, Hiroshi Deguchi, *Technological Innovation of High-tech industry,*JASMIN2000 Spring, 2000. (In Japanese)
10. Hao, Lee, H. Deguchi, Technological Innovation of High-tech industry –Agent based Simulation with Double Loop Learning-, KSS'2000 JAIST, p. 224-229
11. Melanie Mitchell. *An Introduction to Genetic Algorithms.* Massachusetts Institute of Technology.1996.
12. Nelson, Richard R & Sidney G.Winter . *An evolutionary theory of economic change.* Harvard University Press, 1996.
13. F.M. Scherer, David Ross, Industrial market structure and economic performance. Houghton Mifflin, 1990.
14. Schumpeter J. *Capitalism, Socialism, and Democracy.* Harper and Row, New York.1942
15. Takadama,T. Terano, K. Hori, and S.Nakasuka, "Making Organizational Learning Operational : Implication from Learning Classifier System",Cimputational and Mathematical Organization Theory(CMOT),Kluwer Academic Publichers, Vol.5, No.3pp.229-252.1999.

Collaborative Filtering for a Distributed Smart IC Card System

Eiji Murakami[1] and Takao Terano[2]

[1] Yamatake Corporation, 2-12-19 Shibuya Shibuya-ku Tokyo 150-8316 Japan
murakami@pres.yamatake.co.jp
[2] University of Tsukuba
3-29-1 Otsuka, Bunkyo-ku, Tokyo 112-0012, Japan
terano@gssm.otsuka.tsukuba.ac.jp

Abstract. Collaborative filtering, often used in E-commerce applications, is a method to cluster similar users based on their profiles, characteristics or attitudes on specific subjects. This paper proposes a novel method to implement dynamic collaborative filtering by Genetics-based machine learning, in which we employ Learning Classifier Systems extended to multiple environments. The proposed method is used in a yet another mobile agent system: a distributed smart IC card system. The characteristics of the proposed method are summarized as follows: (1) It is effective in distributed computer environments with PCs even for small number of users. (2) It learns users' profiles from the individual behaviors of them then generates the recommendation and advices for each user. (3) The results are automatically accumulated in a local system on a PC, then they are distributed via smart IC cards while the users are interacting with the system. The method has been implemented and validated in Group Trip Advisor prototype: a PC-based distributed recommendor system for travel information.

1 Introduction

Collaborative filtering is a method to cluster similar users based on their profiles, characteristics or attitudes on specific subjects [1]. The techniques are often used in E-commerce applications to recommend some appropriate consumer goods to specified groups of customers [2]. The techniques recommend items other similar users like. Thus, to implement the methods, we analyze ratings of items by users to classify the users into groups, so that users in a group share similar interests. Then, a user is recommended items, which his/her similar users have rated highly and he/she has not looked.

Examples of Collaborative-filtering recommendation are found in the systems: GroupLends[3] and Firefly[4]. Collaborative filtering deals with any kind of contents, because the system need not analyze contents to generate recommendation. On the other side, the shortcomings are summarized in [2] that we need to have enough number of users and rating information compared with the number of items. When the number of users is small, recommended items will become only a small part of the whole items.

S.-T. Yuan and M. Yokoo (Eds.): PRIMA 2001, LNAI 2132, pp. 183-197, 2001.

To utilize the benefits and to overcome the difficulty, this paper proposes a novel method to develop dynamic collaborative for PC-based distributed recommendor systems equipped with smart IC cards as media for personal data assistants for naïve users. By "dynamic collaborative filtering", we mean that the filtering tasks are performed in a distributed environment and that the filtering results are local and gradually spread to the total system via software agents within smart IC cards.

To implement the dynamic collaborative filtering, we utilize Genetics-based machine learning, especially Learning Classifier Systems extended to multiple environments: Organizational-learning oriented Classifier System (OCS) [5]. The concepts of OCS have come from both conventional Learning Classifier Systems in Genetic Algorithms literature and organizational learning in organization and management science literature.

The performance of recent smart IC cards is equal to the one of micro-computer kits about twenty years ago, thus, we can use smart IC cards for a media to implement collaborative filtering systems. The proposed method is implemented in Fairy-Wing: yet another mobile computing system for community computing in a digital city [6]. The system aims at supporting personal information management and information services.

The organization of the paper is somewhat complicated, because this paper addresses the following four topics: (i) Organizational-learning oriented classifier system as a basic mechanism, (ii) a new dynamic collaborative filtering method, (iii) Fairy-Wing with smart IC cards equipped the method, and (iv) Implementation and evaluation of the method into the application: Group Trip Advisor prototype.

This paper describes the four topics in order: the algorithms with OCS, the architecture of the dynamic collaborative filtering, the brief description of Fairy-Wing, the performance evaluation in artificial conditions, and the field tests on Group Trip Advisor prototype for Kyoto City contents. The experimental results have suggested that the proposed method effectively learns the user profiles via OCS and the subjects of the field test evaluate the user friendliness and usefulness of Group Trip Advisor prototype.

2   Organizational Learning Oriented Classifier System

2.1   Brief Description of OCS

OCS consists of the components with problem solving by rule-based reasoning via a set of classifiers, learning by changing the weights of rules via reinforcement learning, rule generation via Genetic Algorithms, exchanging rules among a group of software agents with OCS, and re-using rules for new problems by distributing learned rules to the agents.

Figure 1 shows the OCS architecture extended from conventional Learning Classifier System (LCS) with organizational learning methods. The system solves a given problem with multi-agents' organizational learning where the problem cannot solve by the sum of individual learning of each agent [5].

In OCS, we introduce the four loops of organizational learning mechanism proposed in [7]. Agents divide given problems by acquiring their own appropriate *functions* through interaction among agents to solve problems that cannot be solved at an individual level. This definition implies that the learning for acquiring appropriate functions in some agents is affected by the function acquisition of other agents.

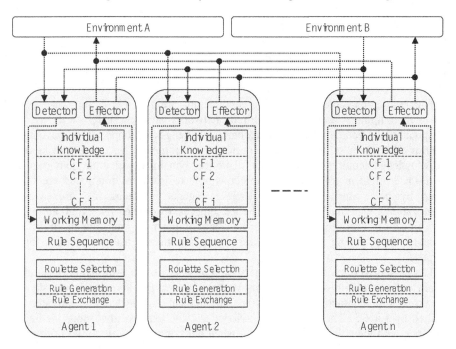

Figure 1 Architecture of Organizational-learning Oriented Classifier System

The agent in OCS contains the following components:

(1) Problem Solver:
- Detector and Effecter: change a sub environmental state into an internal state and an internal state into an action, respectively.

(2) Memory
- Organizational knowledge memory: It stores a set comprising each agent's rule set acquired when agents solve given problems most effectively. In OCS, all agents share this knowledge.
- Individual knowledge memory: It stores a set of CFs (classifiers). In OCS, a CF is implemented by an if-then rule with a strength factor (the worth of rules).
- Working memory: It stores the results obtained in recognizing sub environmental states and an internal state of an action of fired rules.
- Rule sequence memory: It stores a sequence of fired rules in order to evaluate them. This memory is cleared after the evaluation.

(3) Learning Mechanism
- Roulette selection: It stochastically selects one matched rule according to the strength value attached to each rule.
- Reinforcement learning, rule generation, rule exchange, and organizational knowledge reuse mechanisms: They are reinterpreted from the four kinds of learning in [7].

2.2   Collaborative Filtering with F-OCS

The basic idea of the dynamic collaborative filtering from OCS, however, the proposed system F-OCS is extended from the original OCS so that we deal with distributed learning results in smart IC cards effectively. The architecture is shown in Figure 2.

The unique characteristics of the architecture are that (1) it only uses small personal computers with and/or without networks and smart IC cards as their computational resources and (2) the technical challenges are opposed to conventional centralized filtering systems. F-OCS performs the collaborative filtering tasks using the knowledge acquired and/or learned from the dynamically changing environment. An F-OCS agent in a personal computer is able to learn environmental conditions given by both user interaction and Fairy agents in smart IC cards via the organizational learning framework. The learning results of each F-OCS about the sub environment are carried out from the personal computer by Fairy agents in order to exchange them among F-OCSs in the system. We do not use the network for the purpose.

The person who interacts with a personal computer or the information terminal to obtain the specific information wants to know the target knowledge via standard browsers. The interactive activities are automatically collected, accumulated and learned by F-OCS. The acquired knowledge will be used to give more intellectual guidance with the collaborative filtering when other persons come to the information terminal.

Each F-OCS agent contains the functions of machine learning, short-term rule generation, short-term rule exchange, long-term rule generation, and long-term rule exchange. The short-term rules and long-term rules are similar to human's memory system [8]. Each F-OCS agent perceives the problem from the confronting environment. Knowledge is acquired as a result of machine learning, then it is stored into Classifier Store of F-OCS (short-term rules) as short-term rules. Next, when the rules inside the Classifier Store become the most successful ones in this local environment, the corresponding short-term rules moves to a Filter Rule Store (long-term rules) from Classifier Store as candidates of good common knowledge which would be successful for the problem task domain. Rules in the Filter Rule Store are then exchanged via Fairy agents in smart IC cards. They are gradually spread, collected, and accumulated to the distributed environment, and finally they would be successful knowledge for the whole environment. Results of the knowledge stored into Filter Rule Store is not only useful for the recommendor system but also applicable to some other business domains such as marketing research for dynamic data mining [9].

Therefore, F-OCS learns real world environment which constantly changing its state. The goal of F-OCS is that learning series of events generated by users' activity on the interaction with information terminals to browse and seek the information

The classifier system has the following rule sets in its inside.

If<conditions> then <action> weight

F-OCS receives input values from the environment to match the <conditions> part of the rules, then the system makes some responses based on the <action> part of the rule which previously matched with <conditions> part. The reinforce based machine learning is performed by evaluating the fitness determined by the problem domain. The rules which made suitable responses increases their weights from the profits obtained by fitness function.

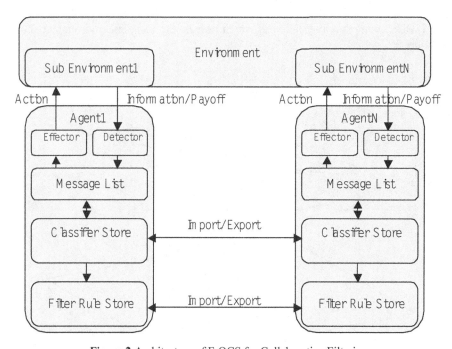

Figure 2 Architecture of F-OCS for Collaborative Filtering

The rule weight management is to evaluate the system responses which come from <action> part of the rule. If the rule makes correctly actions to the environment, the corresponding rule weight increases. On the other hand, the weights of the rules which made bad actions, rule weight decreases, and then useless rules are discarded and replaced newly generated ones via genetic operations. To control the weight management, we introduce the life tax strategy for those rules to decrease their weights then finally they are discarded when the weights will become zero. Thus, the set of rules inside the system always follows the environmental state change by the increasing and /or decreasing the weights. When using for dynamic collaborative filtering or dynamic data mining, we are able to rely on the rules, because their weights are automatically updated according to the environmental changes.

The set of rules are used to give good responses against the environmental changes. As mentioned above, the <action> part of a rule is used both for the immediate response and for responses after the next several steps according to the matching processes with the <conditions> of a rule set. This matching process will generate a chain of executed rules. The response of the system is a result of such a chain of rules execution and is expected to good enough ones even for very complex environments.

Performance evaluation of F-OCS was performed as a preliminary experiment using the data prepared artificially. Test data is shown in Fig. 3. At this time the environment has 2 parameters on the time line (time sequence). One parameter is information ID (web page number). Another parameter is the strength of the interest (interest strength) of a user who interacts with the information terminal. This figure is the simulation results of the user's activity learned by F-OCS. After this evaluation test, F-OCS acquires numerous rules which reflects the complex environment shown in Figure 3.

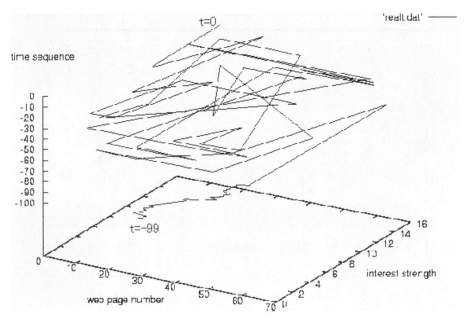

Figure 3 machine learning example for F-OCS

The characteristics of the proposed method are summarized as follows:
(1) Contrary to conventional collaborative filtering techniques, which require very large amount of user profiles in a centralized database, the proposed method is effective in distributed computer environments with PCs for small number of users. We do not require a centralized database or data management.
(2) It learns users' profiles from the individual behaviors of them then generates the recommendation/advice for each people.

(3) The proposed method requires comparatively lower cost hardware resources than the other existing systems.

(4) The filtering results are automatically accumulated in a local system on a PC while the users are interacting with the information recommendation system.

(5) This is attained by the learning mechanisms of OCS, which enable the system dynamically learn users' characteristics on a specific task domain.

(6) The learned results in a local system, or the information on user classification and suitable recommendation for each user class are distributed among all the systems via software agents with and/or without computer networks. That is, the proposed method analyzes the internal rules of the software agents previously used for generating the recommendation and advice for each people then identifying the common rules of the community.

3   Fairy-Wing: Yet Another Mobile Computing System

Fairy-Wing [6] aims at supporting personal information management, information services, and dynamic collaborative filtering in order to interface the people, towns, and digital cities [10]. The main features of the system are that (1) the agents or fairies are small, cheap, and easy-to-use; (2) they are fully distributed among ubiquitous computing environments with and/or without computer networks; and (3) holder-centered information controlling mechanisms. This section describes the architecture of Fairy-Wing and the feasibility of the systems. The Conceptual framework of Fairy-Wing consists of Smart IC cards, Information Terminals, and Information Spaces. In the subsequent sections, we will describe the features of each component.

3.1   Smart IC Cards

The performance of recent smart IC cards is equal to the one of micro-computer kits about twenty years ago, thus, we can use IC cards for a media to implement collaborative filtering systems. Each IC card contains small software agents: Fairies.

Fairy-Wing cards are flexible, easy-to-use, and cheap mobile terminals corresponding to conventional PDAs. The cards contain (1) the security information, or the ping number of card-holders, (2) personal information, which can be masked per data item by users in order to conceal or reveal the individual information, (3) footprints of the user, which maintain past records of activities in a digital city, and (4) local information, which must be transferred among information terminals.

If necessary, each Fairy can be transferred into conventional personal data assistant systems or their own PCs. Furthermore, the shape of the equipments with fairies can be designed in any shapes and forms, for example, they can be like a notebook page, leaflet, button, and/or any wearable style. However, we consider the IC card is a good form, because of the portability and the cost requirements.

All information in the cards is under control of the card-holder, thus, he or she must be responsible for managing and maintaining it. For users' convenience and avoidance of loosing damages, the contents of the IC cards can be freely copied only by the card-holder. When the card-holder loose his or her cards, immediately he or she can distribute the information that the card is no more valid among the digital city. This is easily attained by accessing ubiquitous information terminals. Only the user can do is to inform the specific card ID to the digital city. Then the information will be immediately distributed to the whole city.

3.2   Information Terminals

The users interact with ubiquitous information terminals, which should be equipped with easy-to-use and look-and-feel interfaces for naïve users (for example, touch screens and voice information guidance are desirable). They have a reader/writer for IC cards. The users start the session by inserting their IC cards to the reader/writer. When Fairy-Wings are inserted into the terminals, the terminal will show the most appropriate information to the user based on the stored information in the terminal and the footprints on the Fairy-Wing.

The information terminals are basically client systems connected with information servers in the digital city. However, they are not necessarily networked, if the terminals have enough information for the current users. This is because the fairies contain footprint information, so that the information providing task can be performed in standalone type terminals. This capability will reduce the cost of the system deployment.

3.3   Information Space

The users of Fairy-Wing connect the digital city based on the information of fairies and information terminals. Fairy-Wings are used both in virtual and physical information spaces. For example, in the virtual space shown in a private PC, users can explore digital city malls based on the personal information and buy favorite stuff based on the concepts of relationship marketing. They also gather together to the user community based on the filtering mechanisms. On the other hand, in the physical space, user will have appropriate information or recommendation from digital city via information terminals and/or private PCs, based on the footprint information.

4   Dynamic Collaborative Filtering and Group Trip Advisor

We have developed Group Trip Advisor with Fairy-Wing. To implement collaborative filtering mechanisms in Group Trip Advisor, we have equipped Organizational-learning oriented Classifier System (F-OCS) in it. The system configuration of Group Trip Advisor is shown in Fig. 4.

We use PCs with MS-Windows, Web Browser, and Smart IC card reader/writers and optionally Digital Cameras for user photos. The web browser or F-Browser is used as a user interface to F-OCS.

In Group Trip Advisor, each smart IC card contains the following information:
- Personal information of a card-holder, such as age, hobby, and personal interests.
- The records of card-holder's behaviors gathering through F-Browser: kinds of information and duration of the time he or she was browsing.
- The short-term and long-term rules generated by F-OCS to exchange the rules with another F-OCS when a smart IC is read by another site of Group Trip Advisor.

Because all information of a card-holder required for the learning has been already resided on a smart IC card when he or she uses F-browser, makes Fairies can always learn card-holder's corresponding behaviors. A new learning session will start if a new card-holder comes to the site. Otherwise automated learning via OCS is continuing at each site. In both cases, Fairy-Wing can take a maximum opportunity of learning card-holder's behavior.

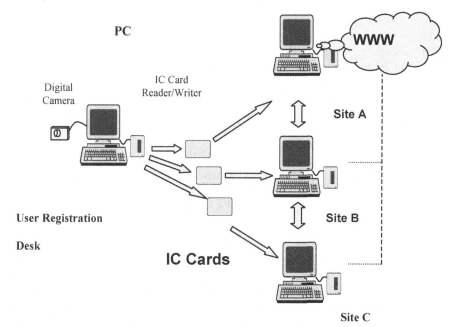

Figure 4 System Configuration of Group Trip Advisor

Users who once registered their basic information in a smart IC card are able to use ubiquitous information terminals. Each information terminal shall recommend users what kind of information is good for them. The information is automatically displayed in F-Browser as HTML documents. Also users are able to navigate the information by themselves without Fairy-Wing assistance through the F-Browser. The recommendation is generated from rules in F-OCS. The rules are divided into short term rules and long term ones. The short term rules are adequate ones in each session and the long term rules are to be commonly used in the whole system.

Fairy-Wing does not necessarily connect to the Internet or other kind of computer networks. The HTML document can resides only on local PC hard disk. Each F-OCS exchanges rules for recommendations among the other F-OCSs through Fairies in the smart IC card when a card-holder visits the other sites. Thus, the recommendations are generated based on the newest learning results among users and information terminals.

4.1   Design of F-OCS

25-bit vectors represent classifier Expressions of F-OCS The information contained in F-OCS classifiers or rules. The contents are:

Age	2 bits
Gender	2 bits
Occupation	3 bits
Hobby	4 bits
Place to go most interesting	3 bits
Preferable type of sightseeing	3 bits
HTML documents viewed in F-Browser	6bit
Minutes of duration time the documents viewed in F-Browser	2bit

Since F-OCS assumes that it receives the contents related to the sightseeing domain. The system utilizes a card-holder's personal information as the input value from the environment. the bits from 0 to 24 with binary expression of 0,1 represent input vectors of F-OCS from the environment.

Strength Assignment for Short-term Rules The condition part of a rule can be represented 1,0, and wild card # in the classifier system. For example, the condition part of a short-term rule is expressed with F-OCS as follows.

$$< condition >= \{0,1,\#\}^{25}$$

The wild card # could be either of 0 or 1. If the <condition> has the more #s, this means the rule will not use the input information well. On the contrary, if the <condition> has the less #s, it will utilize more information from the input. Also the strength values are assigned to each rule to control the applicability of the rule. The strength values are evaluated in the chain of actions of applied rules. The Bucket brigade algorithm is adopted in this system [12].

In the Bucket brigade algorithm each rule makes the bid value if the <condition> agrees with the input value. This bid is determined as follows.

$$specificity=(25-number\ of\ \#)/25$$
$$bid=specificity*k*strength,$$

where, the number of # means how many #s are contained in <condition> part, and k is the constant between $0< k<1$. The specificity values will become larger if the degrees of specialization of a rule is larger, that is, the <condition> of a rule has the less #s.

Genetic Algorithms of F-OCS F-OCS predicts the next behavior of the card-holder from what he/she has done in the previous actions. The genetic operations equipped in F-OCS are the one point cross over with mutation for each of <action> and <condition>. The genetic operations are applied every 100 steps, In each step, F-OCS sets up output values to the environment. Rule selection is performed by the roulette wheel selection. Roulette wheel selection is the method of choosing single rule from rule group based on strength.

$$Pi = F(Si) / \sum_{i=1}^{N} F(Si)$$

i=1...n

where, $F(Si)$ is the strength of an each rule and Pi : is the selection probability of an each rule. In F-OCS, also De Jong's crowding method is applied to keep the diversity of rules [11].

Rule Chain Control in F-OCS F-OCS matches <condition> parts of a short-term rule with the input values from the environments. The iterative process will generate a chain of applied short-term rules. Good chains should be promoted in the whole system in order to improve the adaptability with the complicated environment. However, the chain may become very long and the generation of a chain may go into an infinite loop. The following mechanism is designed to prevent such disasters by extending the idea in [12].

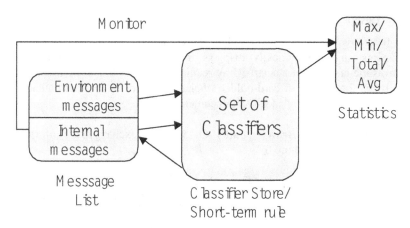

Figure 5 Rule chain control of F-OCS

- Set the number of times of chain execution to 1 in the initial state of machine learning.
- Supervise the state of the strength in the short-term rules.

- When it becomes larger than the specified threshold value determined by the maximum and minimum of the strengths of rules, then increase the number of the chain executions.
- On the contrary, when the strength becomes smaller than the threshold value, reduce the number of the chain executions.

The concept of this mechanism is shown in Fig. 5.

Rule Exchange and Sending Recommended Information   In F-OCS, a fixed number of rules are chosen and distributed to the other F-OCSs. The number of these rules for each agent is as follows.

- The number of rules chosen among the short-term rule group (total 1000 rules) for exchange is 30.
- The number of rules chosen among the long-term rule group (total 1000 rules) for exchange is 34.

These numbers are determined by the memory capacity of the smart IC card. The selected rules are stored in the smart IC in order to transfer the other F-OCSs.

For every 10,000 steps of F-OCS executions, F-OCS chooses only one long-term rule and send it to F-Browser: the user interface of Fairy-Wing. Based on the rule, the F-Browser makes recommendation information. The mechanism is summarized as follows.

Match card-holder's personal information with <condition> part of long-term rules. Apply one of the matched rules using the roulette wheel selection. Display the information generated from the <action> part of the rule. When there are no matched rules, then the most similar rule is applied.

4.2   Design of F-Browser

The functions of F-Browser are that (1) As a user interface, it browses HTML documents, and automatically displays the recommendation information; (2) It Controls the contents of a smart IC by reading/writing both short-term rule and long-term rules, the history of card-holder's behaviors, and (3) It Communicates with F-OCS to show recommended HTML document.

Communication of F-Browser and F-OCS F-OCS exchanges the information with F-Browser shown in Figure 6.

The arrows represent the flow of data. Each of them is explained below. Recommendation information is periodically sent from F-OCS to F-Browser. Once personal information is input to the smart IC card, this information is sent to F-OCS upon request. The card-holder's behavior on F-Browser is recorded and written into each smart IC card. The HTML document IDs and their viewing duration time are recorded. It can save a maximum of 100 histories in a smart IC card. The information is sent also to F-OCS. Since the history records of card-holder's behavior are always saved in the smart IC card, even when a card-holder moves to the other sites, or even when he or she returns to the same site, again, F-OCS can always learn a card-holder's behavior in the same environments. When a user starts a session at one site, F-Browser reads the rules from a smart IC card, and the contents are sent to F-OCS. F-OCS takes these rules as elites then put them into an own short-term rule and long-term rule stores. When he or she closes the session, F-OCS chooses the elitist rule to learn best about the user's behavior, and sends them to F-Browser. F-Browser receives the contents and writes them into the smart IC card.

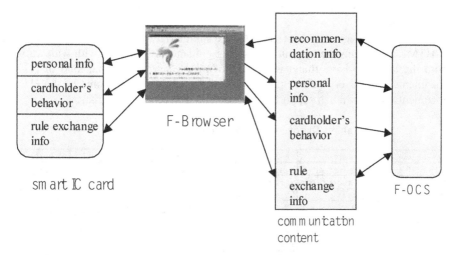

Figure 6 The communication of F-Browser and F-OCS

5   Evaluation of Group Trip Advisor

The proposed method has been implemented in Group Trip Advisor prototype. In the system, users visit some sightseeing places based on the recommendation of the advisor via web browsers. If the users belong to the same group, based on the foot print information, they can get messages of colleagues about sightseeing information at different time and places. Information terminals contain web-browser based interfaces and Fairies are implemented on a thin- and non-contact type IC card, thus can be hold in even a small purse of the users.

To evaluate the performance, we have conducted several experiments from artificial conditions to empirical ones. Because of the limit of the space, in this section, we only describe the results of one of the field tests, in which 10 people have evaluated both recommendation and learning functions of Group Trip Advisor prototype. Then we have analyzed the long-term rules discovered as the common rules of the community of users after the experiment.

The conditions of the experiment were set up as follows.
- HTML documents subjects can browse are selected the information of DigitalCity Kyoto project (http://www.digitalcity.gr.jp/)
- One PC with Fairy-Wing and Group Trip Advisor prototype is used for the ten subjects.
- We have had the two sessions: Training: Subjects ware allowed to freely browse the information provided, during the session, F-OCS has learnt the subjects'

behaviors. Test: Subjects evaluated the recommendations the system has automatically generated.

The experiments have shown that the dynamic and distributed collaborative filtering by F-OCS in Fairy-Wing architecture is effective in such complex real world applications.

The results of acquired long term rules are summarized in Table 1. As the contents of HTML documents were about sightseeing guidance information with wide variety, from the table we have found what kind of people prefers to what kind of HTML documents. Moreover, the strength values of each rule suggest some of the HTML documents are how much supported by people in different characteristics.

Table 1 Discovering the common rules of the community

Age	Gender	Occupation	Hobby	Place to go	Preferable type of	HTML	Strength
21 to 30	F	Office worker	Travel	Kiyomizu temple	Historic spot	13	73.29555
31 to 40	F	Self-management	Others	Ginkakuji temple	Food marketplace	36	64.98769
0 to 20	F	Student	Others	Ginkakuji temple	Food marketplace	50	38.48464
0 to 20	F	Student	Others	Ginkakuji temple	Food marketplace	5	37.17504
31 to 40	F	Office worker	Others	Souvenir shop		37	34.95318
31 to 40	F	Office worker	Others	Souvenir shop		13	33.44566
31 to 40	F	Office worker	Travel	Ginkakuji temple	Historic spot	13	32.02547
31 to 40	M	Office worker	Music	Kiyomizu temple	Historic spot	35	30.98362
31 to 40	M	Office worker	Gourmet	Ginkakuji temple	Historic spot	22	27.11954
21 to 30	F	Office worker	Travel	Kiyomizu temple	Historic spot	51	23.86819
31 to 40	F	Office worker	Travel	Kiyomizu temple	Historic spot	13	20.70117
0 to 20	F	Student	Others	Ginkakuji temple	Food marketplace	13	20.29027
31 to 40	F	Office worker	Travel	Souvenir shop	Food marketplace	43	17.54894
0 to 20	F	Student	Others	Ginkakuji temple	Food marketplace	59	12.39348
31 to 40	F	Office worker	Travel	Kiyomizu temple	Historic spot	59	7.736374
21 to 30	F	Office worker	Travel	Kiyomizu temple	Historic spot	61	6.112746
31 to 40	F	Office worker	Travel	Ginkakuji temple	Historic spot	50	4.366248
31 to 40	M	Office worker	Music	Kiyomizu temple	Historic spot	17	3.741429

6   Concluding Remarks

This paper has proposed a novel method for dynamic collaborative filtering method by Organizational-learning oriented Classifier System and described the architecture of Fairy-Wing: yet another mobile computing system with smart IC cards, and its implementation for distributed PC-based recommendation system Group Trip Advisor prototype. The implementation and experimental results have suggested the proposed method is effective in recommendation systems in ubiquitous terminal environments. Future research includes the deployment of the proposed system and their further extensions.

Acknowledgements

The research is supported in part by a Grant-in-Aid for Scientific Research of the Ministry of Education, Science, Sports and Culture of Japan (C-10680370 and 11792025: Digital City as Social Information Infrastructures). The author thanks to Professor T. Ishida of Kyoto University for valuable suggestions on Digital City Kyoto project.

References

[1] Shardanand, U. and P. Maes, Social Information Filtering: Algorithms for Automating 'Word of Mouth'. *Proceedings of the CHI-95* (ACM Press),1995

[2] Paul Resnick and Hal R. Varian, Recommender Systems. *Commnications of the ACM*, Vol. 40, No.3, p56-58, 1997

[3] Paul Resnick, Neophytos Iacovou, Mitesh Suchak, et al., GroupLends: An Open Architecture for Collaborative Filtering of Netnews. *Proceedings of the Conference on Conputer Supported Cooperative Work*, 1994, p175-186

[4] NetPerceptions Inc., Recommendation Engine White Paper. http://www.netperceptions.com/literature/content/recommendation.pdf, 2000

[5] K. Takadama, T. Terano, K. Shimohara, K. Hori, S. Nakasuka: Making Organizational Learning Operational: Implication from Learning Classifier System. *J. Computational and Mathematical Organization Theory*, Vol. 5, No. 3, pp. 229-252, 1999.

[6] T. Terano, T. Nishimura, E. Murakami, Y. Ishino: Fairy in a Smart IC Card: Interfacing People, Town, and Digital City. in T. Ishida and K. Isbister Eds, *Digital Cities: Experiences, Technologies and Future Perspectives*, Lecture Notes in Computer Science 1765, Springer-Verlag, pp. 378-390, 2000.

[7] Kim, D.: The Link between Individual and Organizational Learning. *Sloan Management Review*, Fall, pp. 37-50, 1993.

[8] H.A. Simon : *Sciences□of□Artificial*, MIT Press,1984

[9] U.M. Fayyad et. Al. : *Advances in Knowledge Discovery and Data Mining*, AAAI/MIT Press,1996

[10] Ishida, T. (ed.): *Community Computing and Support Systems - Social Interaction in Networked Communities.* Springer-Verlag Lecture Notes in Computer Science, Vol. 1519 (1998)

[11] K.A. De Jong: *An Analysis of the Behavior of a Class of Genetic Adaptive Systems*, Doctoral dissertation, University of Michigan,1975

[12] R. L. Riolo: Bucket brigade performance: Long sequence-of-classifiers, genetic algorithms and their applications. *Proceedings of the Second International Conference on Genetic Algorithms*, pp. 184-195, 1987.

Incorporating content-based collaborative filtering in a community support system

Kaname Funakoshi, Koji Kamei, Sen Yoshida, Kazuhiro Kuwabara

NTT Communication Science Laboratories
2-4 Hikaridai, Seika, Soraku, Kyoto 619-0237, Japan
{kf,kamei,yoshida,kuwabara}@cslab.kecl.ntt.co.jp

Abstract. Many systems have been developed to support people in forming communities and communicating with others in the communities. However, community support systems are not only concerned with community formation and communication. Namely, they give people the chance to make use of the communities for personal activities, e.g., they can use other members' knowledge to select information items that are high in quality and conform to the user's individual tastes. Collaborative filtering is a recommendation method that utilizes evaluations given by other users, and is therefore useful for users to obtain desired and relevant information items in a community. In this paper, we present an agent architecture of a community support system with a collaborative filtering method to recommend appropriate information items to users.

1 Introduction

Many community support systems have been developed to help people in forming communities and communicating with others in the communities. However, organizing communities and communicating in communities are only two aspects of community support systems. Socialware, a system which we proposed to support the social activities of network communities, suggests that individuals join communities with various objectives in mind [8]. Accordingly, additional aspects are possible in supporting the activities of people in communities.

In this paper, we focus on information acquisition processes that use communities, and propose an agent architecture and its implementation of a community support system to utilize a community for user's information acquisition activities. In the real world, people use other people's knowledge and opinions to help them select information items, but this is difficult in network societies. In order to solve this difficulty, the proposed system integrates a collaborative filtering mechanism, that draws on the shared knowledge of the community members.

Collaborative filtering is an information search strategy that utilizes evaluations obtained from other users, enabling the user to select information items based on the quality of those items or user's individual tastes [7]. Therefore, collaborative filtering is a beneficial tool for a user for both the utilization of the community and the selection of high quality and relevant items from a large information stream.

S.-T. Yuan and M. Yokoo (Eds.): PRIMA 2001, LNAI 2132, pp. 198-209, 2001.
© Springer-Verlag Berlin Heidelberg 2001

This paper is organized as follows. In Section 2, existing community support systems are briefly discussed. In Section 3, collaborative filtering systems, especially a content-based collaborative filtering method, are introduced, and why and how collaborative filtering should be implemented into community support systems are discussed. In Section 4, the integration of collaborative filtering in the proposed community support system is described. In the remaining section, we describe our conclusions and future work.

2 Community support systems

2.1 Aspects of community support systems

There are many works that aim to support communities on networks [10]. In many cases, network communities rely on communications between members, that is, talking with each other in casual conversation, discussing interests, and exchanging and sharing useful information.

Before communicating in a community, a user wants to understand the surrounding circumstances. That is, the user wants to understand:

- what topics are being discussed,
- what individuals are discussing these topics, and/or
- what other interests these individuals have.

These points have been addressed in some mail user agents and bulletin board systems. Several research works have been conducted on such information that users want to know. For example, Donath proposed the "Visual Who" to visualize the relationship between users' interests [3]. In Visual Who, users are placed on a two-dimensional (2-D) plane according to a similarity of interests. The similarity between two users is calculated based on the number of mailing lists to which they subscribe simultaneously. Users who have similar interests are represented as a cluster of icons, so that users can determine whether a potential community exists. Erickson et al. proposed the Babble system which presents a graphical representation of users and their activities through their "social proxies" [4]. This system shows who is and has been interested in a certain message board. The system can support long-term conversations in existing groups.

In contrast, there is also interesting research focusing on users' personal environments. Besides visualizing person to person relationships, these systems enable people to understand their own information environments. Foner proposed the Yenta system to find clusters of users who are interested in similar topics [5]. The clusters are generated automatically from users' email messages, news articles, and files that the users read and compose. Adar et al. proposed the Haystack systems to make use of a semi-structured database representing knowledge obtained from user activities [1]. According to research on personal information storages, systems will be able to support more user-oriented activities in the future to allow users to share useful information with their neighbors.

2.2   Domain of communities in scope

In this paper, we focus on casual communities on computer networks where the participants exchange and share information on various genres with other users who have similar interests. These communities are sometimes called 'communities of interest' on networks. The community support systems here aim at organizing communities of interest and supporting the communication in each organized community.

From the viewpoint of personal information sharing in communities, we assume the following characteristics of the communities to be discussed.

- The users are not anonymous; they are identified by pseudonyms or their real names. It follows then that all identified users have consistent attitudes.
- The users may know other users' tastes; this does not mean that they should know the tastes of all of the others, but only that they can partially understand the tastes of their acquaintances.
- No authority is recognized by all members; we focus on an information domain where the users' tastes are more important than the quality of items.

Communities with these characteristics are often seen in today's casual network environments, especially with people seeking the communities matching their interests. We now propose a community support system implemented in such a domain of communities.

2.3   Community Organizer

We have been developing a community support system named Community Organizer as a Socialware application [11]. The objective of Community Organizer is to organize communities through the process of information exchange between users. Community Organizer is designed to organize communities based on the following assumptions.

- A cluster of information items (a set of items having similar features) will become the seed of a new community. The cluster will cause people to become aware of the existence of the community and the creators or founders of the items within.
- Allowing people to visualize the growth of the cluster will lead people to consider the growth of the community. When items come out near an existing cluster, this might cause other people to become aware of the activities of the community.

The information items here consist of public messages composed by users and pointers to external information such as World Wide Web (WWW) pages. In the graphical user interface of Community Organizer, each information item is represented as an icon, and the creator of each public message can be identified through the icon.

To visualize communities, the system provides facilities that:

- calculate the similarity between information items having feature vectors with keywords, and
- place the information items on a 2-D plane so that the similarities are reflected.

These facilities provide users with an awareness of the communities; this is the first phase in organizing communities. Each user has an interface to operate the feature vector of the current viewpoint, which corresponds to the center of the plane.

The system provides communication tools for personal messages and public messages. The tools are linked with icons on the 2-D plane to support the communications in the communities. A personal message works as an email article directed towards a specific member, and a public message works as a posting on a bulletin board system. When a user composes a new public message with reference to existing information items, the newly generated message comes out near existing clusters of messages including the referred item and indicates a community activity.

We conducted an empirical experiment on the user interface representations of Community Organizer with the previous implementation of the system [11]. In the experiment, we prepared two versions of a graphical user interface for representing information items to users; one had the 2-D map representations described above, and the other had listing representations like outputs from ordinary information retrieval systems. The experimental results indicated that the 2-D mapped view supported smooth communications among people; at least, the results supported that the representations and implementation of Community Organizer did not disturb the communications of the users.

2.4   The next step in community support

As discussed above, Community Organizer can organize communities and support the communications among their members. However, organizing communities is only a beginning and message exchange is only a part of all community activities. Now we enter the next generation of community support systems, the utilization of communities.

We focus on the information acquisition process of communities so that people can use the communities to obtain their desired and appropriate information in the real world. In other words, we want people to use the knowledge and opinions of others to obtain information effectively. Here we make use of collaborative filtering, a recommendation method that uses the evaluations of other users to select relevant information items. Because it uses the knowledge of other people, the collaborative filtering recommendation method can play an important role in a community support system. That is, a community is an appropriate place to implement collaborative filtering.

Kautz et al. also focused on collaborative filtering and proposed Referral Web, which uses a social network to find individuals and information items effectively [12]. Referral Web uses existing and hidden relationships between people but it does not support people's activities to establish new relationships. Community Organizer is originally designed to support community activities. Therefore, with collaborative filtering, it covers every step in community support, from the creation of a community to the utilization of the community.

3   Collaborative filtering for information sharing in communities

3.1   Collaborative filtering

Information overload is a continuing problem. There is a lot of junk information easily accessible only by keywords (content information) and it is hard to choose information items based on their qualities. As we can see in WWW search engines, although users can select information by the content of WWW pages, they cannot select information by the quality of the information offered. Moreover, users cannot select items according to their particular, individual tastes.

Collaborative filtering, an information filtering system that selects items from the input stream and recommends these items to the user, searches for information items using the evaluations of others [7]. Collaborative filtering enables people to get information items based on their specific tastes, especially in information domains where these tastes are important, for example, casual domains such as music, movies, paintings, etc.

There are several types of collaborative filtering for recommending information items. A basic method is to accumulate the positive evaluations given by anonymous people [14]. In this method, all recommendations are based on the popularity levels of information items. This method is useful in cases where a user's tastes are not critical but there is no way of addressing the user's tastes. Therefore, for domains where individual tastes are important, this method is not appropriate.

To handle a user's particular and individual tastes, we can use the similarities of tendencies in user evaluations. Shardnand and Maes proposed a correlation coefficiency based collaborative filtering method where similarities to other users are calculated based on the information items they evaluated [13]. Herlocker et al. provided an algorithmic framework for collaborative filtering and tested various new algorithms for correlation based methods by simulations on a dataset [9]. In their methods, the correlations between pairs of users are calculated from the items that the users have evaluated. Actually, however, the similarities of tastes between users depend on the genres of the information items involved, that is, even if a couple of members have similar tastes in a certain field, they probably do not have similar tastes in other fields. In a casual community of members discussing various fields, in particular, the contents of the items and the fields that the evaluations cover are important. Delgado et al. used the category information to which an evaluated item belonged, to construct confidence values to other users, although it was not used to select items [2]. We should adopt a type of collaborative filtering that uses genre information both to construct coefficiency or confidence among users and to select items for users.

In some cases, there are authorities in communities and the evaluations given by these authorities are heavily weighted in document selection. This helps users to select items based on absolute qualities and seems to be useful for the recommendation of formal information. However, it does not address communities where the users' tastes are not consistent.

We therefore have three conditions to consider when choosing a collaborative filtering method to implement in a community support system.

- The evaluator of each evaluation is identified. This condition restricts the size of the community involved. It must be small because it is hard to manage evaluations given by a large number of people.
- The contents of all information items are considered. The genre in an evaluation is taken into account.
- No authority is recognized throughout a community. That is, we attach greater importance to the users' tastes than to the absolute qualities of the items.

In the following sections, we introduce a collaborative filtering method that satisfies the conditions above.

3.2 Nakif

We earlier proposed a collaborative filtering method named Nakif, which is a hybrid of content-based filtering and collaborative filtering [6]. The mechanism of Nakif is briefly described below.

Nakif consists of four components: a set of information items, a set of users, a matching facility, and a feedback facility. Each information item has a profile named the "document profile". The document profile for information item h is represented by a pair of a keyword vector $\boldsymbol{kw}_h = (kw_{h1}, \ldots, kw_{hN_{term}})$ and an evaluation vector $\boldsymbol{ev}_h = (ev_{h1}, \ldots, ev_{hN_{user}})$, where N_{term} represents the number of keywords in the whole database, and N_{user} represents the number of users. In the keyword vector, element $kw_{hk} \in \mathcal{R}$ represents the rates at which keyword k is contained in item h. In the evaluation vector, element ev_{hj} represents the evaluation value by user j to item h, where $ev_{hj} \in \{good, bad, \epsilon\}$ denotes the evaluation values for the positive, negative, and neutral evaluations of $good > \epsilon > bad$.[1] Each user has a profile named the "user profile". The user profile for user i is represented by an $N_{user} \times N_{term}$ matrix W^i, where each element $w^i_{jk} \in \mathcal{R}$ represents the confidence in the evaluation given by another user j for keyword k.

Matching is a facility that ranks information items to match the user's preferences and outputs an ordered list, which is provided to the user as a list of recommendations. The items are ranked according to their relevances to the user

---

[1] Although a five-point (or more precise) scale can be used to evaluate items, we use a three-point scale because of the ease in inputting evaluations.

and calculated as follows:

$$match(W^i, \langle \boldsymbol{kw}_h, \boldsymbol{ev}_h \rangle) = \sum_j^{N_{user}} \sum_k^{N_{term}} w_{jk}^i \, ev_{hj} \, kw_{hk} \qquad (1)$$

This function calculates the relevance of information item h to user i. By the function, an item that is evaluated by another member (evaluator) whose evaluations are regarded as reliable (that has a higher value in the user profile) on the keywords of the item has a higher relevance.

When a user gives an evaluation, the document profile and the user profile are modified in the feedback phase. The feedback consists of two parts: modification of the document profile and modification of the user profile. The document profile is easily modified when an evaluation is received. When user i gives an evaluation e_{hi} to information item h, the evaluation vector ev_h of the document profile is modified as $ev_{hi} \leftarrow e_{hi}$.

After the document profile is modified, the user profile is modified by the feedback function as follows:

$$W^{i'} = W^i + ev_{hi} \; \delta \; \boldsymbol{ev}_h^t \boldsymbol{kw}_h \qquad (2)$$

where δ is a constant to control the speed of the feedback. This function works to modify the confidence values of those users who have already evaluated the information item and the information item's keywords.

We conducted a simulation experiment to investigate the performance of Nakif on a set of virtual users and a set of real information items. As a result of the experiment, we could see that Nakif performs more detailed selections of information items [6].

3.3   Collaborative filtering to community support systems

As a community support system, the Nakif collaborative filtering method satisfies the conditions described in section 3.1 and is a useful tool for implementation in community support systems. On the other hand, Nakif uses detailed information on evaluations to provide precise recommendations, so it is desirable for it to be implemented in a domain that satisfies these conditions. We have implemented Nakif as an attachment to the community support system Community Organizer.

4   Integration of Community Organizer

4.1   Overall architecture

Community Organizer was constructed as a system for users to keep all information in their own repositories for the private use of the information. The objective of these repositories is to achieve collaboration in processing public items

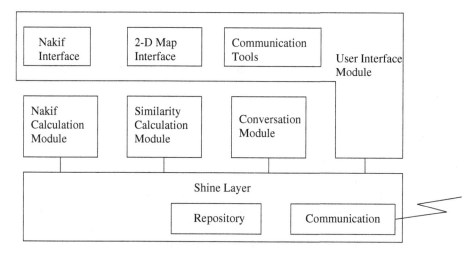

Fig. 1. User agent architecture of Community Organizer with the integration of Nakif collaborative filtering in the Shine multiagent framework. Inside an agent, every two modules communicate through the Shine layer

for each user's private use. Accordingly, we designed Community Organizer as a multiagent system.

We implemented Community Organizer on a multiagent-based Socialware framework called Shine [15]. Shine provides communication and repository facilities, which are commonly used by agents. With Community Organizer, Shine manages all inter-agent communications and the user repositories storing the various user information. We implemented the Nakif-embedded Community Organizer on Shine, using a communication service for sharing evaluation information and using user repositories for storing user profiles and document profiles.

Figure 1 shows the architecture of the Nakif-embedded Community Organizer in the Shine agent framework. The system consists of five modules: user interface module, Nakif calculation module, similarity calculation module, conversation module, and the Shine layer. The Nakif module and the user interface module are discussed in detail in sections 4.2 and 4.3. The similarity calculation module and the conversation module were implemented in the former version of Community Organizer. The similarity calculation module calculates the similarities between the feature vectors of information items. The conversation module manages the communication tools that are used by the users of Community Organizer.

The Shine layer serves the communication and user repository facilities to the application modules. For the implementation of Nakif, the communication component additionally communicates the evaluation information given by other users and the metadata of information items, including the location and the document profile of an item. The repository includes the user profile and the metadata of information items. The user profile and the document profile are used in the Nakif calculation and the location information is used in the recommendation of the item to the user.

Every two modules inside an agent communicate through the Shine layer. For example, when the Nakif module calculates the score of an information item, it sends the result to the Shine layer, and the user interface module is then invoked by the Shine layer to reflect the result.

4.2   Nakif integration

The Nakif module consists of two components: *matching component* and *feedback component*. The matching component reads the user profile and the document profile from the repository and calculates the relevance to the user for each information item by the matching function in equation (1). Then, an ordered list of information items that is ranked by the calculated relevance is created. The produced results, which will be used in the recommendation, are transmitted to the user interface module through the Shine layer as described above.

The feedback component modifies the user profile after getting the user's evaluation of an information item. Each evaluation has a value of *good* for a positive evaluation or *bad* for a negative evaluation. The detailed feedback process is as follows: after each evaluation information is given by the user interface module, the feedback module reads the evaluation information, the user profile, and the document profile of the item from the repository and modifies the user profile by the feedback function in equation (2).

In naive Nakif, the number of users N_{user} and the number of genres N_{term} are predefined and the modification method is not supported. Although there is no facility to change the size of the user profile yet, it is not difficult to implement a size modification procedure into Nakif modules.

Other functions that Nakif requires, such as a function to enable communications with other user agents, and functions to manage and store the user profile and document profile, are expected to be implemented as services of the Shine layer.

4.3   User interface of Community Organizer

The user interface module of Community Organizer provides a graphical interface, as shown in Figure 2, to represent community awareness to its users. The user interface provides mainly four types of windows: a map window, keyword vector window, message window, and profile window. The map window produces a 2-D plane on which the information items are placed according to the relevance (or similarity) between their keyword vectors. The keyword vector window consists of a keyword-value controller to represent the keyword vector of each user's viewpoint. In this window, a user can operate the feature vector (keyword-value pairs) of his/her viewpoint, and the 2-D plane of the map window immediately reflects the modification of the viewpoint. The message window presents the content of each public message and works as a communication tool. The profile window presents the document profile of each information item. This window

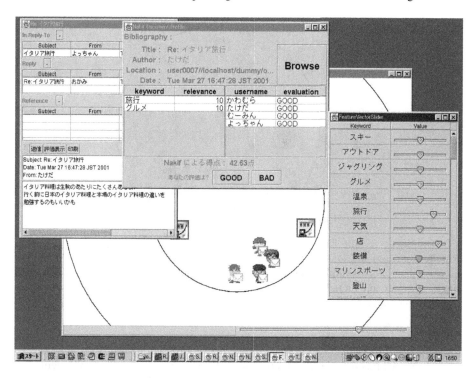

Fig. 2. Graphical user interface of Community Organizer with Nakif integration. The windows from the right at the front are a message window, a profile window, and a vector window. In the back is a map window with icons indicating information items (public messages with human icons and WWW pages with square icons)

consists of keyword-value pairs and user-evaluation pairs for use in collaborative recommendation, and input buttons "GOOD" and "BAD" for user evaluation.

The user interface is managed by the user interface module in the Community Organizer agent. The user interface has three components, i.e., a 2-D map interface, communication tools, and a Nakif interface. The 2-D map interface receives the similarity between every two items and places the icons of the items on the 2-D plane of the map window. The communication tools provide messaging services and manage the inputs and outputs of the message window. The Nakif interface receives an ordered list of items according to the relevance to a user and presents a recommendation to the user on the 2-D plane.

Information items of high relevance in the Nakif collaborative filtering are recommended. Figure 3 shows how information items are recommended in Community Organizer. "Star marks" are used to represent the collaborative recommendations. The number of star marks varies from zero (not recommended) to three (highly recommended). Here, information items represented by icons with star marks to the upper right indicate high recommendations.

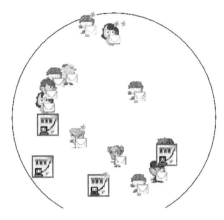

Fig. 3. Recommendations in Community Organizer marked with star marks on the map window. For example, the upper most icon (public message) is marked with a single star (recommended), and the icon to the right of it is marked with two stars (more recommended)

The Nakif interface also manages each user's input of evaluations. The evaluations are produced by the "GOOD" and "BAD" buttons in the profile window. Once an evaluation is given, it is transmitted to the Shine layer, invoking the feedback phase of the collaborative filtering.

5   Conclusions and future work

In this paper, we presented the implementation of a collaborative filtering method in a community support system.

The communities for which Community Organizer is appropriate have relatively small number of users, because all members of a community need to be able to identify each other, that is, members must know each other. Therefore, the computation power is not a critical problem although the calculation time in Nakif increases by the order of $N_{user} \times N_{term}$ for each user.

Several problems remain and require further discussion, especially the system evaluations and privacy issues. The system should be executed by real users for evaluation purposes. The benefit of implementing collaborative filtering into a community support system, or the benefit of a community support system with a collaborative filtering facility, has not been proven through actual use. Tests should be conducted on a casual community of interest, where all users are identified and no authority is present.

We must also consider privacy issues. In the current implementation, the evaluation information of others, the identity of each evaluator, and how each evaluation is conducted, are shown to all users. However, there are many cases where these types of information should not be shown because evaluation information generally reflects the private and personal thoughts and the principles of the evaluator. Deciding whether or not evaluations should be presented according to the characteristics of the community is also a future issue.

References

1. E. Adar, D. Kargar and L. A. Stein. Haystack: per-user information environments. *Proc. of the 8th Int'l Conf. on Information Knowledge Management*, 1999, 413–422.
2. J. Delgado, N. Ishii and T. Ura. Content-based collaborative information filtering: actively learning to classify and recommend documents. *Cooperative information agents II: 2nd Int'l Workshop, CIA '98 Proceedings*, Springer-Verlag, 1999, 206–215.
3. J. S. Donath. Visual Who: Animating the affinities and activities of an electronic community. *Proc. of ACM Multimedia '95*, 1995, 99–107.
4. T. Erickson, D. N. Smith, W. A. Kellogg, M. Laff, J. T. Richards and E. Bradner. Socially Translucent Systems: Social Proxies, Persistent Conversation, and the Design of "Babble". *Proc. of ACM CHI '99 Conf. on Human Factors in Computing Systems*, 1999, 72–79.
5. L. N. Foner. A multi-agent referral system for matchmaking. *Proc. of the 1st Int'l Conf. and Exhibition on the Practical Application of Intelligent Agents and Multi-Agent Technology*, 1999.
6. K. Funakoshi and T. Ohguro A content-based collaborative recommender system with detailed use of evaluations. *Proc. of 4th Int'l Conf. on Knowledge-based Intelligent Systems & Allied Technologies (KES2000)*, 2000, 253–256.
7. D. Goldberg, D. Nichols, B. M. Oki and D. Terry. Using collaborative filtering to weave an information Tapestry. *Comm. ACM*, **35**(12), 1992, 61–70.
8. F. Hattori, T. Ohguro, M. Yokoo, S. Matsubara and S. Yoshida. Socialware: multiagent systems for supporting network communities. *Comm. ACM*, **42**(3), 1999, 55–61.
9. J. Herlocker, J. Konstan, A. Borchers and J. Riedl. An algorithmic framework for performing collaborative filtering. *Proc. of 22nd Annual Int'l ACM SIGIR Conf. (SIGIR'99)*, 1999, 230–237.
10. T. Ishida ed. *Community computing: collaboration over global information*. John Wiley & Sons, 1998.
11. K. Kamei, E. Jettmar, K. Fujita, S. Yoshida and K. Kuwabara. Community Organizer: supporting the formation of network communities through spatial representation. *The 2001 Symposium on Applications and the Internet (SAINT 2001)*, 2001, 207–214.
12. H. Kautz, B. Selman and M. Shah. Referral Web: combining social networks and collaborative filtering. *Comm. ACM*, **40**(3), 1997, 63–65.
13. U. Shardnand and P. Maes. Social information filtering: algorithms for automating "word of mouth". *Proc. of ACM CHI '95 Conf. on Human Factors in Computing Systems*, 1995, 210–217.
14. L. Terveen, W. Hill, B. Amento, D. McDonald and J. Creter. Phoaks: a system for sharing recommendations. *Comm. ACM*, **40**(3), 1997, 59–62.
15. S. Yoshida, K. Kamei, T. Ohguro, K. Kuwabara and K. Funakoshi. Building a network community support system on the multi-agent platform Shine. *Design and Applications of Intelligent Agents: Proc. of 3rd Pacific Rim Int'l Workshop on Multi-Agents (PRIMA2000)*, Springer-Verlag, 2000, 88-100.

A Personal Agent for Bookmark Classification

In-Cheol Kim

Dept. of Computer Science, Kyonggi University
San94-6, Yiui-Dong, Paldal-Gu, Suwon, 442-760, Korea
kic@kuic.kyonggi.ac.kr

Abstract. The World Wide Web has become a source of enormous amount of information. Most web browsers feature bookmarking facilities as a means to harness the vast web space. Users record the URLs of the sites for future visits with bookmarks, but the organization and maintenance of the bookmark file cost users time and cognitive work. A personal agent is an automated program to which users can delegate often tedious or sophisticated tasks. We implemented a learning agent called BClassifier using Naive Bayesian learning method and present the findings in this paper.

1   Introduction

The diffusion of high performance personal computers and the development of communication networks have accelerated the growth of information available on the Internet.. In particular, the World Wide Web has become one of the major services provided through Internet. When searching the vast web space, users use bookmarking facilities to record the sites of interests encountered during the course of navigation. Depending on the browser, this is called either a Bookmark or Favorites.

One of the typical problems arising from bookmarking is that the list of bookmarks, or URLs, lose coherent organization when the list becomes too lengthy, thus ceasing to function as a practical finding aid. In order to maintain the bookmark file in an efficient, organized manner, the user has to classify all the bookmarks newly added to the file, and update the folders. The goal of this study is to implement and test an agent, Bclassifier, which, using machine learning techniques, acquires the knowledge needed for classifying the HTML documents.

Bclassifier analyses the contents of the web documents retrieved from the URLs which are classified under bookmark folders. Thus, the chief source for the training examples for the Bclassifier are the documents explicitly marked by the user. Additionally, the web pages found under categories of Yahoo service are collected and included in the training examples for the purpose of diversifying the subject categories to be represented, and the training examples for these categories as well. The system employs naive Bayesian learning technique which is well-tested, probability-based categorizing technique using supervised learning. In the concluding sections, the

S.-T. Yuan and M. Yokoo (Eds.): PRIMA 2001, LNAI 2132, pp. 210-221, 2001.
© Springer-Verlag Berlin Heidelberg 2001

outcome of this experimentation is outlined and evaluated. A comparison of naïve Bayesian learning method alongside other classifying schemes such as k-Nearest Neighbor and TFIDF is also presented.

2 Techniques for Document Classification

This section presents a brief description of the underlying techniques for learning employed by our personal agent. The three algorithms including naïve Bayesian, k-NN, and TFIDF methods are considered in this study.

2.1 Naïve Bayesian Method

The Bayesian classifier uses a probabilistic method for classification. It is based on Bayesian theorem which can be used to determine the probability that an example belongs to a certain class given a priori probability.[11] The naïve Bayesian method is applied when the attribute values of element w_t that belongs to a class c_j are assumed to be independent from all other possible values. This can be expressed as:

$$p(w_1, w_2, \ldots w_{|v|} \mid c_j) = \prod_{t=1}^{|v|} p(w_t \mid c_j)$$

Thus, the conditional probability for a document d to belong to class c_j can be computed using formula (1).

$$P(d \mid c_j) = \prod_{t=1}^{n} (B_t P(w_t \mid c_j) + (1 - B_t)(1 - P(w_t \mid c_j))) \quad (1)$$

where

$\quad B_t \qquad$: binary coefficient of term w_t in document d

$\qquad\qquad$ (1 if term w_t is present in d , otherwise, 0)

$\quad P(w_t \mid c_j)$: the probability that term w_t falls into class c_j

The conditional probability that a document belongs to the class is computed for each class using the formula (1), and the document is assigned to the class with the highest probability. [8]

2.2 k-NN Algorithm

The k-NN (k-Nearest Neighbor) algorithm is another major text classification method. This method measures the similarity or distance between document Y and each example X stored in the training set using formula (2). Then k most analogous examples are selected and the document Y is assigned to the class that the majority of these k examples belong to.

$$ D_{xy} = \sqrt{\sum_{i=1}^{n} (X_i - Y_i)^2} \tag{2} $$

The i in formula (2) denotes classes and n the number of classes. Value k is determined prior to experimentation using the Cross Validation technique for the purpose of optimizing the performance of the k-NN method. When k equals 1 (k=1), the methods is simply called the NN method.[8][4]

2.3   TFIDF Algorithm

To be classified with TFIDF methods, a document needs to be represented as a vector of selected terms featuring the contents of the documents. Term weights are attached with all the features and the computation of weights is based on frequencies of term occurrences within the document and in the whole collection. TF(term frequency) is the number of occurrences of a term in a document, and IDF(inverse document frequency), penalizes the terms that appear frequently outside of a document. This reflects empirical observations that when the occurrence of a term is concentrated within a document, the term is more likely to have discriminating value than the ones found across the documents. The weight W_i of a term w_i is the product of TF_i and IDF_i [8].

$$ W_i = TF_i \cdot IDF_i \tag{3} $$

W_i : term weight
TF_i : within-document term frequency
IDF_i : inverse document frequency

For the task of classification, a prototype-vector for a class is formulated using the average of TF-IDF vectors of all examples of one class. In order to determine the class for a new document, the system measures the similarity between the document and the class prototype. The document is assigned to the class that shows the smallest value, or angle

3   Related Works

Personal WebWatcher [7] is an agent developed by a team of researchers at Carnegie Mellon University. The system monitors the user's behavior throughout navigation and compiles a user profile by analyzing the web pages the user shows interest in. Having learned what might be pertinent to the user's preference, the system filters the web sites linked from the web page under browsing and dynamically recommends the sites judged to be interesting to the user. InfoFinder [3] produced by Anderson Consulting Co. is another agent system that finds the web documents of interest online for the user by matching web documents against the user profile. Maxims, built at MIT Media Lab, is an assistant agent which learns to categorize email messages on behalf of the user by prioritizing, deleting, sorting and forwarding the email messages. Ringo, which recommends items for entertainment, and NetT, which categorizes news articles, are also recognized as classifying agent systems.[1]

4   System Architecture

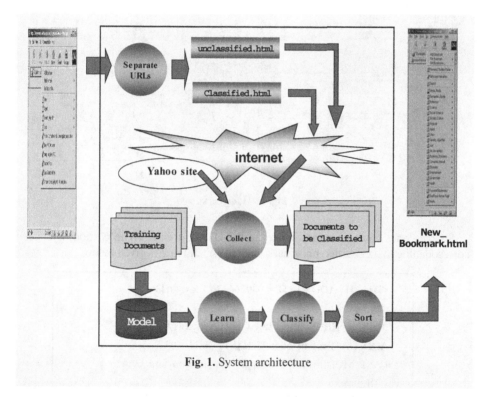

Fig. 1. System architecture

Fig .1 depicts the system architecture of the classifier. Classifying task starts with the bookmark file (bookmark.html), separating the set of URLs classified by the user (classified.html) from the ones simply marked with no label (unclassfied.html). The web documents linked from these two sets of URLS are fetched and stored separately on the local machine.   The web documents found under 14 directories of Yahoo service also are collected.   The documents from classified URLs at bookmarks and Yahoo directories are utilized as training examples, and the documents from unclassified set of URLs are put into the test collection. The classifier assigns the class to the documents on the basis of knowledge acquired through training examples. In the final phase, the newly classified bookmarks are sorted creating a new bookmark file. (new_bookmark.html)

4.1   Separation of the Bookmarks

All the bookmarks listed in the bookmark file on a web browser reflect the user's interest regardless of whether they are assigned to the folders or not. Fig. 2 shows the bookmarks on Navigator browser prior to classifying (a) and the bookmark file's source code (b).

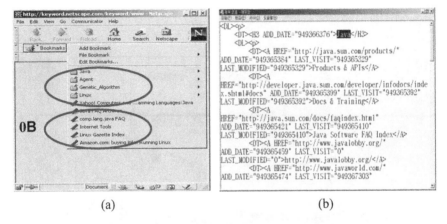

(a)   (b)

Fig. 2. Bookmarks

Source codes contains tagged marks in the HTML format. The portion of codes corresponding to a classified bookmark marked (A) in Fig.2 is given below.

```
<DT><H3 ADD_DATE="949366376">Java</H3>
<DL><p>
<DT><A HREF=http://www.javalobby.org/
ADD_DATE="949365459" LAST_VISIT="0"
LAST_MODIFIED="0">http://www.javalobby.org/</A>
</DL><p>
```

This source code indicates that the URL http://www.javalobby.org falls under the class "Java" by posting tags for heading and <DL>

```
<DT><A HREF=http://www-net.com/java/faq/
ADD_DATE="949367554" LAST_VISIT="949367592"
LAST_MODIFIED="949367523">Java FAQ Archives</A>
```

Naturally, the source codes for unlabeled bookmark (B) http://www-net.com/java/faq/ carries the URL only with no specific name of folder or class. Thereby the classified and unclassified sets of bookmarks can be separated by the delimiter </DL><P> as appearing in the source codes of the bookmark file.

4.2   Collecting Web Documents

For the system in this study, training examples as well as testing data are collected from the Internet. The system parses classified.html and extracts the URLs that are bookmarked and classified by the user. Training examples are fetched from these URLs and stored in the local machine in accordance with the categories marked by the user

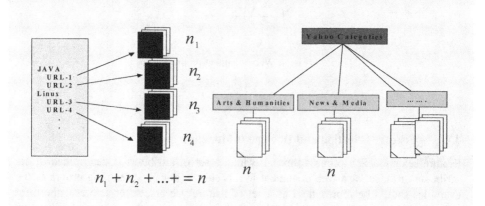

Fig. 3. Collecting web documents

In order to diversify the representation of categories for classification and also to secure unbiased training examples, the documents listed under 14 top categories of Yahoo are collected automatically. When fetching the document, the documents linked from these top-level sites are brought into the local machine to complement the data and to secure sufficient amount of training examples. The training examples obtained from Yahoo categories are stored under the folders bearing their category labels.

4.3   Document Preprocessing

In order to extract features that are most informative of the contents of the web documents to be classified, the documents need to be processed. Consisting of several phases, the preprocessing of text contributes to refinement of training examples and thereby to the confidence level of this experimentation. First, all the tags from the

HTML documents are removed. Secondly, for the purpose of filtering out, terms are matched against a stop word list which enumerates worthless words with a very low discrimination value. Furthermore, through a stemming process, morphological variants of terms are minimized, which in turn reduces the size of unique terms. Fig. 4 describes the preprocessing procedures for web documents.

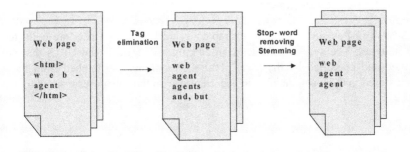

Fig. 4. Web document preprocessing

4.4   Feature Selection and Document Modeling

Feature selection is a process through which a set of attributes is determined to describe an instance, or a web document in this study. For most learning programs the examples should be represented as a set of feature vectors. After selecting the most informative words, the system models the documents as the vector of binary or weighted attributes. For this experimentation, the significance of terms are determined on the basis of information gain. Information gain is a measure of the statistical property indicating the effectiveness of a feature in classifying the training examples. Based on information theory, it is calculated by the expected reduction in entropy resulting from categorizing the examples using this particular feature. [6]

$$V = \{w_1, w_2, w_3, \ldots, w_n\} \tag{4}$$

$$InfoGain(w_i) = P(w_i) \sum_j P(c_j \mid w_i) \log \frac{P(c_j \mid w_i)}{P(c_j)} \tag{5}$$

$$+ P(\bar{w_i}) \sum_j P(c_j \mid \bar{w_i}) \log \frac{P(c_j \mid \bar{w_i})}{P(c_j)}$$

After the information gain for each attribute is computed with the formula (4) and (5), L terms of the largest value from the set of unique words (V) are determined as features.

$$K = \{w_1, w_2, w_3, ..., w_L\} \quad , \quad K \subset V \tag{6}$$

In order to be applied to naïve Bayesian classifier, each web document is modeled as the binary vector of L features as given below. 1 in the vector of binary attributes for a document denotes the presence of the feature in the document, and the opposite case is represented as 0.

$$d_i = (1, 0, 1, ..., 1) \tag{7}$$

4.5   Learning and Classification

The agent system of our experimentation employs the naive Bayesian learning algorithm which is well-tested and known to be the most competitive learning method among text classifiers. The naïve Bayesian classifier is a supervised learning method that requires a large number of training data. In formula (8), C denotes the set of classes.

$$C = \{c_1, c_2, c_3, ... c_k\} \tag{8}$$

The naïve Bayesian classifer computes the conditional probability for a document d_i to belong to each class c_l as formula (9).

$$\rho(d_i) = \{P(d_i \mid c_1), P(d_i \mid c_2), P(d_i \mid c_3), ..., P(d_i \mid c_k)\} \tag{9}$$

The document to be classified is assigned to the class for which the result of computation shows the highest probability according to formulas (10) and (11)

$$P(d_i \mid c_j) = \max_{c_t \in C}\{P(d_i \mid c_t)\} \tag{10}$$

$$C(d_i) = c_j, \quad if \quad P(d_i \mid c_j) \geq T \tag{11}$$

$$C(d_i) = c_{user-defined}, \quad otherwise$$

But unless the probability exceeds a threshold T, the classification is not reliable in terms of preciseness and confidence of the outcome. The system does not assign any category for such documents, leaving the case to the judgment of the user. Besides the naïve Bayesian method, the K-NN method and TFIDF algorithm are also implemented and can be used selectively.

4.6   Sorting and Creation of a New Bookmark File

When the system finishes learning, the folders for 14 categories from the Yahoo service are created and listed in addition to the folders containing user-classified. The unclassified bookmarks are now assigned by the system to the corresponding folder according to the knowledge acquired by the system through learning. The result is shown in the left diagram of Fig. 5. The URLs are sorted by their labels that will appear as folders for bookmarks on the browser.

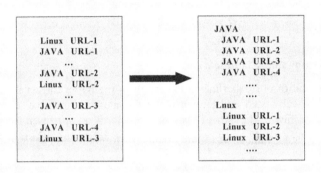

Fig. 5. Sorting

5   System Implementation

The system is implemented in the computer equipped with 300Mhz Pentium II processor, 128M RAM and Linux operating system. The classifiers for this experimentation are implemented in C programming language and the user interface of BClassifier is programmed in Java language.

Shown in Fig. 6 is the user interface when the bookmark classifier is executed. The window for user interface on the upper left corner of Fig. 6 shows the menus for users and the screen when the system is in use. Two windows below the user interface show the position of a bookmark file, folders, a window for General Setting, and a window for Advanced Settings where the user can designate machine learning method, set the number of training examples for each class, and set the threshold. On the right of Fig. 6 is the agent which shows the result of classifying and sorting the bookmarks on Netscape browser.

6   Experimental Evaluation

In this section, we analyze the outcome of classification performed by BClassifier. The tasks of this personal agent for bookmark classification consist of assigning predefined categories to the unclassified documents based on the subject of the docu

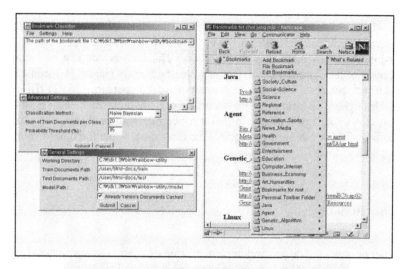

Fig. 6. BClassifier

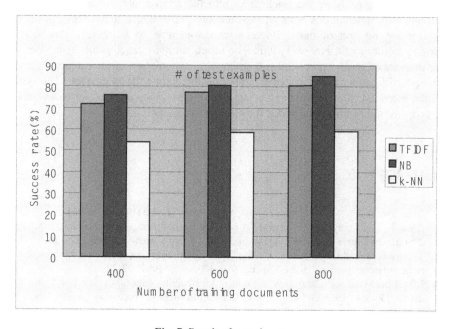

Fig. 7. Result of experiments

ment. 50 documents for each of 14 Yahoo directories were used as training data totaling 700 documents. The training starts with 10 initial training examples, and the number of the examples increases by increments of 10 for every repetition. The performance of the classifier is shown in Fig. 7, depicting the precision rates of three document classification methods. These methods include nave Bayesian, TFIDF, and k-NN techniques.

As a whole, BClassifier proved to be fairly efficient in that two of the three algorithms recorded the success rates all over 70% in three different settings of experiments while the k-NN method is an exception. The success rate is a measure of the effectiveness of the classifier by giving the ratio of correctly classified documents over the total test documents. The naïve Bayesian method outperforms the TFIDF roughly by 5%. Throughout five times of the recursive executions in each settings, the naïve Bayesian shows the least variance in performance rates. In predicting the classes for the documents, the k-NN method requires the most time, while the other two methods are roughly the same.

7   Conclusions

This paper presents the design and implementation of a personal agent called BClassifier. The aim of the system is to assist the user in maintaining the bookmark file by automatically classifying the bookmarks into the appropriate topics for future use. Through experimentations with BClassifier, the performance measures confirm that the learning method of naïve Bayesian is comparable to other text classification learning methods of k-NN or TFIDF. The future study to develop the BClassifer further in terms of greater precision will stress on differentiation of the categories, establishing the hierarchical and associative relationship among the categories. The system will be extended to incorporate an unsupervised classifying method for cases outside the scope of the examples provided for training for each class..

References

1.   Bradshaw Jeffrey M., Software Agent. AAAI Press/The MIT Press. (1995).
2.   Chen, L. and K. Sycara, "*WebMate*: A personal agent for browsing and searching." Proc. 2nd Int. Conf. on Autonomous Agents and Multi-Agent Systems, (1998) 132-139.
3.   Krulwich, B. and C. Burkey. "The InfoFinder agent: Learning user interests through heuristic phrase extraction," IEEE Experts, Vol. 12, No.5, (1997) 22-27.
4.   Lim, Yoon-Taik and Choong-Wha Yoon, "An Evolving Algorithm Based on Cross Validation." Proc of 1999 Fall Conference, Korean Information Processing Society, Vol.6, No. 1. (1999)
5.   McCallum, A. and K. Nigam, "A Comparison of Event Models for Naïve Bayes Text Classification" , AAAI-98 Workshop on Learning for Text Categorization, (1998).
6.   Mladenic. Dunja and Marko Grobelnik, "Feature selection for classification based on text hierarchy". In Conference on Automated Learning and Discovery, Proc. of CONALD_98, (1998).
7.   Mladenic, D., "Personal WebWatcher: Design and Implementation." Technical Report IJS-DP-7472, School of Computer Science, Carnegie-Mellon University, Pittsburgh, USA, (1996).
8.   Mitchell, Tom M., Machine Learning, McGraw-Hill, (1997).

9. Pazzani, M. and D. Billsus, "Learning and revising user profiles: The identification of interesting Web sites", Machine Learning, Vol. 27, No.3, (1997) 313-331.
10. Stuart Russell and Peter Norvig, Artificial Intelligence: A Modern Approach. Prentice Hall, (1995).
11. Zhang, Byoung-Tak, "Learning Agents", Communications of Korea Information Science Society, Vol. 18, No.5, (2000) 26-35.

Scalable Workflow System Model Based on Mobile Agents

Jeong-Joon Yoo[1], Doheon Lee[2], Young-Ho Suh[3] and Dong-Ik Lee[1]

[1]Department of Info. and Comm. Kwang-Ju Institute of Science and Technology
1 Oryong-Dong Buk-Gu Kwangju, Korea (Republic of)
[2]Department of Computer Science, Chonnam National University
300 Yongbong-Dong Buk-Gu Kwangju, Korea (Republic of)
[3]Internet Service Department, Electronics and Telecommunications Research Institute
161 Kajong-Dong Yusong-Gu, Korea (Republic of)
{jjyoo,dilee}@kjist.ac.kr, dhlee@dbcore.Chonnam.ac.kr
yhsuh@etri.re.kr

Abstract. A workflow system defines, creates and manages the execution of business workflows with workflow engines, which interpret workflow definitions, and interact with task performers. As most of non-trivial organizations have massive amount of workflows to process simultaneously, there is ever-increasing demands for better performance and scalability of workflow systems. This paper proposes a workflow system model based on mobile agents, so called *Maximal Sequence model*, as an alternative to conventional RPC-based and previous mobile agent-based (DartFlow) models. The proposed model segments a workflow definition into blocks, and assigning each of them to a mobile agent. We also construct three stochastic Petri net models of conventional RPC-based, DartFlow, and the Maximal Sequence model-based workflow systems to compare their performance and scalability. The stochastic Petri-net simulation results show that the proposed model outperforms the previous ones as well as comes up with better scalability when the numbers of workflow tasks and concurrent workflows are relatively large.

1 Introduction

A workflow is defined as the computerized facilitation or automation of a business process [1]. It is composed of tasks, each of which corresponds to a unit business task or another business (sub-) process. A workflow system defines, creates and manages the execution of workflow processes with one or more workflow engines, which interpret workflow definitions, and interact with task performers [1]. It is common for an actual workflow system to maintain and control hundreds of workflow definitions and tens of thousands workflow processes simultaneously.

We can regard an execution of a workflow process as repetition of three basic steps such that (i) scheduling tasks, (ii) assigning tasks, and (iii) obtaining results until the entire workflow process completes. Workflow engines decide which tasks to perform in the scheduling step. They communicate with task performers to assign tasks in the assignment step. After completing the assigned tasks, the task performers communicate with the workflow engines to report the results.

Most of existing workflow systems such as FlowMark [2], Action WorkFlow [3], FloWare [4], and Exotica/FMQM [5] adopt RPC model-based communications [6] between workflow engines and task performers. Due to the inherent characteristics of

S.-T. Yuan and M. Yokoo (Eds.): PRIMA 2001, LNAI 2132, pp. 222-236, 2001.

the RPC model, workflow engines have to schedule the next tasks for all ongoing workflow processes, and two step-communications for assigning tasks and obtaining results are essential. As the number of workflow processes increases, the scheduling overhead given to workflow engines degrades the system performance significantly. In addition, the two step-communications also impose significant overload on the network bandwidth.

To address this limited scalability, mobile agents have been considered as an alternative to the RPC model-based architecture recently [7]. A mobile agent is a software program that can migrate over a network under its own control and acts on behalf of a user or another entity [8]. Since mobile agents carry the workflow definitions by themselves, they can decide the next tasks to perform without help of workflow engines. Furthermore, workflow engines do not have to communicate with task performers to assign tasks as mobile agents migrate to proper task performers autonomously. It implies that the mobile agents residing in task performers can take loads of scheduling and assigning tasks off the workflow engines.

However, since a mobile agent contains the entire workflow definition, the physical size is apt to be much larger than a simple RPC message. Consequently, the migration of mobile agents over the network causes another communication overhead between workflow engines and tasks performers as well as between task performers.

In this paper, we propose to segment a workflow definition into blocks, and assigning each of them to a mobile agent. The segmentation is called Maximal Sequence model since it groups tasks that can be executed sequentially to the maximal extent. We also build stochastic Petri-net models for three architectural alternatives such that the RPC model, the previous mobile agent model, and the proposed Maximal Sequence model to compare their performance and scalability.

The rest of this paper is organized as follows; Section 2 briefly explains the RPC model and the previous mobile agent model. Section 3 proposes a new approach called Maximal Sequence model along with an illustrative comparison with the previous models. Section 4 presents the simulation results to show the proposed model comes up with better performance and scalability in massive workflow environments.

2 Previous Workflow Systems

In this section, we briefly describe the RPC model and the previous mobile agent model in the perspective of three basic steps (scheduling, assigning tasks, and obtaining results) of a workflow execution.

2.1 RPC model-based Workflow Systems

Fig. 1 depicts workflow executions in RPC model-based workflow systems. A workflow engine decides which tasks to perform in the scheduling step. Assuming that the workflow definition indicates the corresponding task performer is A, the workflow engine communicates with A to assign a task in the assignment step. After completing the assigned task, task performer A communicates with the workflow

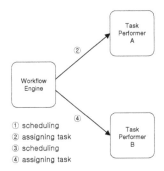

① scheduling
② assigning task
③ scheduling
④ assigning task

Fig. 1. RPC model-based workflow execution

engine to report the result. To decide the next task, the workflow engine again performs the scheduling step. Assuming that the workflow definition indicates the corresponding task performer is *B*, the workflow engine communicates with *B* to assign a task. The entire workflow is executed in this way until the final task is completed.

A fact worthy of note is that the workflow engine solely takes charge of scheduling and assigning tasks. As the number of workflow processes increases, the computational overhead imposed to the workflow engine becomes excessive. Furthermore, communication overhead is also concentrated to the workflow engine. Though distributed versions of RPC model based-architectures are introduced to break up this centralized overhead, the inherent characteristics of the RPC model place limitation in scalability of workflow systems. To overcome this limitation mobile agents-based workflow systems have been considered.

2.2 Mobile Agent-based Workflow Systems

There are some benefits casting mobile agents into workflow systems as follows;
- no need to consult the central workflow engine at every step and hence workloads being imposed on engines can be reduced,
- intelligent routing can be implemented efficiently,
- support thin clients, and
- naturally support heterogeneous environment.

A workflow system may include thin clients such as laptops and PDAs which are connected through unreliable networks. A mobile agent works well in this environment, since network connection is not necessary during the computation. Workflow system environment is fundamentally heterogeneous, often from both hardware and software perspectives. Because mobile agents are generally platform independent, they naturally support heterogeneous workflow system environment. Although there are many advantages of mobile agents in workflow systems, an equivalent solution can be found that does not require mobile agents. Whereas each individual advantage can be addressed in some manners including multi-agent [9][10], a mobile agent framework simply addresses all of them at once.

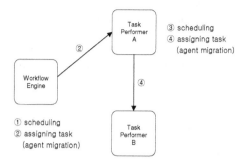

Fig. 2. Mobile agents-based workflow execution

DartFlow, as an example, uses mobile agents for highly scalable workflow systems. Since the mobile agent carries the workflow definition by itself, it can decide the next tasks to perform without help of workflow engines as shown in Fig. 2. In this figure, a workflow engine creates a mobile agent, which contains the entire workflow definition. The workflow engine sends the mobile agent to a task performer (*A* in Fig. 2) that is in charge of the first task of the workflow. After the mobile agent completes the first task, it reports the result to the workflow engine; decides which task performer is in charge of the next task; and migrates to the task performer (*B* in Fig. 2). This migration continues until the entire workflow completes. According to the workflow definition, a mobile agent duplicates and migrates to multiple task performers to execute parallel tasks.

The primary difference of this model to the RPC model is that the scheduling and assigning tasks are not in charge of workflow engines anymore. It implies that the computational overhead is distributed among workflow engines and task performers. In addition, the communication overhead for assigning tasks is also distributed.

Although this mobile agent-based model may seem to resolve the scalability limitation of the RPC model, it has a hidden cost. Since a mobile agent contains the entire workflow definition, the physical size is apt to be much larger than a simple RPC message. Consequently, the migration of mobile agents over the network introduces another communication overhead between workflow engines and task performers as well as between task performers.

3 Maximal Sequence Model

To reduce the communication overhead to move entire workflow definition, we propose to segment a workflow definition into blocks, and assigning each of them to a mobile agent. The segmentation is called Maximal Sequence model since it groups tasks that can be executed sequentially to the maximal extent.

Definition 1. (*Maximal Sequence Path*)
A collection of tasks that can be executed sequentially in a workflow is called a *sequence path* (No AND/OR-Split or AND/OR-Join conditions occur during

sequence path). If a sequence path cannot include another task to be executed sequentially, the sequence path is called a *maximal sequence path*.   □

Fig. 3 shows examples of maximal sequence paths. The workflow consists of four maximal sequence paths, *T1, T2, T3*, and *T4*. Now, we can define the *Maximal Sequence model* of a workflow execution as segmenting a workflow definition into maximal sequence paths; and assigning each of them to a mobile agent. The following algorithm describes a pseudo code of the proposed Maximal Sequence model.

Algorithm *Maximal Sequence Model*:
ELEMENT Maximal_Sequence_Model(*workflow*) {
TASK_QUEUE *q*;
ELEMENT *currentElement*;
  set *currentElement* as the first element of *workflow*;
  do {
    switch (*currentElement*.type) {
    case TASK: add *currentElement* into *q*;
                    currentElement = *currentElement*.next; // next element
                    break;
    case SPLIT: define a set of tasks in *q* as a MSP and delete all tasks from *q*;
                    // MSP : Maximal Sequence Path as in Definition 1
                    for (int i=0;i<# of branches; i++)
                      currentElement = Maximal_Sequence_Model(branch);
                              // branch is assumed to be a sub-workflow
                      currentElement = *currentElement*.next;
                    break;
    case JOIN: define a set of tasks in *q* as a MSP;
                    return *currentElement*; // local *q* will be automatically deleted
    case TERMINATION: define a set of tasks in *q* as a MSP;
                    return *currentElement*;
    } // end of switch
  } while (*currentElement*.type != TERMINATION);
} // end of algorithm   □

The *workflow* in this algorithm is the workflow definition. TASK_QUEUE is a queue for tasks. ELEMENT is an object data type for *tasks*, *joins*, *splits*, or *terminations*. Each branch in a workflow is considered as a sub-workflow. Hence *Maximal_Sequence_Model*(branch) is called recursively in splits. Because the above algorithm is applied to workflow definition during *build-time*, the decomposition of a workflow into blocks makes no effects on the run-time performance and scalability and hence no effects on our simulation.

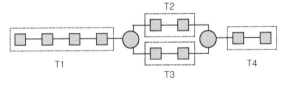

Fig. 3. Examples of Maximal Sequence Paths

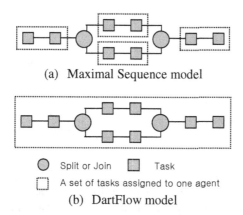

(a) Maximal Sequence model

○ Split or Join   ▦ Task
⬚ A set of tasks assigned to one agent

(b) DartFlow model

Fig. 4. Segmentation of a workflow definition

Fig. 4 shows the difference between Maximal Sequence model and DartFlow model for a same workflow definition. Whereas the DartFlow model makes a single mobile agent responsible for the entire workflow, the Maximal Sequence model creates multiple mobile agents, each of which is responsible for each maximal sequence path. At first glance, the DartFlow model seems to be more favorable to the scalability since a single mobile agent executes an entire workflow without help of the workflow engines. However, the large physical size of the mobile agent with the entire workflow definition leads another performance bottleneck in the communication bandwidth. On the other hand, the Maximal Sequence model can reduce the agent migration overhead at the cost of the increasing number of interactions between the workflow engine and task performers.

4 Experimental Comparisons of the RPC, DartFlow, and Maximal Sequence Model

In this section we construct three stochastic Petri-net models of conventional RPC-based, the previous mobile agent-based (DartFlow), and the proposed Maximal Sequence model-based workflow systems to compare the performance and the scalability. We use *UltraSAN* simulation tool [11] for stochastic Petri-net simulations.

4.1 Preliminaries for Evaluations

Three parameters such as agent migration, assigning tasks, and scheduling time must be considered before the evaluations of performance and scalability. In this paper, we assume that,

'A transmission time of code and/or data is proportional to the size of them'   (1)

The result of RMI performance test [12] shows that our assumption is reasonable. As in Fig. 5, the transmission time of most complex data types is almost exactly

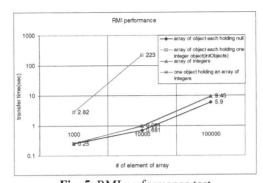

Fig. 5. RMI performance test

Table 1. Agent transmission(migration) rates

The number of tasks assigned to an agent	Agent size (Kbytes)	Transmission rate (Migration)
-	10	1.54
1	20	0.769
2	30	0.485
3	40	0.385
4	50	0.297
5	60	0.256
6	70	0.214
32	330	0.046

proportional to the size of code. By the result of [13], the transmission rate (=1/transmission time) of a mobile agent for 10Kbytes and 20Kbytes sizes is *1.54* and *0.769* respectively. Because the transmission time of a mobile agent is proportional to the agent size (our assumption), we can infer the other transmission rate of a mobile agent for the size of 30Kbytes, 40Kbytes, and so on. In consequence, we can construct a Table 1 that shows the relation between agent size and agent transmission rate (=1/agent transmission time).

In mobile agent-based workflow systems, an agent consists of basic code and context parts. The basic code is an additional overhead for executing agent migration and context management (a code of *scheduling*). A context consists of control data and relevant data for a task. Hence, the size of a mobile agent can be calculated as a following equation,

$$S(Agent) = S(Basic\ Code) + S(Context) * N \qquad (2),$$

where N is the number of tasks to perform and $S(OBJ)$ is the size of OBJ in *Kbytes*. The ratio of basic code and context size seems to effect on our simulations. Each size of basic code and context is assumed to be 10Kbytes in Table 1. The agent size assigned two tasks, as an example, is the sum of the basic code size (=10Kbytes) and the contexts size for two tasks (=10Kbytes*2). Although the context size is assumed to be 10Kbytes in Table 1, various ones are adopted in our simulations later.

Assigning tasks time also must be considered. A context is transferred from a workflow engine to task performers in the assigning tasks step. Our assumption (1) also can be applied to assigning tasks. In case that the context size is 10Kbytes, the assigning tasks rate is *1.54* with the help of Table 1.

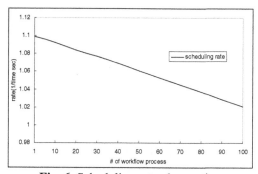

Fig. 6. Scheduling rate observation

Table 2. Values of parameters for a load dependent rate function

$\mu = \lambda(1-x/(B+1))^{\alpha}$	Value	Meaning
λ	Rate of each transition	Constant rate for a single server semantic
B	1000	Buffer size
x	-	Number of customers
α	0.7	Controller for rate change

The last parameter to be considered is a scheduling time. Scheduling time is various depending on the implementation schemes in workflow systems. Because there is no reference for scheduling time, we examined the scheduling time with a sample mean method [14] in a workflow system of Hanuri/TFlow [15]. Fig. 6 shows the results of our observation.

In the simulations, it is reasonable to increase the service rate when the queue length is large. Transition rates are always changing depending on the number of current customers (that is queue length). Therefore, measuring an exact value of the load dependent rate is difficult. The load dependent rate or state dependent service rate is generally computed as a function of the queue length, the maximum buffer size, the arrival rate of customers, and a current load [16]. We used $\mu = \lambda(1-x/(B+1))^{\alpha}$, $0 < x <= B$ as a load dependent rate function. The parameter α is used to control how fast the service rate can change with the queue length, x. Parameter B is the maximum buffer size that customers can enter. Parameter λ is a constant arrival rate of customers (they are mobile agents). Parameter values for a load dependent rate function are summarized in Table 2.

4.2 Petri-net Models

Petri-net models for RPC model, DartFlow model, and Maximal Sequence model are shown in Fig. 7. Although only three tasks are shown for simplicity reasons, simulations are performed on the various workflow structures. All of models in Fig. 7 consist of a 'workflow engine', 'channel', and 'task performer'. N workflow instances are executed. A workflow engine sends messages or mobile agents (in assigning tasks step) to task performers depending on the computing paradigms of RPC model and mobile agents-based model through the channel.

Now we describe the Petri-net model for RPC model, DartFlow model, and Maximal Sequence model.

Table 3. Parameters for the RPC model-based workflow system

Transition	Rate	Type	Semantics
Scheduling	1.1	Exponential	Load dependent
AssignTask	1.54	Exponential	Load dependent
ReturnResult	15.4	Exponential	Load dependent
SetContext	19.2	Exponential	Load dependent
UpdateStates	7.69	Exponential	Load dependent
Init	1.0	Exponential	Load dependent
Task	1.0	Exponential	Load dependent

RPC model

Fig. 7(a) shows a Petri-net model for RPC model. The roles of workflow engine in this model are scheduling, setting contexts for task assignments, monitoring workflow status. They are implemented with *Scheduling* transition, *SetContext* transition, and *UpdateStates* transition respectively in Fig. 7(a). The channel is a physical network that a workflow engine can communicate with task performers. RPC messages and returning messages are transferred through channel. Transmission of RPC messages and returning messages are implemented with *AssignTask* transition and *ReturnResult* transition respectively. A workflow engine assigns a task to a task performer by sending a context containing control data and relevant data. The roles of task performers are execution of assigned tasks. This is implemented with a *Task* transition.

Now let's consider the execution scenario with the Petri-net model for RPC model. At first, a workflow engine in this model reads the control data and the relevant data from workflow definition. They are used to build a context (*SetContext* transition). After finishing *SetContext* transition, the contexts that enable a task performer to execute Task1 (by *Task1* transition) are delivered (*AssignTask* transition) to a task performer. After completing Task1, the task performer returns (*ReturnResult* transition) the results to the workflow engine. A workflow states manager (*StatesMngr* place) stores the returned results. After completing three tasks (*Task1*, *Task2*, and *Task3*) a workflow is destroyed (*DestoryInstance* transition). This simulation is completed after N workflow instances are destroyed. Transition rates for RPC model-based workflow systems are summarized in Table 3. *Scheduling* and *AssignTask* transitions are already justified before. The value of *ReturnResult* transition is fixed as *15.4* not only in RPC model but also DartFlow and Maximal Sequence model. *SetContext* and *UpdateStates* transitions are also observed as *19.2* and *7.69* respectively in executions of Hanuri/TFlow. Because *Init* (initialization for a workflow execution) and *Task* transitions are not sensitive parameters we defined its values as *1.0*. The transition type is assumed to be exponential because of its memoryless property [16].

DartFlow model

Fig. 7(b) shows a Petri-net model for DartFlow model. The roles of workflow engine in this model are to create agents and to monitor the status of workflow executions. They are implemented with *CreateAgent* transition and *UpdateStates* transition respectively. The mobile agents and task results are transferred through channels. Transmission of agents and results are implemented with *Migration* and *ReturnResult* transitions respectively.

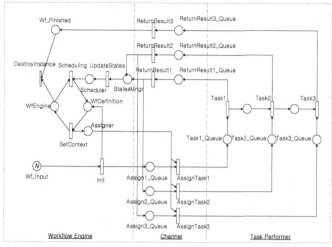

(a) RPC model-based workflow system

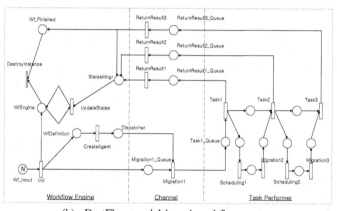

(b) DartFlow model-based workflow system

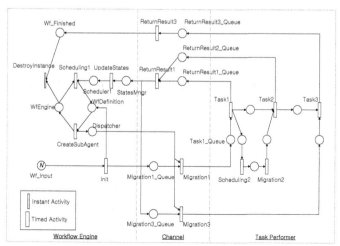

(c) Maximal Sequence model-based workflow system

Fig. 7. Petri-net models for RPC, DartFlow, and Maximal Sequence Model

Table 4. Parameters for DartFlow model-based workflow systems

Transition name	Rate	Type	Semantics
Scheduling	1.1	Exponential	Load dependent
Migration	0.046	Exponential	Load dependent
ReturnResult	15.4	Exponential	Load dependent
UpdateStates	7.69	Exponential	Load dependent
CreateAgents	19.2	Exponential	Load dependent
Init	1.0	Exponential	Load dependent
Task	1.0	Exponential	Load dependent

A fact worthy of note is that there are *Scheduling* transitions in the task performers because the mobile agents residing in task performers can take loads of scheduling and assigning tasks off the workflow engines.

Now, let's consider the execution scenario with the Petri-net model for DartFlow model. A workflow engine creates (*CreateAgent* transition) a mobile agent, which contains the entire workflow definition. The workflow engine sends (*Migration* transition) the mobile agent to a task performer that is in charge of the first task of the workflow. After the mobile agent completes the first task, it reports (*ReturnResult* transition) the result to the workflow engine and decides (*Scheduling* transition) which task performer is in charge of the next task. Then, it migrates to the next task performer. This migration continues until the entire workflow is completed (*DestoryInstance* transition).

Parameters for DartFlow model-based workflow systems are summarized in Table 4. *Scheduling, ReturnResult, UpdateStates, Init*, and *Task* are already justified in the RPC model. Based on the result of [13], the rate value of *CreateAgents* transition is decided to be *19.2*. The value *0.046* of *Migration* transition is an example for an agent having 32-tasks (A context size is assumed to be 10Kbytes).

Maximal Sequence model

Fig. 7(c) shows a Petri-net model for Maximal Sequence model. Although it is similar to the one of DartFlow, diverse values of *Migration* transition as shown in Table 1 are used to Maximal Sequence model depending on the agent size which is determined by the number of tasks. Each maximal sequence path of workflow definition is assigned to a mobile agent during *CreateSubAgent* transition. Created agents migrate (*Migration* transition) to the task performer and execute (*Task* transition) assigned tasks. After completing tasks the mobile agent returns task results to the workflow engine. The next maximal sequence path is determined in the scheduling step of the workflow engine. This is implemented with a *Scheduling* transition in the workflow engine. The simulation continues until N workflow instances are destroyed (*DestroyInstance* transition).

The parameter values are same with Table 4 except that the *Migration* transition is determined by the number of tasks of each maximal sequence path as shown in Table 1.

4.3 Evaluations and Analysis

From now on, we evaluate the performance and scalability of RPC model, DartFlow model, and Maximal Sequence model with diverse parameters such as the number of branches of a workflow, the number of tasks of a maximal sequence path, the number of workflow processes, and the ratio of context size in a mobile agent to reflect diverse workflow system environments.

Relation between workflow structure and average turnaround time
The performance is evaluated on the diverse workflow structure. We change the workflow structure by increasing the number of branches of a workflow and/or the number of tasks of a maximal sequence path. In this simulation we fix up the number of processes as 100 and 1000. A pair of split and join is the main reason producing a complex workflow structure. If the number of branches is increased the total number of tasks composing a workflow definition is increased. As a result, the number of remote interactions in RPC model and the agent migration overhead in DartFlow model and Maximal Sequence model are also increased.

Fig. 8 shows a relation between the number of branch and the average turnaround time. In case that the number of workflow process is 100 (referred to in the text as small-scale workflow systems), the average turnaround time of DartFlow model and Maximal Sequence model are not more efficient than RPC model. But in case that the number of workflow process is 1000 (referred to in the text as large-scale workflow systems), the average turnaround time of DartFlow model and Maximal Sequence model are more efficient than RPC model. These results also say that RPC model is more sensitive to the number of workflow process than the other models. In case that 1000 workflow processes are concurrently executed, RPC model is more sensitive to the number of branch than the other models. The bottleneck in a centralized workflow engine caused more sensitiveness of RPC model to the number of workflow process. On the other hand, DartFlow model and Maximal Sequence model distribute overheads of workflow control (scheduling step, assigning tasks step) to the corresponding task performers. This result is true of the case that the length of maximal sequence path in a branch is increased as shown in Fig. 9 (The length of maximal sequence path is defined as the number of tasks in a maximal sequence path. The length of maximal sequence path *T1*, as an example, in Fig. 3 is 4). As in Fig. 9, Maximal Sequence model outperforms DartFlow model and RPC model in a large-scale workflow system.

As the number of branch and the length of branch are increased, the number of tasks of a workflow is also increased. Consequently, we can say that Maximal Sequence model gives better average turnaround time than the other models when the number of tasks of a workflow is increased.

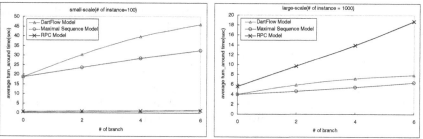

(a) the number of workflow process = 100   (b) the number of workflow process = 1000
Fig. 8. The number of branch vs. average turnaround time

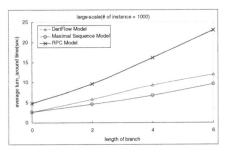

Fig. 9. The length of branch vs. average turnaround time

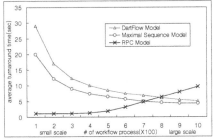

Fig. 10. The number of workflow processes vs. average turnaround time

Relation between the number of workflow process and average turnaround time
In this simulation we evaluate the performance and the scalability of RPC model, DartFlow model, and Maximal Sequence model on the diverse number of workflow process. This simulation is performed on a workflow structure having 32 tasks and 5-splits. Fig. 10 shows the relation between the number of workflow process and average turnaround time. As in Fig. 10, RPC model gives more efficient average turnaround time than DartFlow model and Maximal Sequence model in case of small-scale workflow systems. On the other hand, in case of large-scale workflow systems, it gives worse average turnaround time than DartFlow model and Maximal Sequence model.

The scalability in this paper is an oblique of a performance graph. DartFlow model outperforms any others in the perspective of scalability because it has the least slope. RPC model provides the worst scalable method because it has the largest slope. We can see that the scalability of Maximal Sequence model is almost similar as one of DartFlow model. Although DartFlow model is the most scalable method, it has a significant problem as shown in the following simulations.

Relation between context size and average turnaround time
In this simulation we compare the average turnaround time of RPC model, DartFlow model, and Maximal Sequence model by changing the context size of an agent. In the equation (2), we fix up the basic code size as 10Kbytes but the context size of the agent is changed. Fig. 11 shows a relation between context size and average turnaround time.

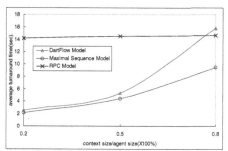

Fig. 11. The context size vs. average turnaround time

This result shows the inefficiency of DartFlow model. In case of the context size is large, DartFlow model is worse than Maximal Sequence model. Worse than all, it requires more average turnaround time than RPC Model. Hence, DartFlow model does not provide better performance than Maximal Sequence model in case that the context size is large enough. However, Maximal Sequence model gives better performance than RPC model even in the case of large context size.

Until now, we compared the performance and the scalability of RPC model, DartFlow model, and Maximal Sequence model-based workflow systems. By the experimental results of above, we can say that Maximal Sequence model not only gives a better performance than other models but also preserves the scalability of DartFlow model. So, Maximal Sequence model increases the performance and scalability in massive workflow process environments.

5 Conclusions

This paper has proposed a new workflow execution model based on mobile agents. Whereas the DartFlow model, which is the first workflow execution model based on mobile agents, makes a single mobile agent take charge of an entire workflow definition, the proposed model segments a workflow definition into blocks, and assigning each of them to a mobile agent. The segmentation is called Maximal Sequence model since it groups tasks that can be executed sequentially to the maximal extent. We have also built stochastic Petri-net models for three architectural alternatives such that the RPC model, the DartFlow model, and the proposed Maximal Sequence model to compare their performance and scalability.

The advantage of the proposed model is that it has mobile agents residing in task performers take the computational and communication overheads off workflow engines, and helps to avoid excessive overhead for agent migration. As the stochastic Petri net simulation has shown, the proposed model outperforms the DartFlow and RPC-based models as well as comes up with better scalability especially when the workflow definition contains a large number of tasks and many workflow processes execute concurrently.

Acknowledgments

This work was partially supported by Korea Science and Engineering Foundation (KOSEF) under contract 98-0102-11-01-3.

References

1. WfMC: Workflow Management Coalition Terminology and Glossary- WfMC Specification, 1999.
2. Frank Leymann, and Dieter Roller: Business Process Management with FlowMark, Spring Compcon, Digest of Papers, pp 230-234, 1994.
3. Action Workflow website: http://www.actiontech.com/
4. FloWare website: http://www.plx.com/html/floware_scaleable_workflow.html
5. G. Alonso, C. Mohan, R. Gunthor, D. Agrawal, A. El Abbadi, and M. Kamath: Exotica/FMQM: A Persistent Message-Based Architecture for Distributed Workflow Management. In IFIP WG8.1 Working Conference on Information System Development for Decentralized Organizations, pp 1-18, 1995.
6. B. Nelson: Remote Procedure Call, Ph.D. Thesis, Carnegie-Mellon University, Pittsburgh, PA., CMU-CD-81-119.
7. Ting Cai, Peter A. Gloor, and Saurab Nog: DartFlow: A Workflow Management System on the Web using Transportable Agents, Technical report, Dartmouth College, 1997.
8. Colin G. Harrison, David M. Chess, and Aaron Kershenbaum: Mobile Agents: Are they a good idea?, Research Report, IBM Research Division, T.J.Watson Research Center, 1995.
9. D. F. Judge, B. Odgers, J. Shepherdson and Z. Li: Agent Enhanced Workflow, BT Technical Journal, 16:3, pp. 79-85, 1998.
10. K. Myers and P. Berry: Workflow Management Systems: An AI Perspective, Technical Report, Artificial Intelligence Center, SRI International, Menlo Park, CA, 1999.
11. D. D. Deavours, W. D. Obal II, M. A. Qureshi, W. H. Sanders, and A. P. A. van Moorsel.: UltraSAN Version 3 Overview: In Proceedings of International Workshop on Petri Nets and Performance Models, 1995.
12. RMI Performance website: http://java.sun.com/products/jdk/rmi/archives/0436.html
13. Manfred Dalmeijer, Eric Rietjens, Dieter Hammer, Ad Aerts, and Michiel Soede: A Reliable Mobile Agents Architecture, In Proceedings of the Int. Symposium on Object-Oriented Real-Time Distributed Computing, 1998.
14. Alberto Leon-Garcia: Probability and Random Processes for Electronical Engineering, 2nd Ed, Addison-Wesley Publishing Company, 1994.
15. Kwang-Hoon Kim, Su-Ki Paik, Dong-Su Han, Young-Chul Lew, and Moon-Ja Kim: An Instance-Active Transactional Workflow Architecture for Hanuri/TFlow, In proceedings of International Symposium on Database, Web and Cooperative Systems, 1999.
16. Donald Gross and Carl M. Harris: Fundamentals of Queueing Theory, 3rd Ed. John Wiley & Sons Inc., 1998.

Author Index

Lecture Notes in Artificial Intelligence (LNAI)

Lecture Notes in Computer Science